Erdoğan Onur Ceritoğlu
Salvaging Buildings

Architecture | Volume 79

Erdoğan Onur Ceritoğlu, born in 1983, is an architect, artist, and urban researcher. In his artworks, he re-contextualizes urban life through a material-driven experience and socially engaged art practices. He participated in residencies and exhibited his works internationally. His academic research focuses on informal labor, the materiality of waste, and reuse in architecture. He has a PhD from Brandenburgische Technische Universität Cottbus Senftenberg, Germany.

Erdoğan Onur Ceritoğlu

Salvaging Buildings

Reclaiming a Livelihood from the Excesses of Istanbul's Mass Urbanization

[transcript]

Zugl.: Diss., BTU Cottbus-Senftenberg, 2022, u. d. T.: Çıkmacıs: Reclaiming a Livelihood from the Excesses of Istanbul's Mass Urbanization

This publication was supported by funds from the Publication Fund for Open Access Monographs of the Federal State of Brandenburg, Germany, and by Hans-Böckler-Stiftung

Bibliographic information published by the Deutsche Nationalbibliothek

The Deutsche Nationalbibliothek lists this publication in the Deutsche Nationalbibliografie; detailed bibliographic data are available in the Internet at http://dnb.d-nb.de

First published in 2023 by transcript Verlag, Bielefeld
© Erdoğan Onur Ceritoğlu

Cover concept: Kordula Röckenhaus, Bielefeld
Cover illustration: Erdoğan Onur Ceritoğlu
Proofread by: Mark Farrier
Printed by: Majuskel Medienproduktion GmbH, Wetzlar
https://doi.org/10.14361/9783839469248
Print-ISBN: 978-3-8376-6924-4
PDF-ISBN: 978-3-8394-6924-8
ISSN of series: 2702-8070
eISSN of series: 2702-8089

Printed on permanent acid-free text paper.

To Merih, Tevfik, Lia and Gian Derya

Contents

They're tearing apart the house next door. They're like butchers: They separate out the meat (useful parts such as glass, doors, tiles, etc.) and throw the bones (bricks, plaster, mortar, etc.) into a truck and dump it somewhere down the road.
—from a short story cited in (Atay 1991, 76; my translation)

List of Acronyms

ANT	Actor Network Theory
ANAP	The Motherland Party
AK Party	The Justice and Development Party
CDW	Construction and Demolition Waste
COOPCENT ABC	Cooperativa Central do ABC
DDT	Dithiothreitol
DfD	Design for Deconstruction
IBB	Istanbul Metropolitan Municipality
ISTAÇ	Istanbul Environmental Protection and Waste Processing Cooperation
OPDS	Organismo Provincial para el Desarrollo Sostenible
PVC	Polyvinyl chloride
TOKI	Turkish Housing Development Administration

Abstract

Turkey's demolition waste management is, to a great extent, dependent on *çık-macıs* (reclaimers) who salvage condemned buildings for raw materials and architectural elements. Its urbanization history is full of key moments marked by building demolitions, which became a necessary material resource for informal urbanization. As early as the 1970s, the çıkmacıs helped the *gecekondus* [squatter houses] by supplying second-hand building materials and construction loans. They managed to turn a lack of infrastructure into an advantage and remain very adaptable to the ever-changing conditions of neo-liberalized urbanization. They depend on solidarity networks and other informal resources.

Assemblage thinking helps to redefine the concept of informality, understand the relational dynamics between various actors, and focus on the agency of materials. The empirical data gained from 'follow the thing' ethnographic research in Turkey and Georgia reveals the double lives of çıkmacıs who move between village and city. Additionally, by following the example of a reclaimed window frame's journey from Istanbul to Tbilisi, we can more clearly see the second-hand trade network in the context of urbanization and incremental architecture. In the context of waste's materiality, the empirical part of the research shows the symbiotic relationship between *çıkmacıs* and the discarded demolition materials.

1. Introduction

As we stepped out of the scrap collectors' truck, I realized that the left-over furniture was stacked in front of the apartment building: a rug, a wooden side board, a damaged mirror, a bathroom scale, some old-fashioned chairs and a few knickknacks in plastic buckets. Showing me the stack, Engin said, "these will be taken to the flea market." Then he exclaimed: "Nothing goes to waste!" He added that he had already sold the reclaimed PVC frames to a second-hand wholesaler from Black Sea Region. The garden looked trashed. The trees were removed. Before entering the building, I noticed that it was named, ironically, İstikbal Apartmanı [Future Apartments]. On the ground floor, I saw that they stored some of the reclaimed materials and building components like windows and doors. There was a note on a salvaged kitchen cabinet with the name of the second-hand buyer written on it. There was a bed on the floor. Next to it, there was a TV on a chair. It was as if someone was temporarily living among all those stacked materials in that room. I heard some deep banging sounds coming from the staircase. I decided to follow the sound. The air smelled burnt.

At the bottom of the stairs was a propane tank. A hose attached to the cylinder extended up the stairway. I followed the hose. On the stairs, I saw some graffiti in Arabic written with red paint. I assumed that it might have been done by the refugee worker from Syria I met earlier. From time to time, streams of sparks were falling from the elevator shaft next to the stairs. I could see inside it because the elevator door was removed. I followed the hose to an apartment on the 3rd floor where the front door had also been removed.

As I went into the apartment, I encountered a worker who asked me how I entered the building. He warned me that the site was dangerous. I noticed that he wore non-construction clothing just like myself. I mentioned that I came with Engin. After that, everything was fine. He told me he was his brother and continued cutting off metal pipes from the heating system. I asked if he knew about

the beating sounds coming from above. He answered that somebody had already started demolishing the building with a sledgehammer. I pointed to the cast iron heater and asked what they would do with it. He explained that he would sell it to a metal scrap dealer. He added that he cut up the elevator into pieces too. While he worked, small fires began to appear on the surface of the wall. The blowtorch's flame left burn marks on the wallpaper. I noticed the yellow mattress foam lying beneath the foot of the worker was also burned.
—from my fieldnotes, entry on 08.10.2016.

Throughout my five years of fieldwork research in Turkey, I often encountered scenes similar to the one described above. It was a time when demolitions were increasing because of urban renewal and the state authorities were not addressing the issue of the overflowing building waste.

With resources depleting as quickly as they are today, reuse has become one of the biggest environmental sustainability topics in urban planning and architecture. As a practice, it has been going on for a long time in Turkey, where not only does there not exist any state structure for handling the massive debris from decades of building demolitions, there is not even any proper material recycling infrastructure. What is worse is that the Turkish government also declares waste pickers illegal.

Within this vacuum created by state negligence, various unrecognized groups of people stepped in and created a livelihood out of this salvage work. These people who will be the main protagonists of this book are referred to as çıkmacıs (singular çıkmacı: reclaimer/reclaiming in Turkish).

There is a saying in Turkish to describe this sort of work: *ekmeğini taştan çıkartmak*, "make your bread from a stone." The construction site is rough; the working conditions are precarious. The phrase is about being persistent in doing the hardest jobs for the lowest income. *Çıkartmak* means extracting in English. The term "çıkma" means "dismantled or second-hand" and, by adding the "-cı" suffix, the word represents a profession: building salvagers. The çıkmacıs' livelihood emerges from an absence of resources and infrastructure. By stepping into this absence, they have adapted to gaps in the margins of capitalism.

1.1 Bread from a Stone: Material Reclamation in Turkey

This book focuses on building salvage, informal waste management and circulation of second-hand materials in Turkey, a country where 6.7 million buildings are structurally weak to survive an earthquake and thus are, according to a Turkish parliament report (Turkish Parliment (TBMM) 2021), slated to be seismically retrofitted or newly rebuilt. In reality, this means that most of the buildings will be demolished and this leads to the question of what to do with the building materials that are scrapped or have been declared waste.

Demolition is the total removal of buildings without any material reclamation. It 'subtracts' the dwelling from the cityscape so that the site can be developed "creatively" by architecture and construction companies (Easterling 2014). Deconstruction, on the other hand, is a thorough and detailed dismantling of construction elements. Material reclamation or building salvage is a kind of mining of the construction materials and architectural elements. This demolition waste often consists of massive, heavy materials such as concrete, wood, asphalt, gypsum, metal, brick, glass, plastic; salvaged building components (doors, windows, and plumbing fixtures); and materials from clearing sites (trees, stumps, earth, and rock).

In the European Union in 2018, almost 36 percent (813 million tons) of waste was generated by construction and demolition activities (EUROSTAT 2020). In the same year, 800 million tons of construction and demolition waste (CDW) was produced in the USA (USA Environmental Protection Agecy 2018). The equivalent statistics in Turkey are not available because the state turns a blind eye on the CDW issue. Over the last decade in Turkey, demolition always seems to accompany new urban development which focus on inner-city slums.

Since the 1960s, rapid informal urbanization for profit in Turkey has had many negative results. Previous tectonic movements of the earth resulted in several historical disasters that destroyed residential areas along with their occupants. Such a history shows that the built environment is weak and dangerous. Due to the fact that the housing stock has already fulfilled its physical and economic lifespan, the demolition of these buildings is utilized by urban developers, state apparatuses, construction companies, architects, and private dwelling owners. For the last two decades, the AK Party government channeled its economic and political agenda towards urbanization and construction of the cities. Hence, the current situation created an economic opportunity to vitalize the construction industry and adapt it to neoliberal dynamics.

Along with this adaptation came the dispossessing of informal dwellers by inner-city slum clearing processes, the privatization of public spaces, and other unjust profit-driven development. Top-down urban regeneration plans overlook the actual need of dwellers because they are associated with urban renewal projects based on large-scale real estate investments. In this scenario, demolition means an immediate solution to eradicate the existing environment rather than a comprehensive plan for building deconstruction or the strengthening of apartment blocks. The housing-stock regeneration has to be privately financed since the state's financial resources are limited. Homeowners are responsible for deconstructing and reconstructing their apartment blocks. To afford this, the state prefers to change zoning laws that result in higher buildings.

In these demolitions, much waste is produced, and much is unmanaged by the city authorities because a circular economy, in which markets have incentive to reuse products, is still only an emerging concept in Turkey. In recently modernized or post-colonial countries, waste lies in a gray zone between the formal and informal sectors. Collection and separation of waste creates a significant livelihood for new rural migrants and refugees. Therefore, waste management is a heterogeneous process, in which formal and informal actors cooperate (Tuçaltan 2018). On the formal side, private recycling factories process plastic and metal waste and some municipalities have waste sorting facilities. On the informal side, self-organized waste and scrap collectors gather and separate the same materials and sell them to the factories. In the end though, state municipalities want to eliminate these street collectors and impose their own collection operations and sorting facilities, which has the effect of limiting job-seeking labor and marginalizing street collecting.

Within the context of this study, a 'construction project' includes both demolition and the making of a new building. General contractors, who manage this process, sell the scrap materials to *çıkmacıs* who, in turn, dismantle, collect, classify, and store them. Recyclable materials are sent to factories, and building components are sold on the second-hand market. *Çıkmacıs* extract PVC window frames, doors, radiators, kitchen counters and sanitary equipment as second-hand components. They also remove lighting hardware, plumbing fixtures, copper electrical cables, taps, and metal pipes; dismantle elevators and central heating systems for metal recycling. They even collect furniture and household items from the previous tenants to sell at a flea market in Kadıköy.

Çıkmacıs operate in an environment in which no regulations exist. They have an informal labor structure and constitute a heterogeneous assemblage including scrap collectors, demolishers, private businesses, governmental institutions, laws, second-hand components and other nonhuman actors. Plus, they have been operating since the peak urbanization began in major Turkish cities, that is, since there was a sudden demand for affordable materials needed to build *gecekondus* (literally 'put up overnight' buildings). Historically they emerged from a rapid urbanization that was shaped by sociomaterial processes in the 21st century. Additionally, demolition and the second-hand sector have been an income resource for migrants as they are now for refugees. The critical debates in this book concern informal labor; metabolic cycles of reuse after demolition processes; urban transformation's role in creating second-hand surplus; second-hand trade and the agency of materials in dwelling construction.

Figure 1.1: A supply yard in Istanbul

Source: Author's own

1.2   The Goal of this Study

This study examines the demolition activities of *çıkmacıs* within the context of historical developments and urban renewal in Istanbul. In terms of the creation of CDW, it is essential to discuss the material life cycles as Istanbul was built up, unbuilt, and rebuilt in different eras of rapid urbanization.

Current urbanization trends will be compared with past activity in order to identify the adaptation processes of these urbanization assemblages. By reflecting on present-day urban regeneration, the study investigates how *çık-macıs'* unrecognized reclaiming activities result from an excess of earthquake-driven projects. More specifically, it investigates these activities by examining sectoral distinctions in the gray zone between formal and informal processes.

This book focuses on the livelihoods of *çıkmacıs* as informal workers in the construction and recycling industries. This is a significantly neglected field in architecture studies. Using low-tech deconstruction processes, the *çıkmacıs* reclaim recyclable and reusable materials from buildings slated to be demolished. They have been active but formally unrecognized actors throughout several different urbanization periods, especially in Istanbul, from its informal urbanization in the 1960s to its current neo-liberal development. Such employment is precarious, especially in low-income geographies with peak migration, rapid urbanization, and cheap labor. *Çıkmacıs'* are migrant laborers. Never completely rural or urban, their lives are wedged between the city and the village. Thus, the study's objective is to investigate the social and economic relations that create networks of labor between the city and the village.

In addition, there will be an analysis of the second-hand trade between Istanbul and other places. An analysis of human and non-human agency is essential for determining the market mechanisms at work in the supply and demand chain of affordable reclaimed materials. The second-hand market functions through supply yards. It is essential to analyze the spatial properties of these yards and their network's rapid growth in their particular context. There is more demand for affordable materials in economically depressed rural areas. Many villagers repair their houses with second-hand construction materials: roofs made out of used wood beams, façades assembled with old PVC frames and metal doors, kitchens built with used cupboards, and floors covered with reclaimed plastic parquets. In those zones, there are more precedents for adaptive reuse in architecture. The afterlife of these materials, including their reuse and movements, is important in terms of addressing sustainability. That is why I trace the ways these materials are reused in new constructions: I document how the materials are disassembled and reassembled into different architectural forms and seek what sort of socio-materiality is reproduced in the 'new' dwellings.

Both human and nonhuman actors within their relevant networks need to be assessed. For example, the non-human agency of earthquakes substantially affects urban planning processes because, in the context of Turkey, they are a threat to the poorly-built environment. Within only a few minutes, an earthquake can destroy cities and transform geographies. Another example are the hazardous materials used in constructions, such as asbestos. They endanger human and no-human lives when they are carelessly dismantled during demolitions. Supply yards accommodate CDW and the people who benefit from its revaluation. A theoretical approach that acknowledges such sidelined agencies can help develop institutional sensitivity toward the idea of sustainable buildings, safe work conditions and environment protection.

1.3   The Unrecognized Future of Waste Management

Existing CDW management research primarily focuses on environmental engineering issues and is heavily influenced by the field of circular economy (Yuan and Shen 2011). Labor conditions in low-income countries or the agency of salvaged construction materials are rarely discussed. There is, for example, remarkable work on the salvage of end-life of ships traded to the Global South for their scrap value (Gregson et al. 2010). However, ethnographic-architectural studies of building salvage practices are noticeably lacking. This is especially unfortunate due to the pressing need for more research into this aspect of the construction sector, especially in regard to climate change, resource exploitation, and CO_2 emissions.

I highly benefited from the guiding research on waste pickers that document the informality of struggling workers in the Global South (Portes, Castells, and Benton 1989; Gidwani 2015; Dias 2016; Gutberlet et al. 2017; Corwin 2018). The linkages between waste picking and building salvage guide the understanding of informal economy and precarious livelihoods. The existing literature on informal waste management is focused on waste paper collectors and how they are influenced by global markets (Dinler 2016); urbanization processes around dump sites; and ethnic struggles of informal workers (Tuçaltan 2018). Regarding CDW, the research emphasizes the emerging sector that deals with excavation work (D. Öztürk 2019). Research on material reclamation and second-hand markets is, however, absent. Referring to this knowledge gap, the study aims to answer the following questions:

- How is CDW produced and managed during the urban renewal process in Turkey?

- o   How are material reclamation and demolition interrelated?
- o   What are the current urbanization dynamics behind the increasing de-molition activities?
- o   How was CDW reused in the history of Istanbul's urbanization?

- •   What are the human and nonhuman actors within the material reclama-tion process assemblage?
- o   How do *çıkmacıs* organize themselves as unrecognized labor?
- o   How are second-hand businesses networked through supply-yards in Turkey? How do these shape *çıkmacıs* livelihoods?

- •   How can waste be conceptualized as a socio-spatial process in terms of its impact on çıkmacıs' livelihood, urbanization and environment?
- o   What kind of materials are actively influencing the reclamation pro-cesses?
- o   What is the agency of second-hand components in construction?

Based on these questions, this study discusses waste material excess as a result of urban renewal, its informal management, and its vital materiality produced by demolition processes and second-hand trade.

The approach of the study contributes to a shift in perspective in architec-ture and urban studies toward distinguishing between human and non-hu-man actors, formal and informal sectors, and rural and urban linkages and livelihoods. In an era of rising energy prices, material scarcity, greenhouse gas emissions, and climate crisis, the issue of demolition and waste in the building sector is very urgent but also very neglected.

1.4   Assemblage Thinking and the Agency of Waste

In the milestone book, A Thousand Plateaus: Capitalism and Schizophrenia, by Gille Deleuze and Félix Guattari (1987), a rhizome—a philosophical term and metaphor—is a root-like structure that ceaselessly creates heterogenous con-nections between different things, entities and circumstances. It is used for describing relations, connectivity and difference between things. A rhizome establishes assemblages that are non-hierarchic constellations. According to Manuel DeLanda, an assemblage is a rhizomatic and heterogeneous system consisting of active singularities and it represents horizontal organizations for understanding complexity and the layeredness of collectives (2006, 14). The opposite—structuralist manifestations—imposes tree-like hierarchies (arborescent) that are shaped by predominant power relations based on human agency. In Actor Network Theory by Bruno Latour (2007, 63), assembling involves the transfer of agency from an individual to a network composed of people, objects, and stories. Multidirectional and complex understanding of 'the social' takes into consideration the agency of non-humans to alter human-centered, linear and dualistic conceptualizations.

This study focuses on concepts based on assemblage thinking like 'thing power' (Bennett 2010), 'trans-corporeality' (Alaimo 2010), 'living waste' (Bell 2019), and the notion of 'cosmopolitics' by Isabelle Stengers (Blok and Farias 2016) in order to conceptualize how a nonhuman agency shapes the world. This concept is used as a framework for articulating critical imaginary that progresses through relational and generative urban formations (McFarlane 2011, 219). For instance, the occurrence of the 1999 Earthquake in the Marmara Sea is regarded in the literature as a natural phenomenon that assembled and reassembled the urban structure of Istanbul (Angell 2014, 667).

Within this framework, the neoliberal urbanization is not taken as a global and overarching development but rather as a trending situation or economic arrangement that influences particular instances of urban change (Simone 2009). The structure of the political economy is not regarded here as generalizable or pregiven. Urban renewal policies, for example, are assembled not only through economic and political bodies, but also through particular moments in household meetings; policy documents; procedures at demolition sites; earthquakes; the accumulation of second-hand PVC frames; or even unexpected opportunities and juxtapositions in everyday life situations.

This book attempts to better identify the emergence of different processual strategies and survival tactics of marginalized urban dwellers adapting to global urban change. For instance, the circular economy cannot be regarded as a new concept in the Global South. Since resources are limited, more or less nothing goes to waste in subaltern geographies (Gidwani and Reddy 2011). That's why the neoliberal approach is not inclusive enough to identify *çıkmacıs* and their interaction with the materiality of waste, such as how they are salvaging building materials without a formal model. The concept of circularity in material reclamation processes in Turkey seems to be efficient and successful in the absence of bureaucratic rules or waste management procedures. Informal actors are more active and creative as they form a symbiosis with existing formal waste management systems. However, neoliberal policies and integrating models automatically eliminate the heterogeneity existing within distributed agency systems (McFarlane 2011b). By contrast, assemblage analysis introduces sociomaterial interaction that promotes multiplicity, co-functioning (symbiosis), emergence, gathering and networking (Parnet and Deleuze 2002; McFarlane 2011a; Farias and Bender 2011).

The implications of assemblage thinking are revealed by ethnographies of everyday practices through thick description[1] (McFarlane 2011a, 210). In my study, a thick description will illustrate the alternative uses and everyday opportunities that construction waste enables. It gives a different perspective that links the everyday to materiality. This perspective reveals the linkages between *gecekondu* urbanization and current neoliberal urbanization. Different transformations of the city led to the emergence of *çıkmacıs*. In both trends, they survive by flexible labor strategies, trade infrastructure, their connection to their village, and the second-hand construction elements' agency. In order to view this agency as an emerging process that is spread across the social and the material, assemblage thinking necessitates careful study of the significance of diverse materials within assemblages (McFarlane 2011b).

Çıkmacıs create an infrastructure that is produced from their material and social relationships. In theory, this is comparable to relational infrastructures, which are everyday organizational strategies for arranging labor, allocating resources, and recognizing success in the Global South (Simone 2015, 34). The infrastructure is facilitated by the relational movement of people, matter, feelings, and information. In this environment, waste is a valuable resource that highlights the vitality of matter versus human-centric conceptualizations (Bennett 2010; Gregson et al. 2010; Bell 2019). To provide an alternative political and economic perspective and highlight the distributive agency, 'assemblage thinking' is used as a framework to understand the livelihood of *çıkmacıs* and their relationship with materials and architecture. The framework of critical urbanism grounded in political economy assists in explaining the interruption caused by the duality between formal and informal processes; however, this gap masks heterogeneous forms in terms of shared agency. On the basis of this dispute, I use political economics to explain how neoliberal politics benefit from urban land rent on the one hand and instrumentalize urban demolitions on the other. As a supporting concept, I use assemblage thinking to zoom in

---

1   Thick description is a technique used in anthropology to describe and understand the multifaceted meanings of human activities, relationships, and environments.

on the features of socio-material connections in building salvage and construction of rural dwellings. In other words, the critical political economy's primary issues remain crucial for an ontological analysis of capitalism's effect on land commodification and urban change. Nonetheless, by focusing on assemblage thinking as a fundamental analytical and empirical paradigm, the book expands into new areas of inquiry such as nonhuman agency and ethnographic studies of survival maneuvers by the urban poor.

The top-down urbanization has already eliminated the existence of *gecekondus* and their social habitat in the 2000s (Erman and Eken 2004). Such ignorance will most likely eliminate the *çıkmacıs* too. Their importance is insignificant to mainstream architectural and urban development of the city. In order to break this narration, the conceptual framework aims to highlight the agency of objects and materials. However, the political economic perspective is still taken as a consequence of a historical urban development that creates second-hand surplus from demolitions. In a setting lacking guidelines or legislation for demolition, the study problematizes how construction materials were reclaimed during Istanbul's demolition and by whom. The notion of assemblage is crucial for envisioning shared agencies that reside in entities like tectonic movements, second-hand components, second-hand building supply yard[2] networks, and unrecognized labor.

What kind of materials are recycled and reused and where are they traded? What are the origins of unrecognized reclamation labor that link the recycling and construction industry? To answer these questions, it employs ethnographic methods to observe the *çıkmacıs* and follow second-hand components in the second-hand market. The fieldwork expands to a multi-sited ethnography by mapping trade routes and supply yards. Further, it figures out the trajectory of building components in an extended supply chain. To identify their role and skills in material reclamation processes, an ethnographic fieldwork was done starting from the Kadıköy district in Istanbul where the middle-class apartment buildings were being demolished and rebuilt intensively. There, I could observe the way that the building components are distributed out of Istanbul through second-hand trade networks.

The findings show that *çıkmacı* reclamation runs in two directions: reuse and recycling. In the first case, the building parts are revalued as second-hand commodities. They collect them and distribute them to other parts of

---

2   In the rest of the text, I will refer to these places as supply yards. These yards were once called *ardiye* in Turkish.

Turkey. The existing literature on *gecekondus* shows that they are not a new phenomenon. When Istanbul was urbanizing rapidly with *gecekondus*, *çıkmacıs* (as demolishers) were providing materials reclaimed from inner-city demolitions to *gecekondu* dwellers. They constitute an unregulated second-hand market networked through migratory associations and personal connections. Because of the removal of *gecekondus*, which provided affordable material demand, they were forced to trade their second-hand components to buyers outside of Istanbul in rural places where building permits are not strictly controlled.

In the second case, they provide non-reusable parts of the buildings to recycling factories in terms of recycling. They are subcontracted for gathering plastic and metal as raw materials for industries grounded in the circular economy. Yet even still, they suffer from precarious conditions and are vulnerable to exploitation. In addition to mapping the supply chain, some of the *çıkmacıs* maintain a dual livelihood divided between scrap collecting and farming. In the urban centers, job-seeking rural and refugee migrants find informal seasonal jobs in scrap collection and demolitions. As a social and economic precaution, they limit their farming practices to the other half of the year.

As demolition activities increase in large urban areas, the second-hand supply yards expand into places where affordable materials are needed because of economic shortages. Hence, such demand comes from low-income households in rural areas and small cities where they themselves build or repair their buildings incrementally. In the near future, the excess of CDW has to be thoroughly reconsidered since material resources are increasingly understood as limited, not endless. Arguably, the formal waste sector will organize the demolition discard management, or an alternative scenario could be imagined, namely, one with the characteristics of an urban commons. However, the agentic future of the *çıkmacıs* is uncertain, especially in terms of how they can adapt to such systematic formalization and privatization.

I hope to contribute to the body of knowledge regarding building demolition, reclamation, unrecognized nonhuman actors, informal labor, and transitional livelihoods between urban and rural. This book addresses the current limitations of research in this area and provides practical and conceptual knowledge to academics and professionals who operate in architecture and urban studies. Beyond its outreach, research is limited by the accessibility of demolition sites, time restrictions, and geographical borders. Due to unregulated and precarious situations, I could not always enter some construction sites. The research was also conducted at a time when the number of demolitions was increasing. Multi-sited ethnography also has constraints since second-hand elements were spreading to unreachable spaces where the investigative power of one researcher is not enough.

Before summarizing the research chapters, I will explain how the research project began as an art project. This preliminary part of the research is essential for understanding my multi-scalar orientation. Consequently, my involvement with reclaimed objects resulted in an unexpected outcome.

1.5 Preliminary Research and Artistic Practice

My first encounter with çıkmacı supply yards was in 2011 when I was an assistant for Mike Nelson, an artist from the United Kingdom. He was making a large installation at the Venice Biennial, imitating the Büyük Valide Han, a historical caravanserai in Istanbul. I was hired as an assistant for him. We were visiting supply yards located on the periphery of Istanbul to find second-hand building components. It was a long excursion between the Asian and European sides of Istanbul to collect second-hand materials. Later, this collection was sent to Venice to construct the British Pavilion.

With Mike Nelson, we drove around Kağıthane on the European side of Istanbul, where old factories were demolished in 2011[3]. We stopped to see the ruins of factories covered with rusted metal, corrugated roof material, and various other structural remains. Our peripheral exploration by car was critical for mapping the çıkmacı supply yards and depots because the periphery was unreachable with public transportation. When we noticed supply yards by the side of the road, we stopped and bargained with the owners for old stuff. During these visits, I was making an inventory of second-hand components. These were industrially produced construction products from the 1980s. Additionally, we encountered some antique building salvagers. The antique depots

---

3   This area was a demolition site for urban renewal projects after the district was deindustrialized. Currently, what is there is a university campus, some shopping malls, offices and residences all of which adhere to the multi-functional development plan. In this district, some old çıkmacıs supply yards are still located along the main road. They are still operative but not like they used to be due to the competitive demolition market and the construction economy in crisis. The yards were owned by the building wreckers who were active during the deindustrialization demolitions of big and small industries along the Golden Horn. They were suppliers of affordable housing material for gecekondu dwellers which used to work in the factories in Kağıthane district.

were located in Zeytinburnu on the Asian side. They stored aged wood from old barns in the Black Sea region of Turkey. Besides that, they salvaged wooden building parts from old traditional buildings in the villages: ceilings, staircases, doors, and built-in furniture. These construction elements were historically more significant compared to what we found in the supply yards. Because of their antique value, they were expensive, and interestingly they were eventually exported to the US.

After assisting Mike Nelson with his project, I revisited those supply yards located on squatted land for my master's research. Further, I made architectural survey drawings of spaces to show the spatial configuration. Some of the large depots' mappings were an earlier version of the diagrams in Chapter 6. I mainly used the 'excursion with the car in the periphery' as a mapping method. In this way, I could find retail hubs, individual supply yards, and depots where çıkmacıs and demolishers created their self-organized zones.

As a part of my master's thesis, I showed three artworks related to building reclamation in the exhibition entitled Tadilat (Remodel) (Ceritoglu 2011). My first work in the collection was mapping the four supply yards I visited in 2011. As preliminary research, the creation of property plan sketches, as a part of my visual notes, illustrated the spatial organization of demolished buildings and supply yards. In addition to this sketching, detailed photographic documentation was made to create a sense of place.

As a second work in the graduation exhibition, I made an installation out of salvaged doors from an old apartment flat. Earlier, I reclaimed these doors from a renovation project where I managed the construction process. The conceptual approach of the artwork was based on the materiality of salvaged doors; however, the production process reflected my involvement in the salvage process. Through my active participation, I was in the field as a professional architect. While designing and managing the construction workers in the application process, I focused on how the dismantling processes of existing building components were performed. All the interior materials were replaced because they were unwanted by the owner. Yet, I reclaimed some of the construction elements to make an installation. By observing and filming the actions of these workers, I documented the deconstruction process, which consisted of dismantling, discarding, and various transportation activities. My involvement in the project enabled me to meet construction workers, conduct preliminary participant observation research, and thus better understand salvaging. These earlier discoveries and artistic research created a knowledge and methodological ground for my latter ethnographic fieldwork on çıkmacıs.

The concept of my next exhibition, "Demolishdemount" in 2014, focused on the building demolitions and urban renewal project in Fikirtepe. The video created for it, entitled "Demolition Feast, 2014", documented the ongoing demolitions. It showed how the excavators broke the concrete, extracted the reinforcement bars from the rubble, and collected them into large 'balls of string' that were then transported out. Later, these scrap balls were sold to a scrap dealer who traded metal with recycling factories. While filming on the construction site, I observed how the scrap collectors did their reclamation. Then, I conducted accompanying interviews with the excavator operators and managers during their lunch breaks.

Figure 1.2: Rebar Balls, 2014 at Sabancı Museum

Source: Murat Germen Archive

My investigation of materiality continued with "Rebar balls, 2015" in which I exhibited a one-ton metal string ball made out of scrap reinforcement bars (Figure 1.2). The aesthetic properties of such an object were my priority because it carried a visual code encrypted with urban renewal, decaying buildings, demolition, and the increasing amount of CDW. For this work, I visited a scrap dealer who gathered all kinds of metal before sending it all to a recycling factory. The ball was purchased at a price calculated with a foreign currency rate. Throughout this process, I made a video about the selection, negotiation, and transportation process. During the production of the work, I met some scrap collectors who became my informants in the study. After the exhibition, I sold the scrap ball back to the supply yard owner at the same metal currency rate. The concept of my artwork refers to the agency of the discarded construction objects that is also discussed in chapter 7.

Through renovation and remodeling projects, I got professionally involved in reclamation. Such wasting via architectural obsolescence (Abramson 2017) highly influenced my line of practice-based research in a multi-disciplinary setting combined with urbanism, architecture, and art. Before engaging in ethnographic fieldwork, I got familiar with the context of the study through my master's thesis and professional practice. This preliminary research prepared me for the ethnographic fieldwork that concentrates on informal labor, building reclamation, recycling and materiality.

1.6 Summary

Employing assemblage thinking resulted in figuring out how to show the relationship between the social and material in the context of Turkey's çıkmacıs. Waste entails unwanted materials and marginalized labor. For this reason, this book focuses on the material, social, and political agency of nonhumans. By doing so, it shows how the networked spatialization of supply yards are replicated places where unwanted things accumulate. As a result of this analysis, the assemblage of çıkmacıs brings together three different empirical themes: the role of human labor, second-hand trade, and the agency of materials. The first relates to the informal labor structure and reclamation processes. The second focuses on commodity exchange through second-hand valuation assemblages. The last argues for the independent agency of different materials and construction elements.

Chapter 2 reviews the theorization of waste in the existing literature to gain a philosophical background for acknowledging its agentic ontology. In this chapter, waste will not be conceptualized as a passive entity but rather as a nonhuman agent that influences micro and macro systems within urbanism. It offers an alternative to the theory of waste that distances it from the human and sees it as only a by-product. This alternative perspective introduces a conceptual framework that reveals how waste's agentic materiality influences political and social processes (Gregson et al. 2010; Hawkins 2010; Bell 2019). With the notion of thing-power (Bennett 2010) and Actor-Network Theory (ANT), it inquires into vital materiality debates around waste. It then delves into the spatialization of waste and looks at the debates on assemblage urbanization (McFarlane 2011a; 2011b; Blok and Farias 2016) and its criticism (Brenner, Madden, and Wachsmuth 2011). Incremental construction is taken as a precedent for such assembly. Additionally, it reviews the literature about informal labor as infrastructural maneuvers (Bayat 2000; Simone 2015). Lastly it focuses on issues around unacknowledged waste labor: formalization, adaptability, privatization, cooperatives, and labor safety.

Chapter 3 is the methodology chapter. It explains the evolution of the project from its initial beginnings as artistic research to its culmination as a Ph.D. in urban studies that utilizes ethnographic methods. It locates a thick description of micro-urban situations in assemblage thinking to decipher human and nonhuman relationships (McFarlane 2011a). In addition, it offers brief information about the long-term duration of the research and the follow-the-thing approach that leads to multi-sited ethnography (Cook 2004; Marcus 1995). Low-end commodities (Hulme 2015), the end-life of ships (Gregson et al. 2010), and waste trade (Balayannis 2020) are discussed in these studies. It introduces cross-disciplinary methods combining ethnography and architecture. These are participant observation, architectural surveying, interviews, and documentary photography. Going further, it sheds light on the research process that questions the ethical and reflexive position of the researcher while doing the fieldwork. To this end, it also introduces the issue of the changing status of the researcher. Finally, it describes how abductive reasoning is employed as a conceptual tool to structure the research process and analysis of empirical data to create a theory. Structurally the empirical findings are grouped into three parts to express the importance of the symbiosis between people, matter, and space in material reclamation.

Chapter 4 is the context chapter that gives a historical background to Turkey's urban renewal and the utilization of demolitions. It contextualizes the role of demolitions in Istanbul and specifically in the district called Kadıköy; it looks at this though the lens of four particular urbanization processes: the commodification of land in the Ottoman Empire; state-led national developmentalism in the early days of the Turkish Republic; liberalization of the economy in the 1980s; and neoliberal development in the 2000s. Later, it focuses on the privatization of land in Istanbul and urban development in Kadıköy in the last days of the Ottoman Empire. The commodification of land explains how Modern suburban houses replaced Ottoman mansions in Kadıköy. It explains the role of the *çıkmacıs* for the emerging *gecekondu* urbanization. They supplied second-hand components to informal squatter constructions. The transformation of single-floor houses to multi-floored apartment blocks (*apartmentalization*) through urban centralization is described in the contemplation of *gecekondu* and middle-class housing upgrades. It focuses on the different political and economic agendas behind the utilization of demolitions in mentioned periods and highlights the significance of material reclamation, especially during *gecekondu* urbanization because of its circular logic in reusing materials.

Chapter 5 is the first empirical part of the research and introduces the labor activities of *çıkmacıs*. It briefly introduces their form of livelihood while contemplating the literature on informal waste management. Then, it evaluates waste management in Istanbul as being heterogeneous because it has both informal (waste pickers and scrap collectors) and formal (municipality and recycling factories) actors. *Çıkmacıs* are determined to be invisible actors among scrap collectors and demolishers who salvage end-of-life buildings. Next, the building demolition processes and material reclamation are explained. Besides this, it documents the labor structure, including family members and refugee workers. It continues by describing the dual lives of a *çıkmacı* family that alternate between material reclamation and farming. The seasonal mobility of labor displays a circular pattern that connects the rural and urban and reflects migration patterns. Finally, it pinpoints what constitutes their dual livelihoods: precarity, relationality, and adaptivity.

Chapter 6 proceeds as the second empirical chapter about the trade activities of *çıkmacıs* in the second-hand market. It discusses the conceptual issues around supply yards as places of second-hand accumulation like location, experience, entrepreneurial success, distribution geography, and customer profile. The spatial organization of yards is illustrated with diagrams. The main empirical objective is to study the differences in supply yards between Istanbul, Ankara, Kayseri, Nevşehir, and Niğde. For this reason, the chapter is outlined according to geographical location. The first is dedicated to yards located in the Asian and European parts of Istanbul. Then, demolition yards in Anatolian towns are described. Finally, the findings on Georgian second-hand traders that visit these yards to export them to Tbilisi are presented.

Chapter 7, the last empirical one, focuses on the materiality of waste in order to determine the nonhuman agents in the assemblage of material reclamation. First, it bridges waste theory literature and Latourian actant ontology, which is also contextualized within assemblage thinking. The active properties of materials in health, construction, and environmental terms are identified as an aspect that influences the human body. Second, it examines the PVC window frames recovered by building salvage processes. It also discusses the agency of asbestos emissions that authorities, and even workers, often overlook in the construction sites. The PVC frames are discussed as a renovation phenomenon in Turkish households. The recovery processes of PVC through recycling processes and its effects on the environment are critically described. The dangers of asbestos exposure in demolition sites are explained in this subchapter. Third, it gives examples of dwellings in which second-hand elements are used. Reclaimed materials play a strong role in the design processes of incrementally constructed dwellings in a wide range of geographies (Greene and Rojas 2008; McFarlane 2011b; Dovey 2014). With the aid of incremental urbanism, a city may grow as its inhabitants or builders make their way through quickly changing circumstances while juggling a lack of resources. The construction process is ongoing, adapting to the skills, materials, cultures, and resources that are available.

The conclusion, Chapter 8, summarizes the book's theoretical and empirical chapters while mentioning research restrictions. Additionally, it underlines the contribution to academic knowledge methodologically, theoretically, and empirically. Plus, it highlights the practical implications of the study. It ends with proposals for future research in this field.

2. Theoretical and Conceptual Framework

This book follows and theorizes *çıkmacıs'* salvaging practices in Turkey in relation to the agency of waste as a second-hand resource. The *çıkmacıs'* activities are key to understanding how urban waste renewal processes, by negotiating the borders of urbanization, can impact more expansive geography. Through the lens of sociomateriality, I investigate how discarded building components are used in incremental constructions in rural parts of Turkey. This theoretical engagement has a three-part structure based on separate but intersecting scholarship. The chapter begins with a theory of the overlooked agency of waste; followed by an exploration of its spatialization and association with 'assemblage urbanization'; and it concludes with a delineation of unrecognized forms of labor.

2.1 Theorization of Waste

> Waste is the dark, shameful
> secret of all production.
> Preferably, it would remain a
> secret.
> *(Bauman 2011, 27)*

Theories of waste focus on the material and its social life through social, cultural, and economic valuation systems (Thompson 1979; Appadurai 1986; Gregson and Crewe 2003). Scholars agree that waste is a transitory period and category rather than the end of a life cycle. However, some conceptualizations (Douglas 1966; M. Thompson 1979; Scanlan 2005) are based on a problematic preconception of a divide between waste and humans. It is perceived as an exteriority. They fail to mention waste's relationality and sideline the fact that economically disadvantaged people in the Global South live in closer proximity to it. Additionally, waste studies have a tendency to give agency and authority only to humans. Nevertheless, these theories are primarily linked to economic, cultural, and social codes centered on the Global North (Bell 2019). These codes are part of a system that assembles and classifies things according to their appropriateness to human values:

> Where there is dirt, there is a system. Dirt is the byproduct of a systematic ordering and classification of matter, in so far as ordering involves rejecting inappropriate elements. The idea of dirt takes us straight into the field of symbolism and promises a link-up with more obviously symbolic systems of purity. (Douglas 1966, 35)

With this 'purity system', once waste is discarded, the system no longer cares about it. Another concept of Mary Douglas is that dirt is matter-out-of-place implies some kind of transgression. Waste represents a "residual category [of things] rejected from our normal scheme of classifications" (ibid, 45). Where there is a human valuation system, there are boundaries that keep waste outside. To keep waste outside we need waste management systems that need maintenance.

Different societies marginalize or exclude people as waste. However, according to Zygmunt Bauman (2011, 3), "wasted lives" are the intrinsic result of modernization and an unavoidable companion of modernity because they are an "inescapable side-effect of order-building ... and economic progress". There is a symbolic contamination inscribed on informal waste laborers that represents them as downgraded elements of society. They are labeled in such a way even though they contribute to the circular economy and sustainable consumption (Morrison 2015). For instance, garbage pickers, trash collectors, and informal recyclers in the majority of the Global South tend to deal with the dynamic identity of waste and move it on its circular trajectory of reuse.

In Michael Thompson's book *Rubbish Theory*, the politics of value is interpreted as a system that depends on time and space (1979). Thompson suggests that the exchangeability of a thing beyond its market value relies on that thing's particular usage history. He refers to a valuation system made by human consciousness that separates things into the categories of what is useless and what is not. To that end, he proposes three types of objects determined by human justification: transient, durable, and rubbish (ibid, 4). Thompson distinguishes between transient objects, which lose value over time, and durable objects, whose worth improves over time. Rubbish lies in-between transient and durable objects and represents a temporary and covert state without time and value. In the rubbish category, things are in a neutral space without any worth where they can be rediscovered and evaluated for a new use and moved into the durable object group. His subsequent theory suggests that rubbish as a category allows for translations in use and value. The condition of unworthiness is tied to temporality, which means the ability of items to transit across these categories. In addition, time is a crucial concept in recognizing and negotiating waste (Viney 2014; Allon, Barcan, and Eddison-Cogan 2020). If there is too much emphasis on the categorization and territoriality of waste, it becomes likely that one will lose sight of the critical role that time plays in shaping our perceptions of, and interactions with, discarded things. Referring to Douglas' definition, Viney argues that waste is "matter out of time" (Viney 2014, 2).

Thompson (1979, 148) explains that the transition between categories is motivated not by the fundamental features of objects but by new and unforeseen uses and functions ascribed to them by humans. The person-and-thing relations in his theory are limited to those categorizations based on temporality and the cultural evaluation of things. Other factors like creative practices or the inextinguishable properties of toxic waste are missing. The transitory practices in the arena of human activity are essential for reviving value since rubbish is not an endpoint but rather a pivot point. However, the value again depends on human judgment in Thompson's theory. It disregards waste's independent activeness to alter habits or practices because it also exists in time.

Scanlan (2005) puts forth another kind of distancing argument that acknowledges the separation from nature and humans as well as the creation of modern society out of its cleansing and discarding activities. Such disassociation was created within high-income societies at the time when technological developments in urban sanitation designated a city with a modernist ideal order (ibid). Within such an orderly system, the consequences of our own waste are black-boxed with municipal waste management and the recycling industry with its sustainable rhetoric of a circular economy. His arguments ignore the way waste is also managed by informal means or self-managed systems in low-income geographies. There, through inventive recycling processes, waste is turned into functional materials. It is part of networks, services, and infrastructure produced in spaces beyond the confines of the planned urban settings.

In summary, the literature on waste discussed in this section was based on a disconnection between human and nonhuman agents; the creation of a passive and active duality; and ordering systems. However, in peripheral geographies, human activities and their byproducts are more intertwined. A more fruitful theory of waste can be developed if we focus on the experiences of individuals whose existences are defined primarily by their livelihoods structured around waste. In the following, I discuss approaches that support the active participation of materials, the dynamic relationship between humans and waste, and how waste could be redefined through these discussions.

2.1.1 Waste as Active Matter

More recent studies eschew dualist conceptions of waste in favor of more relational perspectives (Gregson and Crang 2010; Hawkins 2010; Bell 2019). This socio-materialist approach attempts to overcome the distanced binarism between humans and waste (Hawkins 2010). Such an evaluation of waste is rooted in theories that employ flat ontological perspectives, putting humans on the same level with nonhumans and considering the agentic and performative qualities of materials (Latour 1988; Bennett 2004; Alaimo 2010; Ingold 2012). These 'new materialism' theories acknowledge the transformative power of nonhuman. Ingold suggests that materials (2012) have fluctuating properties because they change under the influence of the surrounding environment. In an attempt to theorize the interactions and entanglements between human and matter, Stacy Alaimo pursues a "trans-corporeal" relationship between the human body and waste (2010, 3).

The concept of waste needs to be expanded through an investigation of the consequences of waste's role in places where people and waste closely interact on a socio-material level. Bell offers a counter concept of "living waste" that roots "itself in lived experiences of waste; in empty-belly or peripheral contexts; in human lives and other-than-human life forms; and in understandings of waste in all its materiality and agency." (Bell 2019, 117). In the following section, I begin with an overview of Latour's actant ontology in order to disclose the importance of nonhuman agency and to highlight the role of waste and its materiality.

2.1.2 Actant Ontology

Reclaimed material or a salvaged heating system can have an impact on the architectural planning and construction of a rural house. Recycled PVC frames can become a part of the circular economy. The incineration processes can damage the environment through the recycling processes. An earthquake, abandoned building, or PVC frames can play an essential role in urban renewal projects. Latour's actant ontology theory can help us better comprehend how everyday things, impending natural disasters and technology have agency in political and economic processes.

According to Latour, an actant is a source of action that may be human or nonhuman within a network (Latour 1988). In its interactions, it is effective, capable of doing things, and purposeful enough to create an impact, cause consequences, or influence the trajectory of events (Latour 2007). Further, in his definition, an actant has the ability to alter and act on other entities based on relationships within a network. Each actant in the network has an effect on the manner in which the network functions. The material form of individual actants contributes to the establishment of linkages within a network: the physical properties concurrently define and constrain the modes in which exchanges may occur and emerge. Things, artifacts, devices, technologies, texts, algorithms, institutions, and humans are not comprehended as separate and independent features that belong to different fields or vocabularies but as interconnected actants interacting with each other through mutual relationships (Law 1992).

The actant's competence is inferred from its performance rather than any predetermined assumptions before its activity. In this respect, performance is critical to analyzing a network since the longevity of the actant is only valid when its performance is repeated in recognizable patterns. By describing a more distributive agency between human and nonhuman actants, Latour establishes a language for the numerous ways to reveal different forms of things and their distinguishing roles in a network. The ANT brings together natural, cultural, and social bodies, both human and nonhuman, organic and inorganic, material and immaterial (Latour, 2007). His strategy is to balance the distinctive agency of humans. He emphasizes specific nonhuman entities inside a network of relationships other than human subjectivity while highlighting their material qualities or unique, effective powers. At the same time, he proposes a horizontal analysis to stage human and nonhuman actors for the formation of networks. This horizontal analysis distributes agency to each assemblage element.

Latour expand the consideration of objects beyond their conventional role in fulfilling human needs (ibid). In the context of this study, employing a Latourian perspective allows an investigation of how reclamation procedures of construction waste are entangled in specific material capabilities that function to bring the matter into the present and arrange particular meanings and values around it. Moreover, Latour emphasizes contingency and performativity of materials in political processes (2016, 16). For instance, asbestos emissions from construction ignored by the Turkish government) become part of political and public debates (Odman 2019). Methodologically, this approach allows an exploration of how salvaged materials are reactivated in specific second-hand markets as valuation networks that try to bring matter back to life and arrange specific interpretations and values. The second-hand window frame salvaged from the city takes part in the assemblage of a rural house through the *çıkmacı* supply yard network.

There are three forms in which actants interact with networks: intermediaries, mediators, and immutable mobiles (Latour 2015). Intermediaries are actants that do not alter the network as it passes through them. Being transparent, they are capable of transmitting inputs without leaving a mark. Predictable by the cause that creates them, they replicate the input. Mediators always have an effect upon what passes through them. Due to this, they modify the form, function, and meaning of the network wherever they are associating. Immutable mobiles are actants that preserve their form or configuration while moving through and over the networks. To put it another way, they can be replicated indefinitely across a network without changing. They also have the power to enlarge the network into different territories and spaces.

To give an example of these three forms within the context of this research, intermediaries are the urban renewal projects that continually create building scrap material. Mediators are *çıkmacı* and their yards. After deconstructing and sorting out the parts (all of which are regarded as waste) of the building, they put some of its elements back into use through their second-hand trade network. The second-hand market expands its territories through supply yards as immutable mobiles where reclaimed materials are distributed.

Tim Ingold finds Latour's emphasis on nonhumans limited because it only addresses the agency of matter inside an assemblage (Ingold 2008). Latour's ANT is focused only on the mutual and interactive collaboration of actants within a network of functional totality. Counter to this, Tim Ingold (ibid) refers to the individual agency (singularities) of materials that are independent from a network and to the singular transformations of materials throughout their lifespan. Ingold (2012) stresses the individual signs of activity, growth, or reactivity, for example, in the dematerialization processes after the production of the object. What needs further attention is waste's material composition, what other materials are moved around, and what exactly are the dynamic properties that make discarded things flow.

For Ingold, things remain active in their material form after their fabrication because the elements that compose them continue to be involved in the circulations of an external medium, like air, which simultaneously announces their decay and enables their regeneration (Ingold 2007). By decay or decomposition of their structural substance, materials have properties that are animated by their surrounding medium's impact. For instance, waste can decay or change in form due to its material composition or exposure to air. Or, a metal roof can change color after years of exposure to sun, air and water. In demolition, workers are the medium that decomposes the building's structure into materials, and they activate asbestos or other substances from construction components:

> We see the building and not the plaster of its walls, the words and not the ink with which they were written. In reality, of course, the materials are still there and continue to mingle and react as they have always done, forever threatening the things they comprise with dissolution or even dematerialization. (Ibid, 9)

Based on this, the properties of materials cannot be defined as stable and fixed but rather as processual and relational. Material properties could only be determined as a consequence of time or one of the mediums activating it. Latour and Ingold create an opportunity to understand the agentic properties of nonhumans: Latour explains that agency is distributed in a network, and Ingold suggests agency should be based on individual actions and the capacities of things. Their contribution is the philosophical ground for the next discussion on waste as an animate entity with agency.

2.1.3 Waste and Thing Power

> Materiality is a rubric that tends to horizontalize the relations between humans, biota, and abiota. It draws human attention sideways, away from an ontologically ranked Great Chain of Being and toward a greater appreciation of the complex entanglements of humans and nonhumans. (Bennett 2010, 112)

Thing power refers to the potential of everyday man-made things to transcend their status and, as Jane Bennet puts it, "to manifest traces of independence or aliveness, constituting the outside of our own experience" (ibid, 15). Bennet claims things outside human subjectivity are capable of asserting themselves, that they have the ability to influence people. Humans prefer to believe that they are the only ones who manage the world of things. She asserts that 'thing power' will engender a whole new type of human culture, for example, one that uses more environmentally and materially sustainable methods of production and consumption (ibid). She discusses a pile of debris she encountered on the street as a case study to explain the effect of discarded objects that are no longer perceived as useful or valuable. Rising from a pile of trash, the potential of matter is "the curious ability of inanimate things to animate, to act, to produce effects dramatic and subtle" (ibid, 6). However, she clarifies that the need to discard things to make place for new ones diminishes the thing's worth. Still, she says, a thing "continues its activities even as a discarded or unwanted commodity" (ibid, 6).

Thing-power asserts that matter has the capacity to surpass humans through its liveliness, but it can only be fully functional in the context of an assemblage (Hawkins 2018). The unique features of waste components are enacted through actions, and their surprising capabilities or liveliness may emerge when they interact with humans and nonhumans. For instance, *çıkmacıs* vitalize construction waste as second-hand commodities that are later used in incremental rural constructions. The thing-power of waste is utilized by *çıkmacıs'* transient activities.

Another critical theory that could be useful for a nonhuman-agency perspective on waste is trans-corporeality, which represents the unbreakable bond between the human and nonhuman (Alaimo 2010). Referring to new materialism and material feminism, she argues that all embodied beings are connected to the material world through reciprocal relationships and transformative interactions: "Imagining human corporeality as trans-corporeality, in which the human is always intermeshed with the more-than-human world, underlines the extent to which the substance of the human is ultimately inseparable from the environment" (ibid, 2). In order to make moral efforts to protect animals, plants, and nature, she argues that the environmental justice movement should distance itself from the centrality of a separately-existing human subject. Further, ethical sensitivity and environmental awareness should stem from an excruciating and baffling interdependence and coexistence, that is, a being transcorporeal, a being a part of the active material world (ibid). Trans-corporeality allows us to rethink material agency in order to apprehend "the often unpredictable and unwanted actions of human bodies, nonhuman creatures, ecological systems, chemical agents, and other actors" (ibid, 2). Trans-corporeality links to ethical discussions that problematize our interaction with waste.

In the book, *The Ethics of Waste* (2010), Gay Hawkins examines the way humans experience waste via their senses, feelings, and emotional interactions without ever withdrawing from it or denying it. She claims that although the disruptive presence of waste can endanger humans, it can also shape them by altering their habits and corporeal practices, especially the ones that determine their levels of attachment to what is discarded. To prove her point, Hawkins makes an analysis of gleaning, repair, and creative reuse practices. In her comments on Agnes Varda's documentary entitled *The Gleaners and I* (Varda 2000), Hawkins (2010) sees gleaning as an ethical stance against the excessiveness of waste or an act of self-sustainability within already existent cultural practices and habits. In another case, she concentrates on an Australian Aboriginal community's methods of 'making do' such as through gleaning or scavenging. These activities also suggest reusing whatever is available to utilize. A kind of 'creative reuse' system can thus emerge in less commodity-oriented cultures like these. There, the materials themselves take part in an authority structure that previously was a 'humans only' zone. The polarizing waste-human interaction could be the reason for the current environmental waste crisis:

> While environmentalism recognizes this in the demand that everybody "reduce, reuse, and recycle," this is only the beginning of the story. The imperative to manage our waste better or avoid the 'waste stream' altogether doesn't really get to the heart of how we might come to live differently with things. (Ibid, 76)

In the Global North, the sorting of waste into separate bins in households is considered adequate enough to count as ecological awareness. It is essential to underline the fact that these are volunteer workers donating their collecting and sorting labor to the recycling industry and energy production plants (ibid). Prior to the industrial revolution and before the waste collection managed by state, waste was an internal problem of the household. Resources were scarce, reuse was prominent, and people were more aware of the labor behind the manufacturing process. They knew how difficult it was to produce commodities.

Hawkins uses earthworms as an example of the art of transience (ibid, 119). Through their biological functions, the example of earthworms may have an ethical resonance, as seen by their ceaseless work in breaking down substances.

Her worms demonstrate how waste could be reused productively and assist the decomposition and renewal of substances. The same analogy could be made between the earthworms and building salvagers. Salvagers break apart buildings into individual elements to be used for other architectural projects but they cannot fully recover the energy and matter as well as saprophytes can (Lynch and Southworth 1990).

In her discussions about the accumulation of plastic products, Hawkins points out how the ethics of critical scholarship on single-use plastic has postulated its over-production and over-use (Hawkins 2018). Single-use plastic facilitates practices of disposability that are based on the forgetting of a material's afterlife (ibid). However, the concept of disposability contradicts the immutable and permanent materiality of plastic waste. In this future, all plastics, including construction PVC, should be discussed from the perspective of their materiality because their everlasting presence and toxic recycling processes are considered to be the cause of many environmental, spatial and geographical problems.

2.2 Geographies of Waste

The variety of compelling new materialist studies discussed above emphasize the transient aspect of waste's materiality and its association with people, space, and processes (Bell 2019). In the new materialist paradigm, there are no hierarchies, systems, or mechanisms that create dualistic boundaries between the natural and social world. Instead, there are relational processes that are the tangible results of the material effects of natural and social interactions. Waste is involved in the construction of new identities, interests, and daily politics. It resides in between those interactions as a broader result of consumption, circulation, and renewal activities like "food sharing, scrap metal collection, curbside scavenging and recycling, clothing reuse, reversible materials, building repair and repurposing and e-waste art" (Allon, Barcan, and Eddison-Cogan 2020). By focusing on trade, repair, and maintenance practices at the bottom of the waste commodification chain, researchers can better understand the transformative cultural and social processes derived from these new concepts of waste. Of course, close contextual encounters within urban space and places of exchange are also needed.

2.2.1 Second-hand Trade

Space is a complex vessel and repository, a transitional gap where things can be revalued. These gaps, according to Hetherington (Hetherington 2004), serve as places where an object's worth may finally be decided. However, in these places we distance ourselves from things that seem to be at our disposal. Examples of these places include a basement, attic, garage or even the recycle bin icon on a computer desktop:

> The gap is the space where things are held in a state of denying their wastage—where they are held at our disposal for a second time so that we can attain a settlement with their remaining value. (Ibid, 170)

The remaining values of things are stored in these gaps in order to be put into their secondary life cycle. For example, waste from previous production can pile up in the auto salvage yards, where valuable items can be retrieved from it, such as those with use-value and exchange-value (Soderman and Carter 2008, 20). Flea markets also function as spatial lacunae peripheral to conventional retail spheres and capitalist consumption patterns.

> We show here how car-boot sales [U.K. term for 'flea markets'] are located on the margins of, indeed often beyond, conventional understandings of re-tail space, and that they are placed there through the workings of regulatory power – a power that in this case is about protecting existing, often monop-olistic, market environments through processes that both seek to 'other' car-boot sales and constrict the spaces in which they might operate. (Gregson and Crewe 2003, 20)

Building salvage yards and flea markets are both located on the periphery of ur-ban areas. Those 'outer locations' set the framework for value creation and de-termine the geographic boundaries of second-hand zones. The second-hand sites are the product of possibilities and entrepreneurial imaginaries that work with and occasionally against the landscapes of power created and controlled by first-hand market capital (ibid). Remarkable transitional second-hand ex-change spaces are revealed in Gregson and Crewe's book, *Second-hand Cultures*, where things are trapped in time and space, waiting for revaluation, with life cycles that are prolonged almost infinitely. Flea markets in the Global South are often pushed to the social and geographical periphery of urban areas due to their waste trade, their association with informality, and the fact that the populations who attend flea markets are often socially and economically neglected and excluded (Seale, 2015).

In the ship-breaking examples that follow, a beach on the coast of India becomes a transitional gap for revaluing discarded commodities with divergent reuse activities. In conceptualizing waste and materiality, Gregson and Crang (2010) question the connection between waste and its management as a technological accomplishment. Waste has been understood primarily through the lens of its treatment and management practices. They argue for a paradigm shift: waste is a social construction and not just a category (ibid). The classification of waste as a stable entity fails to recognize the performative and dynamic function that disposal plays. Their case studies show that ship breaking practices enable the undoing of ships. In their research situated in Chittagong-Bangladesh, Gregson and others focus on end-of-life ships that no longer function as vessels but rather as thousands of tons of scrap steel (Gregson et al. 2010). In their work, Sitakunda beach is analyzed as a kind of lab where materials are transformed into new commodities through dangerous and poisonous processes. They argue that discarded ships are brought to this place from different regions across the globe because the "arts of transience" are so eloquently situated on that beach, and also, the dismantling of waste is loosely regulated there (Hawkins 2010, 123). The art of transience represents ethical concerns about sustainability that are based on everyday transactions. According to their research, through informal practices of transience, ninety-nine percent of the ships' materials are recycled into steel reinforcement bars for concrete used in construction in the Bay of Bengal. This is done by:

> Confining attention to movement up the value chain... and, paying attention to point of sale commodities, following the things research works to stabilize things in the still life of the object form. This stabilizes the object by stilling material and placing it utterly at the command of capital. Flatter ontological perspectives such as vital materialism acknowledge that it takes much to hold things together and that material is both agentic and performative. (Gregson et al. 2010, 853)

As Gregson and others suggest, salvaging, deconstruction, and revaluation processes all include creative material appropriation and alteration in the 'chocky-chocky' furniture industry in the beaches of Chittagong. These researchers claim that witnessing materials in transitory states enables us to have a critical idea of the effort required to keep them together and break them apart.

The ontological thesis of their study emphasizes the intrinsically unstable properties of toxic waste materials. The breaking down of end-of-life ships reveal that things are assemblages that can always be dismantled. They conclude that every material has the capacity to be reassembled; nevertheless, some materials like asbestos should probably be stabilized and disposed of as wastes, regardless of how much maintenance effort it takes to do so in low-income contexts.

Waste is a dynamic and unpredictable material. Its transformative properties cultivate growth and development through its movement and formation. The unforeseeable identity of waste materials depends on their temporariness and capacity to create unexpected and unpleasant consequences. Such repercussions of waste appear in the case of the decomposition and production history of asbestos (Gregson, Watkins, and Calestani 2010; Mazzeo 2018). For example, building demolitions before the asbestos ban endangered waste workers and neighborhood dwellers' health in Turkey, which draws attention to the differences in waste management politics between the Global North and South. Waste regimes in the Global South allow divergent practices to emerge but ignore the environmental and health risks.

In a different debate, Gregson and others use a performance-based reading in regard to the disposal of asbestos (Gregson, Watkins, and Calestani 2010). They suggest broadening the concept of vital materialism from an ethical understanding of "generosity and enchantment" to "principles founded on respect, humility, responsibility, and astonishment towards those materials that most threaten human life" (ibid, 1165). The performativity of materials changes depending on human actions. For instance, asbestos is inactive in a building's wall or a ship's engine room, but after a disposal or salvage process alters its material state, it becomes active and agentic and endangers human health. It is primarily harmful within the zone of disposal and salvaging activities. Furthermore, the unregulated disassembling of large-scale commodities—by dismantling, carving, splitting, or pulling apart—is a transformative practice that includes a dissolution of form that animates other constituent materials. This concept of waste calls for seeing the material's life and capability as dynamic, association-forming, and dispersed across the material world.

Secondary lives of discarded commodities enable the achievement of new livelihoods through entrepreneurial activities. The presence of such materialities and active aspects of waste can lead to the creation of government management and planning mechanisms for controlling urban growth. Such growth is shaped through governmental policies and infrastructures relating to repair and maintenance:

> The city is able to reproduce itself because of never-ending activities of repair and maintenance, which are not just incidental but provide a good part of its dynamic, as they continually rinse away breakdowns. (Graham and Thrift 2007, 7)

Waste and its accompanying salvage businesses take place in peripheral spaces although they are needed for rinsing away breakdowns in the center. These locations are yet again examples of the 'distancing from waste' rhetoric. They are commonly deprived of the proper regulations that control and manage the process of material transformation and reuse. Often these salvage processes activate dangerous aspects of the materials that, in turn, damage human health and the environment. However, these clandestine places also provide somewhere that materials can be creatively reused.

2.2.2   Assemblage Urbanization and Incremental Construction

> The materials themselves are multiple and of differential lifespans, from the relative obduracy of red brick through to the throw-away character of stop-gap materials like sackcloth or polyester... Different materials within the assemblage are more or less stable, while some parts can have multiple uses and spend large periods of time unused, such as small storage tanks for times of water shortage, sandbags stored in anticipation of the monsoon or stored bricks for post-monsoon housing repairs. (McFarlane 2011a, 216)

Spatialization of the everyday depends on a variety of materials in constructions that have multiple functions. 'Assemblage urbanization' is a term that refers to how salvaged materials are gathered to create informal architecture. Here, it is essential to highlight the 'hippie modernism' of the 1970s. It was based on the idea that self-help and ad-hoc construction were integral parts of architecture and design (Jencks and Silver 1972). In critical urban theory, assemblage thinking is used to identify the socio-materiality of urban life and the relationships that construct it empirically (McFarlane 2011a; 2011b; Acuto 2011; Farias and Bender 2011; Simone 2011; Dovey 2012; 2014; Blok and Farias 2016). Coming from Bruno Latour and Isabelle Stengers, the concept of *cosmopolitics* plays a very supporting role for assemblage urbanism (Blok and Farias 2016). It reveals new ethical methods for co-constructing a shared environment with objects, infrastructures, and collectivities that coexist with humans. First, I look at the basic definition and properties of an assemblage to explain the social and material complexity of material salvage.

An assemblage is generated through its constituent components. A socio-material constellation of interrelationships between human and nonhuman parts equally participates in the whole without any hierarchy. Its philosophical meaning stems from a translation of the French word, *agencement*, which means 'layout, arrangement or alignment'. The term mainly stems from the philosophy of Deleuze and Guattari (Deleuze and Guattari 1987). According to Gilles Deleuze, an assemblage is a multiplicity made up of several heterogeneous forms; it creates ties and relationships between systems across different realms and is continuously subject to transformation (Parnet and Deleuze 2002, 132). As a tool for explaining social complexity, assemblage thinking is used as an anti-structural term that refers to emergence, heterogeneity, peripherality, and ephemerality (Marcus and Saka 2006; Farias and Bender 2011). The cartography of the *çıkmacıs'* assemblage is very complex but it can be seen as the convergence of the following actors: reclaimers (scrap collectors and demolishers), demolition discards (waste), urban transformation projects, laws, regulations, second-hand markets, supply yards, refugees, migration networks, cooperativism, communication, earthquake, transportation infrastructure and many others.

Through transformation, the dynamics of assemblages change in different phases at any point in time. The concept of territorialization and deterritorialization designate the transformation and the dimension of the assemblage (DeLanda 2006). Any procedure which breaks down or changes the boundaries of space or "increases internal heterogeneity is considered deterritorialization" (ibid, 13). As an example of such deterritorialization, demolition activity is a pertinent process in that it decomposes the materiality of a building assembly, downgrades the worth of building components, and supplies a surplus of discarded materials.

To differentiate between different assemblages and their transforming phases, De Landa introduces two parameters to analyze social structures: territorialization and coding (ibid, 13). By adding two adjustable variables, he parametrizes the assemblage concept to eliminate binary oppositions and dualities that polarize conceptual approaches for explaining social ontology.

Territorialization, that is, stratification, describes how well the identity and border of a social body are defined:

> The conflict between communities, in short, tends to sharpen their bound-aries and to force them to become less tolerant of internal differences. This causes the assemblage to rigidify and homogenize; that is, to increase its degree of territorialization. (Ibid, 126)

A particular assemblage can be a deterritorialized system with loose borders. First, the relationships between its components blend with each other. Second, code is an indicator of how much a syntax or algorithm influences a social en-tity (ibid). The syntax in social bodies emerges as rules, regulations, and laws that lead to dichotomies like formal and informal. One way that assemblages work as wholes through "relations of exteriority" is that they have individual capacities to interact with each other (ibid, 10). Exteriority means that com-ponents may be disconnected and inserted into a new assembly. Their proper-ties are emergent. For example, reuse practices enable discarded materials to be reassembled into another body in a geographically, socially, and economi-cally different setting. Dwelling, as a verb, can make new arrangements that displace and replace construction materials. Dwellings and other assemblies coexist to form the urban, which is a multiplicity:

> This process of socio-material engineering involves the translation of var-ious materials into new uses over time, including roofs that become, first, floors for sleeping then, later, spaces for renting out and ladders that shift from being access points to the roof to stairs for a new family living in a newly built shack on the roof... materials, such as the ladder or the corru-gated metal sheets, operate as functional systems that coordinate differ-ent domains, from the spaces of the shack to the aspirations and desires of the inhabitants and the availability of money and materials. (McFarlane 2011b, 658)

The incremental construction process of a favela dwelling in Paraisópolis (a neighborhood in São Paulo, Brazil) is interpreted in terms of assemblage ur-banism (ibid). Their dwellings are made from a colorful assemblage of cement and found objects like children's toys and discarded pieces of plastic and metal. He suggests that just such a socio-material assembly of discarded things begs the questions of what additional knowledge of the city it may provide, of how these activities of gathering, composing, aligning, and reusing could add to our understanding of urbanization. That is why McFarlane's study of a dwelling created by informal activities may indicate that urbanization is a gathering and assemblage process, an alignment of social and material activities.

In particular, he contends that the idea of assemblage is crucial for comprehending the spatially associated, productive, and processual character of the city. Generativity is defined as the momentum of capital accumulation within the unpredictable juxtapositions that define urban space. For instance, informal and formal urbanization's juxtapositions bring together the urban life in the Global South. The spatiality of an assemblage is formed by arbitrary proximities, disruptive occurrences, and regular everyday cycles of work, ambiance, and communality in addition to past and present capitalist dynamics. Therefore, the city could be conceptualized as multiple assemblages of everyday and imagined urbanisms supported by emergent infrastructural practices that deal with materials. This idea is based on the hypothesis that certain powerful agendas or groups can disperse and realign the elements of individual urban assemblages, but not with any pre- given spatial or temporal templates (planned urbanism) (McFarlane 2011a, 224). As an example, he points out that the favela as an urban setting is territorialized, deterritorialized, and reterritorialized by the municipality and international NGOs or other aid institutions as well as its residents. Such transformation is materialized within the dwelling level through the agency of discarded or affordable materials.

To demonstrate the significance of assemblage discourse in his research, McFarlane notes how particular materialities play an essential part in the configuration of urban inequality within the poor's everyday lives (ibid). For a subaltern cosmopolitanism that provides the new basis for new urban commons, such material networks may be seen as essential resources that construct the domesticity of informal settlements:

> The materialities of the home—whether in the form of housing objects ranging from sackcloth and corrugated iron to brick, breezeblock, and hydroform, or infrastructures of drainage, sanitation, water, or electricity—play a central role in the everyday lives and hardships faced by the poor. Housing within informal settlements is typically—though not exclusively—constructed individually and incrementally, using locally available materials, and often clustered in ways that depend on closely shared roofs, walls, and infrastructures. Infrastructures and the housing materials themselves often change, are added to or discarded over time, revealing

a complex rhythm of assembling and reassembling that is central to the form and nature of domestic life. (Ibid, 216)

Assembling and reassembling processes of materials in incremental urbanism is closely associated with the agentic roles of reused and recycled materials. These construction processes consider materials a resource separate from industrial recycling, that is, not as a raw material but as a necessary object that reflects the urban inequalities and uneven distribution of urban resources. Squatters build their homes by collecting materials from "local construction debris, riverbeds, manufacturing waste, or patches of tree cover" (ibid, 216). It is crucial to underline the role of materiality in how urban informality is made, unmade, and remade by these apparatuses. Simultaneously, relational practices are the embodiment of foresight that senses how to make the next maneuver with the incremental accumulation of potentials and possibilities:

> The surface... is a de-signed built environment, an act of fabrication in both senses of the word – i.e., something that is put together from available materials and something that need not tell the "truth" of a given situation, whether that situation refers to the process through which the built environment was constructed, what it was intended to be used for, or what use can be made of it. (Simone 2015, 26)

The harmony of the surface with its patchwork combination depends on the complexity of its social layers. The surface renders explicit not just harmony in terms of an economic or spatial evaluation but also the way that particular socioeconomic classes can improve their surroundings (ibid). For example, building practices in Turkey rely on collage, composition, and gathering methods. Inhabitants of post-colonial areas have had to rely on their incrementalist and relational practices of survival. They have the ability to salvage the components of the urban surface, which is a hybridization of their physical surroundings, livelihoods, social connections, and socioeconomic status. Such gradual and interim development, which relies on small investments and the cheapest available materials, characterizes construction and repair activities in the Global South (Greene and Rojas 2008; McFarlane 2011b; Silver 2014; Dovey 2014).

McFarlane adopts the notion of assemblage thinking by offering three conceptual categories: descriptive orientation, rethinking agency, and critical imaginary (McFarlane 2011a, 2). First, he claims that ethnography is a descriptive orientation and methodological tool that investigates dynamic processes and everyday practices in-depth and with thick description. In paying comprehensive and empirical attention to relational conditions of actants in which socio-material assemblages are formed, urban researchers can better grasp how current urban inequalities are shaped in everyday life. A significant contribution that assemblage thinking could bring to critical urbanism is the revealing of ethnographies of specific urban resources. For instance, to redefine waste as an urban common would reveal the emerging uses and possibilities of materials. Furthermore, it would provide a new viewpoint that could bring together the complexities of daily life and issues of broader economic change.

Secondly, he discusses that agency is distributed to all actants within the assemblage, not only to an overarching system or structure. Such a framework goes beyond conventional interpretations of human influence by acknowledging the significance of things such as infrastructure, waste, dwelling, etc. For McFarlane (ibid), urban socio-materiality is not a passive backdrop to urbanity but actively shapes cities. This everyday socio-materiality also reflects urban inequalities and possibilities that arise from such conditions. Through deploying a multitude of coexisting actants, assemblage thinking facilitates the discovery of new findings by expanding the socio-technical horizon to include "policy documents, housing and infrastructure materials, placards, banners, and picket lines, new and old technologies, software codes, credit instruments, money, commodities, or material conditions of urban poverty, dispossession and inequality" (ibid, 215). With this distributed agency perspective, heterogeneous demolition waste management can emerge as a resource for constructions peripheral to the development of urban areas.

Lastly, McFarlane argues that assemblage thinking has the potential to revitalize the urban imaginary through the adoption of a progressive cosmopolitanism. It suggests a more inclusive urban commons built on mutuality, solidarity, and opposition. Encouraging new methods of linking criticism with political activism, a form of a right-to-the-city, he sees assemblage as "collage, composition, and gathering" that "implicates a privileged us with an exploited they and uses that as a basis for collective recognition, forging solidarities and resistance" (ibid, 221–222).

Major criticisms of assemblage urbanism and its ontological assumptions are made by authors who believe that assemblage thinking is decontextualized in explaining the critical urban concepts without utilizing critical urbanism based on political economy (Brenner, Madden, and Wachsmuth 2011; Rankin 2011; Tonkiss 2011). It doesn't pay attention to the "context of contexts" and doesn't fully understand how capitalism shapes modern cities:

> In particular, the descriptive focus associated with ontological variants of assemblage urbanism leaves unaddressed important explanatory questions regarding the broader (global, national, and regional) structural contexts within which actants are situated and operate—including formations of capital accumulation and investment/disinvestment; historically entrenched, large-scale configurations of uneven spatial development, territorial polarization and geopolitical hegemony; multi-scalar frameworks of state power, territorial alliance formation and urban governance; and the politico-institutional legacies of sociopolitical contestation around diverse forms of dispossession, deprivation and discontent. (Brenner, Madden, and Wachsmuth 2011, 233)

Brenner et al. challenge three critiques of assemblage urbanism (ibid). The first criticism is directed toward the micro-focus on socio-materiality from an ontological perspective; they claim that this neglects the influence of the global economic power relations that structure and influence urban life. Second, regarding these urban topics, they find that the ontological perspective of assemblage thinking is abstract and indefinite; it is disconnected from the critical issues that urban political economy problematizes. Third, instead of focusing on certain institutions and social dynamics, their assemblage thinking highlights the importance of nonhuman actors (ibid). It proposes ambiguous forms of material and human relations and anonymous political powers as a way to understand the constitution of urban inequality, precarious living conditions, and uneven development. They conclude that it's vital to use assemblage thinking's methodological experimentation and intellectual risk-taking to build a critical urban theory that is still based on the geopolitical economy. However, for McFarlane, assemblage thinking is not about setting up a new ontology for critical urbanism. Rather, he prefers a strategy that combines assemblage thinking with other critical, activist, and underrepresented practices through highlighting urban life, thick description, and politicized radical commons (McFarlane, 2011c, 738). Rather than replacing political economy, assemblage thinking calls for a new understanding of capitalism as the result of socio-material processes. Simone finds the socio-material in the "surfaces of urban life" (Simone 2011, 357).

Simone's remark aims to lead the assemblage debate away from abstract issues and toward notions that attempt to understand urban living empirically (ibid). He is concerned with the reductionist methods that approach the topic only in terms of capitalist accumulation and exploitation. However, his point is not that political economy approaches are irrelevant, but rather that analysis of capitalism does not lead to a complete description of urban sites, in particular to what he refers to as surfaces and urbanization customs (ibid, 362). Simone interprets assemblage thinking as an observation method focusing on urban life in particular locations and comprehending how urban life is carried out. He does not interpret urban surfaces only through the perspective of control, commodification, and dispossession of capital. He observes them through more repetitive, complex, and obscure processes of adaptation and collaboration. To reinforce his point, he refers to the Tanah Abang textile market in Jakarta. He identifies the market as a multi-layered surface that, while being made up of a dominant controlling class, overarching politics, and commodification, also has, at the same time, the affiliations and collaborations of its people and trade practices that share common opportunities, experiences, memories, risks, and struggles within and beyond the surface level of the market surface:

> There are surfaces of compliance, orderly distributions of space, opportunity, and costs, of obeisance to formal authority and surfaces of continuous rehearsal. Here, the market becomes an occasion to reiterate memories of association and to provisionally explore new ones; where the buying and selling is the mechanism and incentive to chart out transactions and affiliations that 'shift things around'—materials, opportunities, connections, information, affects—that provide a critical supplement to people's urban lives. (Ibid, 363)

In explaining relational practices that revolve around market spaces, Simone remarks on repair services and the trade of second-hand items (Simone 2015). His empirical studies often focus on markets where such informal practices accumulate. Below the surface of urban life in Tanah Abang's market dynamics, the interplay between the formal and informal is interpreted as a certain strategic mode: he describes the level of accessibility as contingent upon how one navigates the market's happenings and activities (Simone 2011).

A comparable notion of such a dynamic setting resides in Rahul Mehrotra's concept of "kinetic city" as "ephemeral urbanism" versus the "static orderly city" (Mehrotra, Vera, and Mayoral 2017, 17). In the cities of the Global South, as opposed to the two-dimensional modern ways of building cities, he states that the temporary quality of the kinetic city derives from incremental and informal urbanization. The environment is usually built with recycled and adjustable materials like "plastic sheets, scrap metal, canvas, and waste wood"; a typical example of this would be local marketplaces that accommodate street vending, festivals, and pop-up dwellings inhabited by marginalized people (ibid, 18). Unlike cities constructed with steel and glass using the futuristic designs of utopic urban planners, most emerging cities are built from clay bricks, straw, recycled plastic, pumice blocks, and scrap wood (Davis 2006, 19). Living with waste is a daily reality for people and communities in the Global South. Waste is linked to physical and social precarity, deteriorating living circumstances, and economic restrictions and support processes (Bell 2017). Waste is turned into useable resources via adaptive recycling methods in which people's networks, services, and infrastructure are expanded beyond the confines of the contemporary modern city: "In this way a kinetic city recycles the static city to create a new spectacle, new conditions, and unexplored possibilities" (Mehrotra, Vera, and Mayoral 2017, 19). The transience of the city is not only fixed to the materiality of the space but also to the movement of its people. The flux of the kinetic city relies on functioning infrastructures that connect urban and rural.

For instance, introducing circulatory urbanism, Echanove and Srivastava discuss a concept of acknowledging a commuter urbanity that rejects the static city and the perception of the duality between rural and urban that includes accessible movement and communication in-between (Echanove and Srivastava 2014). They defend the urban-rural continuum because of its historical economic and social dependency on seasonal labor. Their perspective is based on the fact that, no matter how far away, they keep their connection with where they come from, their village. To put it differently, various social dynamics are shaped over time, such as social networks; religious and familial relationships; and shared labor skills and knowledge bases (Simone 2015). To a great extent, the achievement of circular urbanity relies on these social systems and the prioritization of infrastructural needs that authorize the individual's mobility. Without the entrepreneurial initiative of the people and accessibility of urban infrastructure, it is questionable whether or not the villagers could continue to exist on the margins of the megacity.

Assemblage urbanism reads this heterogenous whole in a flat non-hierarchical perspective that possesses the value of being a distributed agency.

Second-hand markets could be analyzed using the concept of assemblage urbanism because they are made up of human and nonhuman actants and their connections. A network of things and practices forms a relational whole that functions heterogeneously. It works with the potential, emergent, generative and contingent characteristics of the assemblage. While second-hand markets are still attached to the historical accumulation of capital, they are also open to unpredictable outcomes. For instance, informal ship-breaking activities enable a second-hand furniture sector. This sector is an outcome of the global waste trade and everyday survival strategies of economically-excluded communities. Favelas or *gecekondus* are built as the result of the multiplication of social and material processes. In this context, discarded materials are in a transitional state in which waste is not a category but a sociomaterial construction of the environment. Furthermore, incremental construction processes of informal dwelling display practical (real) and imagined (ideal) urbanization juxtapositions. As Simone (Simone 2011) argued, assemblage urbanism is a heuristic tool to understand the urban surfaces containing reassembled materials, unexpected possibilities, experimental maneuvers and prospective experiences.

In my book, socio-materiality of waste and relational aspects around dwelling production are interpreted into the material, labor, and economic relationship (second-hand market) that shows how unrecognized forms of income generation are constituted around the waste. Generally, waste scholarship associates informality with infrastructural labor and its relationship with formal management systems. Next, I will discuss informality as a mode of relationality between the unrecognized actors of infrastructural assemblage.

2.3 Waste Labor

As a concept, urban informality therefore cannot be understood in ontological or topological terms. Instead, it is a heuristic device that uncovers the ever-shifting urban relationship between the legal and illegal, legitimate and illegitimate, authorized and unauthorized... that serves to deconstruct the very basis of state legitimacy and its various instruments: maps, surveys, property, zoning and, most importantly, the law. (Roy 2011, 233)

The informality of building salvage is not an indicator of a unique economy or recycling market. It is a complex bundle of political, economic, institutional, and material processes across time. It should not be regarded as a pre-given and stable category because it is ever-transforming and dynamic. The margins between the formal and informal are territorialized and deterritorialized by the trade routes of the unregulated second-hand market. Codes represent dominating political and economic power facilitated by regulations and laws. They include a set of principles or policies that determine the relationality between the informal labor and formal market dynamics. These margins constantly interplay with each other, forming divergent networks and relationships. Altering the informal and formal dualisms, assemblage thinking can explain the shifting lives of people dealing with poverty who are continuously going into and out of informality. Changing laws, government regulations and waste management systems often cause building-salvage practices to find heretofore unrecognized new valuation systems through the trade of CDW.

2.3.1 Infrastructural Maneuvers

Within modernizing processes of economic, social, and cultural systems, the people who are coping with urban poverty in the Global South already find it hard to adjust to market structure, contracts, exchange values, speed, and bureaucracy. In addition to these struggles, it is important to interpret informalization as a spatial, societal, and economic adaptation process. Informalization of urban life is influenced by global economic integration schemes, the deregulation of prices in the real estate market, the weakening of welfare resources (reduction of social programs, subsidies for common goods), and clientelist privatization (Bayat 1997, 20). To discuss the shift from socialist and populist regimes to liberal economic policies in the context of Middle Eastern cities, Bayat argues that the increasing number of marginalized urban poor are based on processes of financial restructuring, economic integration, informalization, and social exclusion (Bayat 2000). To tackle this, economically disadvantaged individuals slowly find their own strategies of survival. To acquire the basic necessities of their lives (land for shelter, urban collective consumption, informal jobs, business opportunities, and public space), individuals and families engage in modestly quiet and collaborative livelihood strategies that are informal and sometimes illegal (Bayat 2004, 257).

Bayat's assessment is informed by Michel de Certeau's (Certeau [1984] 2013) idea of the 'practice of everyday life' as a collection of methods that are capable of dismantling the authoritarian structure of power and discipline. He is intrigued by the spontaneous and disorganized spatial outcomes of the marginalized. What Bayat means by "the quiet encroachment of the ordinary" is the urban poor's life-long and subtle search for social and economic security, a search that navigates the overarching dynamics such as globalization and financialization; the ultimate goal is to maintain or look for autonomy in unaffected circumstances and environments (Bayat 2000, 536). This encroachment by subaltern people results in the emergence of street politics that fundamentally change the city (Bayat 1997). While describing 'the habitus of the dispossessed', Bayat (2007, 580) argues that urban life is epitomized by adaptability, pragmatism, negotiation, and an endless battle for survival and self-development. These kinds of interventions are searching for an exit from the globalized economic order (ibid).

Comparable in some respects, Abdoumaliq Simone (2004; 2006; 2015) relates how residents in an African city establish habits and routines that help them become resourceful despite the lack of available infrastructure. The key to overcoming such a crisis is to "multiply" the functionality of "documents, technologies, houses, [and] infrastructure" regardless of what materials need to be appropriated for production; and this shows their capacity to mobilize people "with different skills, perspectives, linkages, identities and aspirations" (Simone 2006, 358). He refers to these practices in non-binary terms, defining them as 'relational infrastructures' produced by community associations as well as relationships that constitute the possible ways of inhabiting cities:

> These relationships are not just social events or descriptors of exchanges and transactions. They are not simply embodiments of sentiment or vehicles for organizing work, expenditure, attention, and recognition... Rather, they are materials themselves to be articulated in various forms in order to construct circulations of bodies, resources, affect and information. They are vehicles of movement and becoming, ways of mediating the constantly oscillating intersections of various times, spaces, economies, constraints and possibilities making up city life. (Simone 2015)

Thus, such infrastructure is not just the incarnation of particular materialities and operations but also a layer of exchanges and associations that exercise their own capacities in unexpected patterns. Infrastructure with its relational attributes acts as an assemblage. Infrastructure is a physical entity and a collection of social functions and relations. However, as has been well noted with respect to Southern cities, the locus of infrastructure continues to be fragmented because it is characterized by intermittent processes, resources, and temporality (Amin 2014; Simone 2015).

These maneuvers for the organization, expenditure, and recognition of work facilitate the circulation of bodies, resources, affects, and information. Simone (2015) suggests that collaboration and commonality are the key identifiers of how relational ties are constructed to create ways of income generation. According to him, the adjoining businesses can be deployed as a cohesive organization, pooling resources like equipment, connections and manpower. The transactional entrepreneurs are recognized as co-residents connected to one another by ethnicity, diverse habitation histories, traditional kinship relations and various networks of work organizations or economic orientations.

Besides the aspects of relationality discussed by Bayat and Simone, there is a great deal of related theoretical work within the context of informal labor that will be addressed in the next section.

2.3.2 Informal Waste Labor in the Global South and Turkey

The critical approach to the political economy of informal waste labor denounces the dualist tendency to separate the informal and formal sectors; instead, it sees the two as deeply associated with each other (Portes, Castells, and Benton 1989). Informal waste collectors are an unenviable part of post-colonial economic development and the transition away from an agriculture-based economy in the Global South (Gidwani 2013; 2015). Some see them as constituting a secondary sector attached to the formal market like the reuse and repair economy in India (Corwin 2018). This economy depends on global commodity markets that regulate material prices (ibid). Others discuss the vulnerability of informal labor in the environment of 'accumulation by dispossession' that is a consequence of urbanization (Gidwani and Reddy 2011). Another study, from Kavya Michael and others, analyzes informal labor as an 'arrival occupation' for the refugee and migrant population in Bangalore, India (Michael, Deshpande, and Ziervogel 2019).

More significantly, informality is embedded in waste systems based on the coexistence of heterogeneous socio-technical forms (Gidwani 2015). In a heterogenous waste regime, some of the researchers highlight the function of cooperatives that need strong support from the government in order to continue their micro-entrepreneur status in the Global South (Dias 2016; Gutberlet et al. 2017). By emphasizing the social and human resources aspect and taking into account various forms of collective organization, such as waste collector cooperatives, Dias and Gutberlet (2017) address livelihood commoning, security, social agencies (NGOs), social support, participatory policy-making, and decent working conditions. In other words, they address those socio-technical forms of waste collection that adapt to the governing system through the cooperation of dispersed actors (individual waste pickers). This resembles the concept of an assemblage, in that it "is a mode of ordering heterogeneous entities so that they [can] work together for a certain time" (Müller 2015, 28).

The existing research on waste pickers in Turkey is based on the conflicts between informal waste pickers and the state, recycling sector, and new regulations (Dinler 2016). A further study by Tuçaltan discusses the changing waste regime in Ankara and the coexistence of waste pickers with the formal waste management system (2018; 2019). In another study, the waste pickers' mobility in the city is examined by observing their territorial negotiations (Altay and Altay 2008). In yet another study, in Istanbul, the visual representation of waste pickers is politicized by using documentary video and photography (Şen and Artıkişler Kolektifi 2014).

The research on self-employed waste pickers in Turkey follows their confrontation with new state regulations and recycling market dynamics. In her dissertation combining ethnographic analysis and political economy, Dinler (2016) investigates how the waste pickers regulate the recycling market labor. In the context of Turkey's informal market, she reveals the local government's attempts to control the self-regulated structure by establishing formal legislation and interfering with the trade by forcibly decreasing recycling exchange rates. Going further, she argues that the solidarity organizations of the waste pickers are crucial for their access to social welfare. In her study, the role of social associations, such as those of kinship or tribe, are a significant aspect of wealth accumulation when it comes to questions like warehouse ownership or where waste is stored. Lastly, she reveals how, from within the global market, the London Metal Exchange also sets the prices in the local recycling market in Ankara (ibid). Her study shows that, by following the currency of metals, the local exchange value of recycling materials (as raw input for the recycling industry) is regulated by global markets. Importantly she suggests that although the recycling market appears independent because of its self-employed and informal nature, the financial institution's rules and policies regulate the dynamics of the market (ibid).

Although the arrival of formal actors and technology changed the labor structure in the early 2000s, informal players have remained an essential feature of Tuçaltan's work on Ankara's waste systems (Tuçaltan 2019). She investigates the connections between urban waste governance and capitalist urbanization in regard to the urban regeneration of landfills. She links the urban transformation of a landfill area with the *gecekondu* squatters around it through their connections with the socio-technical advancement in waste management and municipal investment to create luxurious dwellings. She points out that the destruction of storage spaces belonging to waste pickers forces them to leave the area and sell their collection for low prices rather than ending the informal recycling. According to her findings, waste was transformed from being useless to being a resource. She claims that "urban planning serves as a tool to transform an open dumping site, and this socio-technical transformation became an instrument for the acquisition of land rent" (ibid,10).

The waste paper collectors named themselves the 'papermen' in Ankara (Altay and Altay 2008). Altay's artistic research on the papermen shows that the precious and the discardable can coexist and displace one another. Observing the movements of the papermen and logging them into a diary with his observations, he mapped their movements in Ankara's neighborhoods. His methodology covers the relationships and hierarchy between different types and groups of recycling workers. The hierarchy depends on their kinship and ethnicity (ibid). Another critical artistic research by a collective called *Leftover-works* (Artıkişler) focuses on the papermen from a cinematic perspective that problematizes the representation of waste labor, focusing on their conflicts with the local government, which aims to ban collecting from the streets. Their surveys and interviews in video format reflect upon the oppressive urban politics of AK Party on the poor and refugee workers from Syria (Şen and Artıkişler Kolektifi 2014). Their work shows that documentation based on video and photography is a beneficial medium for ethnographic research. They use activism through media and exhibitions that problematize the rights of informal recycling workers.

The studies on waste collectors in the Global South are also important for comprehending informality as a continuum of the capitalist system in Turkey. Informal labor is an integral part of heterogeneous waste management. In these assemblages, *çıkmacıs* have a different relationship with waste when it comes to its potential to be counted as a common resource because they do not glean from the street, but instead deal in construction scrap. Additionally, they commodify materials in the second-hand market. However, they are vulnerable to dualist and legalist policies since they operate in recycling sectors by collecting and sorting waste.

2.4 Conclusion

This chapter maps different theorizations of waste for assembling a framework to comprehend production and revaluation of second-hand components and recycled materials. Waste is a social matter that originates from interactions with humans and nonhumans (Bell 2019; Bauman 2011). Some conceptualizations of waste ignore the unbreakable and existential relationship between modernity and waste in the Global South and they create distance between humans and waste. By tapping into new materialism and actant ontology, the agency of waste is highlighted to create a ground for focusing on empirical studies based on the global circulation of end-of-life objects revaluation through the secondary sectors. Additionally, the issue of disposability of plastic objects raises ethical considerations on the sustainability of the recycling industry (Hawkins 2009).

My encounter with reclaimed materials transcribes the 'dramatic and subtle' effects of trash piles (Bennett 2010, 6) that precedes practical and aesthetic processes in reclamation building elements. The term, actant, borrowed from Bruno Latour (2007) underlines the agency of discarded matter within a sociotechnical assemblage which interconnects demolition practices, second-hand trade, and building construction. Therefore, the political and social features of recycling are debated around ethical concerns through the concept of disposability that centers ethical behaviors and habits into environmentalism (Hawkins 2010). The conceptual framework of material reclamation apprehends the corporal relationship between waste labor and the materiality of waste.

The formalization of waste infrastructure is a capital venture for profit-driven systems like real estate that feed from the creation and speculation of urban land value. These dynamics further reflect the shifting waste regimes hinged on infrastructure, actors, power struggles, and valorization dichotomies. On the other hand, the notion of assemblage thinking is a ground for portraying an empirical sensitivity to the ways in which waste and people continuously interact, merge, and reconfigure one another to weave the urban fabric of everyday situations. Incremental means of informal dwellings is a gathering process that implies how urbanization is an assembly process and how waste is reused creatively (Dovey 2014). The complexity and dynamics of urbanization as a process are illuminated through temporary and transient socio-material interventions.

The notion of the practice of the everyday is reviewed within studies that conceptualize and politicize livelihood activities and entrepreneurial maneuvers of dwellers (Bayat 2013; Simone 2015). The inner dynamics of urban life appear to depend on social and material relations beyond the political economy's concept of the urban. Informality is defined as the shifting mode of power relationships between institutions, regulations, codes, policies and the efforts of ordinary people. Such scholarship reveals an intricate micropolitics. A strategic provision of makeshift infrastructural systems and spatial practices permits individual dwellers and social communities on the outskirts of rapidly expanding megacities to develop a good affiliation with local and global institutions. The scholarship on informal forms of infrastructural waste labor in the Global South reviewed their emergence into the heterogenous whole (Gidwani 2015; Tuçaltan 2018). Additionally, waste picker cooperatives are seen as the conjoining continuum between the informal and formal processes. My main argument in bringing together such a review is to highlight the ways in which the materiality of waste and human interventions are strongly bound to each other through relational networks.

Nevertheless, I base my research on the *çıkmacıs* who are invisible mediators of such material agency. Their role is two-fold: as part of the secondary sector (Corwin 2018) and as off-the-record migrant workers for the recycling industry (Michael, Deshpande, and Ziervogel 2019). The agentic materiality of second-hand components is vital for places where incremental (Dovey 2014), ephemeral (Mehrotra, Vera, and Mayoral 2017), and assemblage urbanism (McFarlane 2011a) takes place in the Global South and late-modern countries like Turkey.

While the political economy may help to explain the elevated level of discontinuity between formal and informal forces, it is more likely that this seeming discontinuity conceals some type of distributed agency at play (Simone 2011). On the one hand, I utilize political economy to explain the neoliberal politics that instrumentalize urban demolitions for profit. On the other hand, I use assemblage thinking to micro-focus on material aspects of socio-material relations in building salvage and incremental dwelling construction. In the context of the study, the core concerns of the critical political economy remain fundamental for analyzing capitalism's influence on the commodification of land and urban transformation in an ontological sense. Still, by employing assemblage thinking as its central analysis and empirical concept, the study extends into a new inquiry of nonhuman agency and everyday urban life redefined around urban informality.

3. Methodological Reflections

3.1 Introduction

> Ethnography is a theory of
> description.
> *(Nader 2011, 212)*

My involvement with the *çıkmacıs* in Istanbul started with my cross-disciplinary 2012 MA exhibition (see Ch.1.5), which had the goal of gaining new information through practice-based research. As I dwelled deeper into the subject, I became interested in the livelihood of demolition workers and scrap collectors. My further academic pursuit shifted from artistic research to a Ph.D. in urban studies because I also desired to discuss the subject using urban theory. Because urbanization is one of the key factors in how *çıkmacıs* emerged in the city as a profession associated with the development and maintenance of the city, I was interested in ethnography as a methodological tool to capture the social and urban aspects of them.

I consider ethnography an interdisciplinary research method that different disciplines can utilize in their field practices. Assemblage thinking emphasizes a thick description of informal trajectories and diverse worlds (McFarlane 2011a). Further, thick description itself entails a microfocus on the subject of the fieldwork while, at the same time, the researchers analyze and reflect on their own social, cultural, political point of view as well as their personal interpretation on specific context (Geertz 1973, 3).

For example, the research on ship-breaking (Gregson et al. 2010) uses ethnography to analyze the second-hand furniture market. Follow-the-thing methodology is utilized to describe the ways which end-of-life things are utilized to create secondary industry in subaltern places. Ships and furniture are nonhuman elements that validate the agency of things with multi-faceted analysis of ethnographic fieldwork. Simone's conceptualization of relational infrastructures is also a result of micro focus on everyday tactics based on relations between people in the Global South. Additionally, the fieldwork on market spaces conceptualizes repair and maintenance practices constituted by everyday alliances and common aims (Simone 2015). Using concepts that identify "human and nonhuman relationships and affects, assemblage ethnographies uncover new subjectivities that blur 'the boundaries between researcher and researched' and enables both to become active participants in emerging assemblage agencies" (Ghoddousi and Page 2020, 3). During the research, it was necessary to identify the two important actants; humans (*çıkmacıs*) and nonhumans (earthquakes, second-hand construction elements, second-hand markets, supply yards, and urban transformation policies). According to empirical analysis, the assemblage of *çıkmacıs* brings together three different empirical themes:

- The role of informal labor in material reclamation
- Second-hand trade infrastructure: social networks (relational via migration) and supply yards (spatial)
- Materiality of second-hand construction elements in building construction and environment degradation.

Accomplishing the fieldwork requires long-term engagement; a concern for informal knowledge and everyday practices; and the discipline to listen to all aspects of the field (ibid). That being said, I should make it clear that my time in the area was not during an intense period or at a specific location, which is how most conventional ethnographic research is conducted. My fieldwork spanned 4 years between 2015 and 2019 and included several condensed research periods scattered between these years. Prior to that, the preliminary research for my master thesis took place between 2012 and 2014. As a result, I could see the changing second-hand market dynamics through Turkey's unsteady economy.

By following the *çıkmacıs'* trajectory, I was exposed to demolitions and second-hand trade. The mobility of human and nonhuman actors suggested a multi-sited ethnography. In the summer of 2018, I took a month-long research trip to Ankara, Kayseri, Nevşehir, and Niğde, all of which are places where second-hand components are traded. Later I traveled to Tbilisi, Georgia, to find importers of second-hand parts. I transcribed 35 interviews and wrote field notes, including sketches, participant observations, and go-along interview notes each day during my time in the field. Before data analysis, I translated them from Turkish to English. I selected informants—presented under pseudonyms—according to their active participation in the fieldwork, the size of their facilities, the type of activities and their development history.

In addition to profession-based ethnography at multiple sites, I employed the 'follow the thing' methodology (Marcus 1995) to trace the commodity chain of second-hand building components within a regional geography.

3.2 'Follow the Thing' Approach

In 1986, anthropologist Arjun Appadurai coined the phrase 'follow the thing', which was expanded upon in 1995 by another anthropologist, George Marcus. Both urged researchers to conduct multi-site studies based on following things, including their processes of production, trade, use, and disposal. Arjun Appadurai suggests that things should be analyzed by following their configurations, purposes, and movements because he believed that things have their own social lives (Appadurai 1986). Additionally, he claimed that the actual and historical circulation of things cannot be brought to light by an approach limited by the assumption that things have no significance other than through those qualities endowed to them by human transactions, attributions, and motives (ibid, 3). He suggested that "even though from a theoretical point of view human actors encode things with significance, from a methodological point of view it is the things-in-motion that illuminate their human and social context" (ibid, 5). Based on these ideas, I interpret this thing-oriented emphasis as a way to understand the dynamics in the second-hand commodity chain.

George Marcus' (1995) invites geographers to participate in multi-sited fieldwork because of globalization. His call is fundamentally oriented towards exploring the movement of culture, artifacts, and identities in dispersed time-space. Further, he makes clear that "although multi-sited ethnography is an exercise in mapping terrain; its goal is not holistic representation, an ethnographic portrayal of the world system as a totality" (ibid, 99). Marcus' ambitions instead lie in cross-cutting between the local and global to find parts that are both in and out of the system; these parts are represented as subaltern, a term which refers to colonized subjects that are socially, politically, and geographically excluded. For him, fieldwork strategies "following connections, associations, and putative relationships are thus at the very heart of designing multi-sited ethnographic research" (ibid, 97). Moreover, the approach aimed to de-fetishize commodities (Harvey 1990, 418) by linking customers to previously unseen, unheard, unknown, and underappreciated producers from countries all over the world.

David Harvey highlights the importance of revealing globalized commodity changes in order to investigate the exploitation of labor and resources in the Global South (ibid). Following Harvey, Ian Cook and others to conduct a series of follow the thing studies entitled 'Geographies of food: following' (Cook et al. 2006). Specifically, the study on the papaya supply chain "outlines the findings of multi-locale ethnographic research of food globalization, focusing on a supply chain stretching from UK supermarket shelves to a Jamaican farm, and concluding in a North London flat" (Cook 2004, 642). This study's unique multi-locale ethnography identifies all the human and nonhuman actors and portrays their invisible relationships. The research reveals how exploitation at the production sites provokes moral and ethical positions.

Initially, the 'follow the thing' approach was only used to study a restricted set of commodities in a supply chain, primarily within the food and fashion industries (Mintz 1986; Dwyer and Jackson 2003; Barnett et al. 2005). Beginning around 2015, the range of research subjects was expanded to include low-end items and waste; inexpensive China-produced commodities (Hulme 2015; 2017); ship breaking (Gregson et al. 2010); and toxic waste (Balayannis 2020). These approaches, which I will discuss in the following sections, are former studies that inspired my research methodology.

Journeys of Low-End Commodities

In her book, *On the Commodity Trail: The Journey of a Bargain Store Product from East to West*, Alison Hulme traces the trajectory of low-end commodities (e.g., a plastic Buddha statue) from their manufacture origins as raw material in a Chinese landfill through regional factories, international trade centers, distribution networks, online marketplaces, western bargain stores, and finally, to the consumer's front door (Hulme 2015). In her ethnography that traces the backend of the value chain, she identifies the key sites (landfill, factory, container ship, port, and bargain store) and its key players (waste peddler in Shanghai, wholesale buyer in Yiwu, container ship captain, dock worker, store owner, and customer). Her research attempts to encompass a global commodity chain. However, at the end of her study, she notes some untraceable elements of the equation:

[S]low parts of the chain, the older, clunkier mechanisms backing up the mouse-clicking efficiencies of speedy capitalism at the front of the house, the grinding rust of the container ports, with their spilled contents, breakages, illicit cargos (sometimes of people), industrial accidents, and an incessant nature that still breaks workers despite things having changed from previous eras. (Hulme 2017, 159)

Within these ruptures, she refers to things and lives that are lost, altered, dropped, or evaluated as useless, their existence appearing and vanishing in the blink of an eye: "Rupture is so frequently now the norm, a 'flow' of micro-catastrophes at each part of the chain, that serves to make it stronger but polarize the lives of those along its trajectory" (ibid,159).

The most relevant part of Hulme's research for my fieldwork is the first part where she describes the 'dump towns' where the journey of plastic products generally begins and often ends in China. Much of this waste, which comes from both local and western countries, is recycled into tiny pellets, which are melted down and molded into new products in regional factories. She explores the livelihoods of waste peddlers and how they are exploited by various capitalist forces. According to her, following the object across multiple sites brings the researcher into gaps and ruptures in the slow parts of the chain, and a micro-focus on these instances can clearly reintroduce the role and condition of the subaltern within a globalized economic system (Hulme 2015).

Dismantling practices

The second example is the investigation of the shipbreaking industry on Sitakunda beach near Chittagong (Discussed in Ch. 2.2.1) (Gregson, et al. 2010). The ships, which were built in the Global North, are sent to eastern locations like Turkey and the Global South. It is necessary for my 'follow the thing' research to take into account discarded commodities shipped to newly industrialized countries for disassembly or recycling.

This fieldwork focuses on end-of-life ships broken down for their scrap value in Bangladesh. It looks at how local furniture businesses known as 'chock-chocky' reclaim materials from these disassembled ships and rework them into new furniture to sell to middle-class Bangladeshi customers. Their study points out many fieldwork difficulties, such as the difficulty contacting customers who suspect that the study supports the efforts of NGOs to stop shipbreaking. In order to access the households that purchased chock-chocky furniture, they mainly interviewed women. Their study is not entirely positive when it comes to shipbreaking resources. They worry that reuse, recycling, and remanufacturing could have negative effects on where end-of-life things are being discarded or put out of sight. Those effects, unfortunately, result in environmental degradation, climate change, neglect of labor health and safety, unequal distribution of income, and exploitation of migrant and refugee labor.

Gregson and others remark (ibid) that these locations where the process of dismantling and recycling are articulated are places where waste is weakly controlled or unregulated. These places host the movement of unwanted commodities near the end of their useful lives. On the verge of economic expansion and development, the presence of secondary markets like furniture production via shipbreaking is beneficial for establishing local livelihoods. However, it is essential to acknowledge that such integrated circular systems come with invisible costs. Because the release of materials like asbestos or toxic fumes can be hazardous for the dismantlers and the environment itself (Gregson, Watkins, and Calestani 2010).

Toxic Waste Disposal

In an ethnographic study by Angeliki Balayannis a chemical stockpile in Tanzania was 'followed' throughout the process of its removal from its storage location in Tanzania (Balayannis 2020). The materialities of hazardous waste, in this case the pesticide DDT, are highlighted in her landmark research through her examination of common disposal methods and their infrastructure. Hazardous material movements are unjust but legal, and they have complex narratives in their Global North-to-South context. The Global South countries agree to receive industrial or solid waste from the Global North that will be stored or recycled there. For example, England and the European Union still sell separated plastic to Turkey but it is not sustainably recycled there (Greenpeace 2022). In short, in terms of waste disposal, Western capitalism exploits these underregulated countries.

The stockpile of DDT waste was shipped from Greece to an enclosed site in Tanzania in 1987. Later, it was sent back to Poland to be incinerated. Across time and space, Balayannis (2020) broadens the spectrum of relevant parties in waste economies and pays attention to hidden discarding practices. She addresses the removal process by interacting with participants in the Africa Stockpiles Programme (ASP), including government agencies, universities, intergovernmental organizations, non-governmental organizations, chemical producers, and disposal businesses (ibid, 773). What is more, she discusses participants' testimonials and bureaucratic documents on pesticides via interviews, participant observation, photography, and archive study (ibid, 774).

Her way of using assemblage thinking aims to achieve two methodological goals. First, she examines how waste material is transformed through its disposal process. For her, the effectiveness of the disposal activity is always dependent on material aspects, and she argues that maintaining coherence between remotely designated guidelines from the North and local operations is not as simple as it is recorded in the official documents (ibid). This occurs because the local officials in the hosting country do not have strict controls or the regulations are too loose to identify the level of hazard.

Secondly, using reports as evidence of removal, she focuses on bureaucratic representation and its relationship with the materiality of the waste management company (ibid). By doing this, she identifies removal reports as nonhuman actors representing corporate knowledge production and the lack of important contamination and safety details (ibid). Her conclusion puts the ethical superficiality of global institutions and their politics of toxic waste disposal in the Global South into question. The North knowingly sends their nonrecyclable waste to places where the regulations are lax. Plus, they never take any responsibility for the environmental degradation they cause in the South. As Balayannis so aptly observes: while it is physically impossible to dispose of the waste stockpile or eliminate its hazardous damage, it *is possible* to remove it from appearing on any official documents (ibid, 790).

The three examples discussed above focus on fractures, unattended materialities, and transformation of waste disposal practices that end up or start in newly industrialized subaltern geographies. Through their methods, they identify invisible actors; precarious labor; the agency of waste within a global commodity chain; and its negative degrading effects on the environment. I have found multiple commonalities between these precedents of these studies and my own follow the thing methodology.

3.3 Methods for Collecting Empirical Data

To gather empirical materials, I approached my field subject from a cross-disciplinary perspective. This systematic framework combines ethnographic, architectural, and artistic methods. In this subchapter, I describe how I combined participant observation, architectural surveying, interviews and photography.

3.3.1 Participant Observation and Architectural Surveying

Participant observation is a practice in which the researcher immerses themselves in a specific social setting while, at the same time, learning how to occasionally distance themself from that setting enough to be able to objectively observe, think critically, and write about what has been experienced (Bernard 2006). Throughout this process, my sketchbook became an apparatus for collecting spoken and visual fieldwork data found at the demolition site. Because of the mobility of the informants at their work sites, it was very challenging to take notes and follow them. I used an A6 size handbook, and my smartphone helped me deal with this challenge. Sometimes I had to take notes on my smartphone. It was a practical device for blending into everyday situations. I also used the device, with their permission, to take photographs and short videos documenting their activities.

The field notes and visual memos are the central and defining tools that I improved during my long-term fieldwork. At the end of each day, I had to transcribe the notes into clean copies while the visual documentation served as a guideline for remembering and translating the empirical material. The notes are accompanied by sketches of the apartment buildings, photographs of the environments, and videos of labor activity. The field notes and my sketchbook accompanied photographic and architectural surveys. Plus, I wrote category codes on the notes such as economy (value, second-hand trade), migration (rural, urban, refugee), waste management (reuse, recycle), urbanization (environment, urban transformation projects, demolition, *gecekondu*), politics and, labor (safety, livelihood).

My field notes and sketches were visual memorandums consisting of plan layouts of apartments in demolished blocks and supply yards. They documented some modern plan layouts from Turkey's apartmentalization period. If they weren't registered in archives, all the planning details were erased by demolitions. Based on those memos, I calculated an average number of building components that could be reclaimed, mainly interior and exterior façade openings. While visiting supply yards, I drew quick floor plan sketches to be used as visual memos. Later in the data analysis, utilizing satellite imagery by Google Earth, I created 3d diagrams of the scrap yards that showed the uses of the spaces. These drawings enabled me to develop a better understanding of the yard's differences in terms of size and design.

In these early stages of the research, my participation in the reclamation process was limited to being a passive observer. I carried out my own practice as a researcher and architect. From morning till night, I was actively surveying spaces, making notes, and taking photos and videos. Participant observation "provides context for sampling, open-ended interviewing, construction of interview guides and questionnaires, and other more structured and more quantitative methods of data collection" (DeWalt and DeWalt 2011, 3).

During lunch, cigarette breaks, and other pauses, the workers and I shared food and were able to have deeper conversations revolving around labor migration, place of origin, kinship networks, *gecekondus*, the recycling sector, and urban renewal projects. The day-to-day category codes enabled me to create a framework out of the field notes, participant observation, and casual conversations.

3.3.2 Interviews

The semi-structured interviews took place in the *çikmacis'* depots and supply yards in the Altınşehir area located on the Asian side of Istanbul. The guidelines for interview questions were formed by literature on waste collectors and trending academic debates around neoliberal urbanization. I chose my informants based on their background in scrap collection, demolition and second-hand trade activities. I could walk right in and ask about prices of components like a customer, then introduce myself as an academic researcher. In the beginning, it was hard to reach people because they suspected that I was some sort of government official inspecting their businesses. I had to explain my purpose in asking questions. Being an architect and a Ph.D. student softened my presence for them. I talked with most of the owners in Altınşehir. Some of them were more interested and attentive than others. As I was driving through a peripheral neighborhood on the European side, I came across the same type of depot and supply yard agglomerations. Here too, I went into the depots and met people managing their businesses.

In a later phase, I started to visit demolition sites. Most of the time, though, I ran up against a barrier there because the sites are dangerous and entrance to them was frequently forbidden. Besides that, they did not want to waste their time on me. It took me a while to find people who could trust me enough to have casual conversations. After occasional visits, they got used to my presence.

During the demolition of a building behind where I lived, I met a scrap collector named Engin. I regularly visited the site to make observations and have conversations with him while he was working. Then, he introduced me to his labor team, which consisted of his family members or people from his same village. Through Engin's contacts, I met several other scrap collectors. Since I was interested in where the second-hand components were used, I also interviewed some customers of theirs. After a certain number of interviews, the information I gathered was getting fairly uniform so I decided to stop the interviews.

> [E]ven if a researcher does not take a grounded theory approach, qualitative research in general, and participant observation in particular, encourages the continual reassessment of initial research questions and hypotheses, and facilitates the development of new hypotheses and questions as new insights occur as a result of increasing familiarity with the context. (Ibid, 15)

In the beginning, I used my first stage questions for sit-down interviews in Altınşehir. These questions focused on how they obtain second-hand materials and who they sell them to; what the dynamics in the second-hand market are; and what the legal status of their business is. Nevertheless, I realized these questions, based on preliminary observations, were insufficient for guiding the research. The important empirical data remained out of reach because my inquiries were basically constructed from my preliminary observations. For instance, migration, seasonal labor, refugee workers, and the link between informal housing were substantially missing from my collected data. After a few interviews, I realized that the structured ones did not capture the informants' perspectives. Furthermore, the questions were based on the political economy of urban renewal projects that overshadow the alternative potential of small entrepreneurs. They were also based on dichotomies between formal and informal thresholds within the construction market.

This approach did not reveal the informants' actual views. The conversations were stunted because of the leading questions that resulted in too many similar answers. For example, they said they were doing an unimportant job in the construction market, and their participation in the construction sector was often invisible. Throughout the research, I had to often revise my framework as I followed the changing fieldwork. Instead of structured interviews, I gave more attention to participant observation, casual conversations, and go-along interviews. Such exchanges had an open-ended quality that allowed the interviewees time and space to reflect on, and more easily voice, their ideas and opinions.

Most of the sit-down interviews and everyday conversations were un-recorded because my informants were not comfortable with the presence of a recording machine. This was because they wanted to remain anonymous; they worried that their recorded testimonies might be used against them in the future. However, they did give consent to my taking video and photographs.

Every day, I took a detailed record of everyday conversations and inter-views, adding them to my daily jottings. After a day at the demolition site, I wrote up the notes in a research diary. Since the conversations were not recorded, the transcription started at an early phase. During this phase, I took general notes while, at the same time, doing category coding. After improve-ments in my interview experience in the field, I was proficient in guiding the conversations toward research questions (see Ch. 1.3).

These casual conversations at their work sites were crucial for accessing the testimonies of my informants. These conversations not only revealed their po-litical views, which were nationalist and conservative, but also exposed their livelihood, which was sometimes in the form of seasonal work. Also, in some cases, I got to learn how they constructed their houses with second-hand ma-terials when they first arrived. Such natural-occurring oral narratives offered me immediate information about their context, viewpoints, concerns, and dis-cursive practices (Hammersley and Atkinson 2019). In addition to context-set-ting casual conversations, I conducted semi-structured interviews with every participant focusing on specific themes such as migration, labor, recycling, second-hand, trade, and urbanization.

The semi-structured interview questions helped me triangulate the empir-ical data and this, in turn, provided a space for me to expand on some impor-tant topics unfolding in the most recent daily discussions. According to Gal-leta (2013, 45), semi-structured interviews include open-ended questions and other inquiries oriented toward collecting data that is embedded in the infor-mants' experience. Although the informants were not aware of such a frame-work, it is vital to point out that their testimonies are the empirical knowledge that this study is grounded on.

The tacit knowledge and experience of the informants were further col-lected by go-along interviews when sit-down interviews and participant observation were not available. Sit-down interviews often remove informants from their usual context and prevent them from taking part in 'natural activi-ties' (Kusenbach 2003, 445). As a countermeasure, go-along interviews allowed me "to observe their informants' spatial practices in-situ while accessing their experiences and interpretations at the same time" (ibid, 46). Since I was with *çıkmacıs* working in the demolitions or their depots, the go-along method helped me access unrevealed experiences and perspectives. Such go-alongs took place while they were dismantling stuff, transporting reclaimed materials, or cutting out some part of a building. The materiality of their environment was more graspable for me when they were directly engaging with it physically.

This engagement allowed me to speak about the economic and supply changes in the second-hand market and the frequency of demolitions during the four years of fieldwork. According to Hammersley and Atkinson, repeat interviews are significantly beneficial for tracking transformations over time (Hammersley and Atkinson 2019, 97). Such repeat interviews allowed me to connect the adaptive tactics and experiences of the *çıkmacıs* to the changing economic conditions of Turkey.

In sum, I used different types of interviews: semi-structured, go-alongs, and casual conversations. Among them all, go-alongs, which I actually saw as 'work-alongs', were the most useful for gaining practice-based insights. My camera was also there capturing those significant moments.

3.3.3 Photography

Producing still images (photography) is one of the primary tools that I employed to construct an interdisciplinary approach that combined art and ethnographic writing practices. The use of photographs by ethnographers and urban researchers is employed for documentation and survey purposes. It can show how the informants and their environments relate to each other better than written text can. Photographs reflect the perspective of the researcher. They reveal equivocal details and fragments. Besides that, they are evidence that proves the researcher's presence in the field. Pink (2013, 49) defines this function of photography as a visual study diary and note-taking, which reveals how one can respond to the field during the research process; additionally, it hones our vision by framing the specific situation in the viewfinder. For her, the camera may unexpectedly take ethnographers into a deeper relationship with informants and can help one's fieldwork techniques evolve. On any given occasion, these processes are intertwined with the connections formed with the informants as the study unfolds. One of the method questions is how to utilize the images and text together. To achieve this, I will refer to the Marcus' montage concept (1990) and Pink's (2013) 'image captions' in ethnographic writings.

Montage is a film editing technique that combines different film clips together. It is not only limited to filmmaking but also used to make photomontages (composite photographic images). It is basically an editing process that generates new forms of narration in cinema, photography, and literature. When a writer introduces flashbacks, they use a montage effect that sets up an interplay between past and present. George Marcus (1990, 2) proposed that an ethnographic text should be produced using a montage principle in order to better reflect the non-linear narration of ethnographic research and daily life. He means by this that ethnographic texts should contain the views of individuals and academic discourses non-hierarchically. Acknowledging that, I would like to suggest that the photographs represent a simultaneous reality along with the descriptive text, like captions, as if they are being used in a montage of descriptive text, photos, and their captions.

Generally, photographs or images are accompanied by text describing what the image contains, that is, describing *what has been photographed*. Sarah Pink (2013) uses them as binding and capturing elements for extracting meanings and nurturing arguments. She regards the photographs of her participants as realistic depictions. At the same time, their lengthy captions reflect details of the environment that cannot be seen and sometimes they also contain the informant's opinions (ibid, 71). For her, the caption's goal is to get readers to think about their perceptions of the image and recognize how the snapshot and cultural symbols it contains might be understood. In the example below (Figure 3.1), I used an image to introduce a caption text that creates a description and analysis of the environments and people who inhabit them. This caption acts as a vignette linking the scenes and the background story.

In the beginning, it was unclear to my informants what the intention of my work was. My role as a researcher was also uncertain until I published the field photographs in an online magazine. This photo essay was titled 'Kapı yok pencere çok' (Not enough doors but windows) and it depicted several sites and actors in the field (Ceritoglu 2018). Instantly, I shared the essay with my informants, and they read it. The means of photojournalism and visual storytelling helped me make a statement of my critical perspective and my visualization of reality. Fortunately, it helped me to get closer to my respondents. Such usage of photography is discussed by Pink, who extensively used photography in her studies;

Showing photographs to their subjects can provide feedback on the images and their content while also forging connections with members of the 'community'. This can provide excuses or reasons for further meetings, which might include visiting people in their homes and building up connections with them. In this way, ethnographers may also use such photographic practices as ways of communicating about themselves and what they are interested in. (Pink 2013, 78)

The previous distance between my informants and myself turned into a trustful relationship when they saw something concrete in the photo essay and it became clearer what I was pursuing. This online publication highlighted the limited visibility of my informants in the construction sector. It was a helpful tool for meeting new actors in the second-hand market because I could show them this essay beforehand.

The production and usage of images were also executed by çıkmacıs. They were posting photos and videos of the components in online marketplaces where they exhibited their supplies. Some were advertising their demolition work with videos on online image-sharing platforms. These images possessing archival and documentary value helped to identify the variety of components, the places of accumulation, the logistics, the means of transportation, and the involvement of the workers.

As a visual art practitioner, photography is one of the more powerful mediums that I employ. From the earlier stages of my encounter with çıkmacıs, I used the camera to capture labor activities and places where second-hand components were accumulated. During breaks, I showed my informants those photographs. I also surveyed and archived their 'advertisement' photos and videos of salvaged items. These mediums enabled a relational exchange and produced a visual archive of reclaimed materials and the precarious work environment.

Participant observation, field notes and jottings, survey drawings, different types of interviews, and visual documentation are architectural and ethnographic methods that I employ throughout the fieldwork. Such a multi-disciplinary perspective creates distinctive monitoring of demolition and building reclamation in an unregulated context.

Figure 3.1: Jabir, a refugee worker from Afghanistan[1]

Source: Author's own

---

1   He is wearing a hat that he found in an emptied apartment. His jacket is worn out on
     the shoulders. The work shoes and hand gloves are the only appropriate safety clothes
     he wears on the demolition site. He is standing in front of the security barrier made of
     galvanized metal sheets. They reused an elevator door of a salvaged apartment block
     as their main entrance.

3.3.4 The Research Process

According to ethnographer Giampietro Gobo (2008), the ethnographer's presence is initially intrusive because it can cause shame, discomfort, tension, and
anxiety among the community of participants. Reflexivity is a self-controlling
mechanism that entails a critical self-interrogation of the researcher's position
informed by their background subjectivity, identity, and social background
(Stuart 2018, 211). It is a kind of critical awareness of how the researcher's
presence transforms the order of things in a typical fieldwork environment.
To attain this goal, I asked myself questions such as: What is my role in the
demolition sites? How am I perceived by the *çıkmacıs*? Who does and doesn't
give support to my presence? Why and why not? What might be the specific
things limiting my access? Who or what is setting my rules of engagement?

My first goal was to build and establish trusting relationships with my
informants. To accomplish this, I showed up every day at the dangerous and
partly knocked-down demolition site where I took the same risks as my informants, that is, I also did not wear the proper work safety clothes. Even with the
class difference, I was able to establish a non-hierarchical relationship with
them because I was interested in what they were doing. Such a relationship
was unusual for them in the construction sector because architects generally
represent higher positions in the labor order. In general, the empathetic and
ethical concern about the informants' precarious life conditions enables the
researcher to establish trust, which leads to open access and more refined
empirical findings.

My profession as an architect sometimes became useful when they asked
me about building technology. Such exchanges improved my status as a participant. Nevertheless, social distinctions (status, education, etc.) hampered
communication with reluctant informants in several instances. For many
years, I have lived in Istanbul, a city that is changing rapidly from the influence of neoliberal dynamics. As an informed neighbor, I was observing the
developments on my street. The neighborhood where I lived was a middle-
class part of the Kadıköy district that was rapidly being gentrified. When
urban transformation intensified after 2012, I witnessed the way buildings
were demolished one after the other.

When I focused on a specific family, the youngest member, Engin, became
my contact person. He was open-minded and supported me in conducting my
architectural surveys and interviews. I assume this was because we were about
the same age. He was aware of the lack of research and state support in his

field. In terms of visibility, he wanted to reveal the economic difficulties and labor conditions. I share his viewpoint. As an artist, architect and academic, I am very critical of the demolition projects of the AK Party. Further, I became more politically engaged after taking part in the Gezi Park civil occupation and demonstrations[2] in 2013. This movement was against the top-down privatization and neoliberal urbanization. These processes were happening literally right at my doorstep.

When the building behind our shared apartment was announced to be 'under urban transformation', I could observe and document all the stages[3] of demolition and construction of the "Uzay Apartmanı"[4] from my bedroom window. Every day I took pictures and made videos of its disappearance. One day, during the dismantling and reclamation of the building, I went there to ask if I could salvage an IKEA bed frame that I could see from my bedroom window. That was where I met Engin, who was working alone in the building. I could see how he was discarding window frames. After explaining that I was a neighbor, he got friendlier and showed me around the abandoned building. Engin became my main informant and invited me to other sites where he was working with family members.

For the first Tbilisi Architecture Biennial, I was invited to make a pre-event presentation in May 2018. During my visit, by coincidence, I saw a local second-hand supply yard advertised on Facebook. Then, I managed to contact a wholesaler who exported second-hand components from Turkey. Then, I did my first semi-structured interview with a local trader. Subsequent to the interview, I documented several old Soviet apartments in the micro-district of Gldani, whose façades were upgraded by components from the depot. On my second

---

2   On 28 May 2013, a surge of civil disobedience and organized demonstrations erupted in Turkey, firstly in response to the urban development project for Taksim Gezi Park in Istanbul. The park, which is the only green space in the city center, was slated to be turned into a shopping mall and city museum by reviving an old Ottoman military barracks. Thereafter, supportive demonstrations and strikes occurred around Turkey, opposing a broad range of issues, notably among them: urban inequality, freedom of speech, human rights and islamist conservative politics that were causing secularism to deteriorate.

3   The four stages are: the vacating of the premises, putting up barriers with glazing corrugated plate, the dismantling and reclamation of the reusable and recyclable building components, the demolition, the excavation for foundations, and the construction of the new building.

4   All the apartment building names are in Turkish. In this case, Uzay means 'Space'.

visit to Georgia for the main event of the Biennial in October 2018, I recontacted the seller and received free PVC frames for an art installation. In the course of the production, I went to several second-hand supply yards and held detailed semi-structured and go-along interviews with several workers from the yard. In the following year, I revisited them to have an update on how their business was progressing. My occasional visits created a mutual understanding and feeling of trust with the owners. Furthermore, I could observe the changes in the material flow from Turkey to Georgia based on the fluctuations in the sector.

In the second stage of the fieldwork, my aim was to follow the trade and re-use activities of second-hand components (PVC frames, doors, etc.). Based on the empirical data in Istanbul, I visited demolition yards and *çıkmacı* supply yards in the Anatolian cities of Ankara, Kayseri, Nevşehir, Aksaray in Turkey, and Tbilisi in Georgia. During my visit to the Anatolian cities in May and June of 2018, I conducted semi-structured interviews and held participant observations while I was visiting depots several times during my stay. Further, I documented vineyard sheds, country cottages, apartment buildings, and village houses. Each town I visited was undergoing a nationwide urban renewal projects. I investigated the associations between second-hand retailers and customers in order to figure out material configurations. These clues help me to interconnect demolition practices, self-help construction methods, and the trade of affordable materials. I also discovered that the journey of second-hand components did not end in Anatolia but continued on to neighboring Georgia.

3.4 Analyzing Empirical Data

In the analysis phase of ethnographic research, the researchers collaboratively gather codes, analyze data, and choose what data to collect next in order to create a theory as it arises. This process is known as theoretical sampling. The analytical process of acquiring observations and looking for the best assumption (hypothesis) to explain those findings is known as the abductive reasoning approach.

The analysis of empirical data can be described as the process through which data is transcribed, organized, and interpreted to develop theories. Brewer sees it as a process in which one first aggregates what is found into patterns, categories, and descriptive units; then, one can conduct a search for any relationships between them (Brewer 2000). He continues by defining 'interpretation' as the craft of giving meaning and importance to the analysis; he then defines 'presentation' as 'writing up' the gathered information (ibid, 104). During the process of gathering data and analyzing, I employed theoretical sampling and coding throughout.

Abductive reasoning

> Rather than following a predetermined set of research questions in the data collection process, abductive ethnography embraces serendipity and allows intuition to guide the fieldwork. Data analysis begins neither with inductive nor deductive reasoning. By temporarily disassociating the data from their context, specific theoretical debates, and the experience of data collection in the field, the ethnographer is able to play with the data freely and lead this process to a surprising discovery and insight. This discovery is then conceptually articulated through the dialog among the insight, contextualized empirical evidence, and theoretical knowledge. (Bajc 2012, 72)

Using abductive reasoning, I highlighted the emergence of a generated theory from the ethnographic findings. First, I gathered the empirical data and built preliminary insights and hypotheses about it; then, I assessed these theories as I continued doing the fieldwork, and finally, I further developed or abandoned these theories. Based on abductive logic, theoretical sampling is a critical method that entails a back-and-forth strategy between data collection and data analysis (Charmaz 2014; Stuart 2018). Abductive logic fundamentally begins with observation, examines all potential explanations to form theoretical arguments (or hypothesis) about that observation, and then tests those arguments with further observation. This kind of reasoning uses both inductive and deductive models at the same time:

> It is sufficient to understand abduction in relationship to induction and deduction. Induction refers to the process of collecting new data and using it to strengthen or problematize well-established theories. The deduction, on the other hand, suggests a hypothesis about specific observations that are already based on existing theory. From a pragmatist perspective neither induction nor deduction is particularly creative, because neither leads to new theories. Theory generation requires us to move away from our preconceived notions and to create new narratives about the phenomenon we are trying to explain. (Tavory and Timmermans 2014, 2014)

To put it another way, the research is data and theory-driven at the same time. It is a circular logic to explain an observation as research evidence that does not correspond to existing theories. The researcher speculates how this evidence could be explained by forming new hypotheses or theories deductively. But while developing a new hypothesis, the researcher inductively makes new observations based on the same phenomenon. Induction verifies explanations via empirical testing, while abduction proposes explanations that are subsequently codified into deductions.

For example, one of the original research questions was: Are *çıkmacıs* a new phenomenon coming out of the current neoliberal urbanization. After several weeks of gathering field notes, I found out that they used to supply materials for *gecekondu* dwellers in the 1970s. On the basis of that finding, and after going through the theories and studies of *gecekondu* urbanization, I came up with the argument that they must have adapted to several different urbanization periods in Istanbul. When I reviewed the fieldwork, I looked for more empirical evidence of their past and present experiences in second-hand trade: I was curious how they interpreted their role now. As a result, I came up with the more robust hypothesis that their entrepreneurial model seemed to exist in the zone of a self-regulated trade and labor system. Then the research question changed: What is the role of demolitions in the history of Istanbul's urbanization in regard to the emergence of the *çıkmacıs* and material reclamation processes? During this back-and-forth process, coding becomes important to classify empirical data during this interplay between data and theory. Codifying and recording the empirical data (memoing) at an earlier phase enabled me to mature my reflective and interpretive attitude toward fieldwork.

Coding and Analysis

Coding sorts the empirical data into categories to offer evidence for analysis and interpretation (LeCompte and Schensul 2013, 59). Categories are informed by the conceptual framework and research objectives. To achieve the coding process, day-to-day field notes, memos, and transcribed conversations are assembled in a MS Word document. Then, I review them thoroughly and add any missing information with the help of the video and photographic documentation. For example, I write a description of how they dismantle a window frame and then translate all the notes to English.

To illustrate, during a casual conversation with Rıfat, he stated that: "We used to sell second-hand components that we reclaimed from inner-city demolitions to *gecekondu* dwellers in the 1970s". This segment describes the former relationship between self-help housing and the building reclamation activity of *çıkmacıs* in the past. Therefore, it was categorized under *"gecekondu, trade, and urbanization"*. After applying this procedure to all the data, reappearing codes started to appear: economy, migration, waste management, urbanization, politics, labor, and infrastructure. The general coding was carried out during the fieldwork. Later, I added more specific coding throughout the analysis process. From the same example, I labeled Rıfat's statement into sub-codes: "urban transformation, migration, unrecognized labor, *gecekondu* urbanization, urban demolitions, second-hand trade, dual lives, incremental construction, formalization, repair".

After completion, all data was transcribed and categorized thematically to illustrate common themes and contrasts in the empirical findings. These codes were based on the *çıkmacıs'* views of their role in the construction sector and the categories that structured the thesis with assemblage analysis: materiality (recycle, reuse, environmental impacts); labor (migration, seasonal work); trade (networks), and urban renewal projects in general. The value and significance of the codes lie in their demonstration of the commonalities and differences of the *çıkmacıs*. For instance, they all participate in cooperatives or informal labor organizations. Also, differences show how entrepreneurial approaches differ based on specific cases. The market dynamics are not fair to all. For example, Anatolian *çıkmacıs* formed an association with each other as a whole, but the ones in Istanbul compete with each other for territory. In the end, the themes in the codes identified during my first analysis served as a foundation for the presentation in the empirical chapters.

During the fieldwork, I transcribed 35 interviews with *çıkmacıs*, tenants, demolishers, scrap collectors, scrap dealers, and their customers. However, I chose 12 of them in the second round of analysis according to their location, experience, labor organization, professional, and immigration background in the second-hand market. Further, I made this reduction because they are the ones with whom I managed to go into depth with and each of them represent different types, especially in terms of having long-term experience or entrepreneurial success. These subjects were primarily connected to the perspectives of *çıkmacıs* on reuse and recycling, environmental concerns, and labor precarity in the context of urban development in their localities, and more particularly on their influence on seasonal labor structure and second-hand trade. To emphasize the primary results of my study and the study's core argument, I concentrated on testimonies that reflected the many dimensions of urban re-

newal and their legal grounds for producing demolition waste, material reclamation, and second-hand trade in extensive qualitative detail.

They were more involved in scrap dealing from the street than building
reclamation from demolitions. They could switch in-between due to second-
hand supply shortage when the number of demolitions was decreasing. In this
way, they engaged in various processes of valuing second-hand material, from
trading with recycling factories to selling in the flea market. I could observe
how they were flexible in adjusting to different markets and dynamics. Plus,
they still had strong ties with their home village, where they were farming half
of the year. I believe that evaluating such rural connections sheds light on the
seasonal labor theme.

During my analysis, I categorized five different types of *çıkmacıs*: old-
school and experienced, new and entrepreneurial, new and unsuccessful,
resilient, and fading. For instance, the Rıfat and Tezel brothers represent
figures who have experienced demolitions since the earlier gecekondu period;
Serhat and Ulaş are entrepreneurs who are new to the demolition and second-
hand trade; Muslim's story illustrates an unsuccessful business; Demir comes
from scrap dealing and becomes a promoter of second-hand trade; Engin and
his brother are a prominent precedent for family business structure and rural-
urban work; and Halis' and his supply yard depicts a continuation of work as an
inherited asset. In Istanbul, four case studies (out of 8)—Rıfat, Demir, Halis,
and Tezels' supply yards—were chosen for spatial diagram representation
based on their size and complexity. The remaining is portrayed using satellite
images since spatial orientation is not as varied as in the previous four cases.

The overall data analysis process was an interplay between data collection
and theory. From the beginning of the research, category-coding became an
essential tool for mapping patterns and theoretical themes. Theoretical sampling helped me streamline the data collection process while making hypotheses and tracing existing theories. As I continued collecting the empirical data,
I tested these hypotheses in terms of their viability in relation to the everyday
experiences of the *çıkmacıs*.

3.5 Conclusion

The studies discussed in the first section of this chapter have proved useful
for envisioning the flow of low-value commodities and waste in the Global
South. They focus on production cycles and the materiality of these objects in

north-to-south exploitative circular economies. I highlight how such 'multi-sited' ethnography could be done with a 'follow the thing' method. Within the environment of an unevenly developed world, these concepts are able to focus on different localities within a networked trade system.

This study employs an investigation of livelihood practices related to waste reclamation in the secondary commodity chain existing beyond Istanbul's borders. By employing such methodology, I aim to investigate the importance of unregulated labor and nonhuman actors in the reclamation sector. The ethnography of the fieldwork derives from my conversations and observations of scrap collectors. It focuses on their double lives. The multi-sited approach is oriented around seasonal labor and the trade of second-hand components from Istanbul to Anatolia.

Unstructured discussions and spontaneous conversations were also part of the data collection process. The field notes, and day-to-day mnemonics, were accompanied by architectural survey drawings of supply yards and dwellings. I used them to create diagrams to orient the reader to the spatial organization of spaces.

To theorize my empirical findings, I pursued a path grounded in abductive reasoning. First, I started with research questions from the existing literature. After my first analysis of the field work, I realized that my questions were influencing my informant's answers, questions such as "Do you think that your activities are good for the environment?". Then, I shifted my approach. I reconfigured theoretical arguments and research questions in the light of the empirical findings. The reconfiguration process led me to generate new hypotheses about reclamation processes. Based on data triangulation (coding and theoretical sampling), I categorized the actors according to their experience in the sector, entrepreneurial approaches, and management models to be used for structuring Chapter 6. The study reveals a cross-section of these actors from different backgrounds and positions within the market. Throughout this process, I was guided by reflexive questions that problematized my subjectivity as a researcher.

As a support layer, photography became the primary visual tool to document sites and people. In the analysis phase, I combined ethnographic writing and analysis of photography with a montage logic and captions. To achieve this visual narrative in the book's linear structure, I used descriptive captions as a vignette to accompany the photographs.

Besides, it contributes to the unattended field of building reclamation and the flow and utilization of second-hand materials in rural dwellings. While conceptualizing socio-materiality and nonhuman agency, it maps the distribution of materials from second-hand supply yards. Lastly, it describes the resilient character of unrecognized migrant labor bypassing neoliberal configurations by introducing forms of value production different from those of hegemonic capitalism.

4. Setting the Scene: Urbanization through Demolition and Redevelopment

4.1 Introduction

Tracing the history of Istanbul's land commodification and urban demolition is an essential prerequisite for an understanding of material reclamation activities. As a preface to a later empirical analysis, this chapter will mainly focus on the commodification of land from a political economy perspective. The current situation of construction waste excess is associated with the rebuilding of Istanbul apartment blocks that, from the 1970s onward, became the primary housing construction archetype.

Recall that we are here approaching the city as a rhizomatic multiplicity consisting of human and nonhuman assemblages. For example, regarding nonhuman agents, the earthquake in Istanbul changed seismic engineering policies and zoning regulations. These combined to increase the number of apartment building sites becoming real estate assets.

Additionally, *çıkmacıs*—with emergent capacities—have economically adapted to market dynamics and continue to coexist in the construction market. Through their supply yards, they provided affordable materials and even loans for the construction costs of informal settlements; this all happened at a time when there were no government public funds available for housing needs. This chapter highlights how the *çıkmacıs'* activities developed in a time in which neoliberal dynamics were pushing them from central to peripheral positions.

The chapter is structured in four parts. First, it focuses on the commodification of land starting from Late Ottoman modernization of Istanbul. Historically analyzing these processes, I illustrate how apartment blocks became spatial archetypes and significant assets in real estate. Secondly, I describe the urbanization processes of *gecekondu* in the 1950s during the industrialization of Istanbul and rural migration. The chapter continues with the liberalization processes in the 1980s that legitimized informal housing. The last part reflects upon the latest trends in the neo-liberalization period when global capital shifted their focus to large-scale projects, real estate, and finance (Korkmaz and Ünlü Yücesoy 2009). In each part, I describe the urbanization of the Kadıköy district, a middle-class neighborhood in Istanbul where the fieldwork was conducted (Figure 4.1).

Figure 4.1: Location of Kadıköy district in Istanbul

Source: Author's own

4.2 The Commodification of Land in the Ottoman Empire

During the Ottoman Empire, all lands were deemed imperial-owned unless explicitly described as 'private' or assigned to non-Muslim minority congregations. If they paid taxes on them, the peasants could use state-owned lands for agricultural cultivation but were not allowed to possess them as private property. In urban areas though, members of the public could buy property, for example, houses and gardens. Under imperial law, land was something that was given by the empire, secured by the empire, and could sometimes be lost to the empire again (Keyder 1999, 3). Because of this circumstance, land rights depended on the dynamics of a moral economy between minorities, peasants, and the state elite. During the modernization period in the nineteenth century, the Ottoman empire passed new laws to address this situation; some of these laws allowed for the private ownership of land while others placed various limits on land accumulation and trade (ibid, 5).

The urbanization of Kadıköy, where my fieldwork was conducted, is very representative of this land commodification process: In the late 19th century, the improvements in public transportation and the new more liberal land ownership laws were essential requirements for developing Kadıköy as an Ottoman summer resort in the Asian part of Istanbul. The ferry services that connected villages along the Bosporus started to make regular stops in 1843 and later, in 1873, suburban trains connected these services to inner parts of Kadıköy (Akın 2010). After the establishment of the Haydarpaşa-Izmit suburban railway line (Figure 4.2), the areas in the Asian part could develop into resort districts around the suburban stations established by the Ottoman upper class.

Figure 4.2: Suburban train line connecting Haydarpaşa to Tuzla in 1918

Source: (Salah 2013)

The Land Code of 1858 facilitated the transformation of imperial lands around the city into real estate, introduced a title deed of ownership, and enabled the systematization of property records (Bayraktar 2016). By the beginning of the 19th century, almost all of the urban land in Istanbul had turned into public estates[1], which were easier to use for private construction (Tekeli 1996). Additionally, the Construction and Building Law[2] in 1882 enabled the parceling and settlement of agricultural land such as vineyards and orchards on the periphery of Istanbul (Tekeli 2011). It also allowed private property development around mansions with large gardens. In Kadıköy, these were owned by Ottoman state officials, wealthy foreigners, Levantines, Armenians and Greek merchants (Cantürk 2017).

In the early 1900s, urban rehabilitation in Istanbul's historic urban center focused on creating public spaces and road constructions. The first Ottoman urban reform interventions were based on those of the French modernists and focused on developing public parks, transportation systems (roads and tram lines), and sanitation infrastructure (Bilsel 2011). Their strategic plan concentrated on organizing and clearing the inner city rather than foreseeing and preparing for an increase in the population. Demolishers at this time employed themselves in the second-hand trade of wooden and masonry construction materials (Çelik 2007, 241). The structuring of the inner-city through the demolition of public buildings and housing development continued into the early days of the Turkish Republic (1923–1950).

4.3 State-led Developmentalism in the Early Days of the Turkish Republic

In the early days of the Turkish Republic, developmentalism was a potent way to satisfy the pledge of nationalism that accompanied the creation of a new modern state, economy, and culture. As part of that, traditional wooden houses and some historic buildings were demolished to make way for a road construction project that was based on a master plan by the French urban planner Henri Prost. These demolitions were intensified during the regime of prime minister Adnan Menderes who shifted state development funds to Istanbul and away from Ankara, the new Turkish capital. The debris of traditional houses and Ottoman landmarks were used in the construction of new housing in Kadıköy (Bilsel 2011). This material salvage of buildings was inherited from a common practice during the Ottoman period (Türeli 2014). Subtraction and addition

---

1   *Vakıf Arazisi* in Turkish.
2   Ebniye Kanunu in Turkish.

processes, in the form of demolish and develop operations, determined the physical transformation of Istanbul's built environment.

4.3.1 Menderes' Demolition Operations in Istanbul

Since World War I, as part of the nationalizing of the Turkish economy, the state has been seizing the assets of non-Muslim minorities. During the events of 6–7 September, 1955, also known as the Istanbul Pogrom, Greek residents and their buildings were attacked by nationalist mobs. After that, the Greeks—who constructed the main commercial areas of Taksim Square—were forced to abandon their houses and commercial establishments and emigrate out of Istanbul; this came as a result of the nationalist politics of the Menderes government (Ergur 2009). These emptied buildings were then squatted by rural Turkish migrants.

Top-down planning decisions without any site-specific research erased historical neighborhoods. In this period, minority's properties and historical landmarks were erased from Istanbul's urban history (Figure 4.3). These operations, driven by the liberal agenda of the state, left deep and painful scars in Istanbul. Menderes was pro-automobile and supported widespread freeway development and rapid industrialization (Boysan 2011). These motorways connected the industrial areas to a broader transport network. The city's population drastically increased because of immigrant workers.

Figure 4.3: Eminönü demolitions during the Menderes government

Source: Burak Boysan Archive

Immediately after the demolitions were completed and due to the already-altered land ownership laws, the empty land on the side of the new boulevards was made available for the construction of new apartment blocks (ibid). The predominant 'build and sell' (*yapsatçılık*) method of *müteahhits* [construction contractors] emerged during this period. With the build-and-sell system, the contractors bought the land from the owner—who was part of the Ottoman elite—in exchange for a few apartments. Following the Condominium Act of 1965, which permitted individual ownership of apartments (Erman, Altay, and Altay 2004), Ottoman summer estates along the Marmara coast of Istanbul were demolished to build modern apartment buildings in both the Asian and Anatolian parts of the city (Korkmaz and Ünlü Yücesoy 2009).

Meanwhile, the Kadıköy suburbs continued to be a summer resort. The traditional mansions of the 1910s had already been replaced by modern masonry villas in the 1930s and 40s. The first zoning plan allowing three floors was passed in 1952 (Berkmen and Sırma 2019). The bureaucrats of the new Republic and the post-war bourgeoisie shared the residential district with the second-generation descendants of the old Istanbul families and the remaining non-Muslim minorities (Derviş et al. 2009). The opening of public beaches in Suadiye, Caddebostan, Moda, and Fenerbahçe in the 1930s reinforced Kadıköy's reputation as a resort, and, up until the 1960s, the large former estates were being divided into smaller parcels for two-story modern villas (Ekdal 2004). Soon these villas would be replaced by apartment blocks with structurally insufficient building stock that would later become second-hand components for current urban renewal projects.

4.3.2 Phase 1: Apartmentalization in Istanbul

The housing demand of the middle-class in Istanbul was met primarily by the construction of multi-story apartment blocks on privately-owned land in holiday resort districts. In Turkey, apartmentalization resulted from external influences, the shortage of financial resources, and the lack of accessible urban land (Balamir 1994, 29). In the 1960s, tremendous public pressure was exerted to lift construction restrictions so as to allow the ownership of Ottoman-era properties to be divided among shareholders (Keyder 1999). The result was the transformation of many single-mansion plots into several three to ten-story high apartments (Figure 4.4). Up until the Condominium act allowed individual apartment deeds, ownership was based on cooperative possession made up of owners (Bilgin 1988). In the 1960s, the emerging middle class dreamt of owning an apartment in a new building rather than having a detached house in the suburbs because apartments represented modern ways of urban living (Bozdoğan 2010).

Figure 4.4: An apartment block that was built after demolishing an old house on Bağdat Street in Kadıköy

Source: (Arkitekt 1976)

The construction of middle-class apartment buildings was usually financed by provincial entrepreneurs with sufficient capital. The *müteahhits*, were predominantly from the Black Sea region, which had a tradition of seasonal migration to Istanbul since the 19th century (Keyder 1999). Furthermore, they had connections to mobilize a construction team, usually made up of workers from their hometown, and they could build without an architect (ibid, 21). In the Kadıköy district along the Marmara Sea, some property owners, heirs of the state elite, hired a *müteahhit* to demolish an abandoned Ottoman mansion and build a 6-story apartment block in its place. The contractor took half of the apartments in the block to finance the construction costs. Before construction was finished (preferably while the foundation was laid), the *müteahhit* was trying to sell the apartments to supply more financial resources. Indeed, prospective middle-class buyers paid installments to the contractor in the absence of an organized credit market for housing purchases (Işık 1995, 43). This method of construction financing (*yapsatçılık*) was the only available type.

The technical standards of the apartments were uniform: the contractors usually copied from a model that had been implemented before; and thus, hiring an architect was deemed unnecessary (Keyder 1999). The construction crew consisted of low-paid manual laborers who were rural migrants mainly skilled in farming. Practices that increase the exploitation of informal labor, such as employing workers with an extremely low hourly wage without insurance, or any social security, were frequently encountered in *yapsatçılık* (Işık 1995, 44). During the 1960s, the materials were manufactured locally by a construction industry where demand was proliferating. Quality could never be a concern as long as a protectionist foreign trade regime made importing materials impossible (Tekeli 1978). The low quality of the housing stock built in this period was considered to have a severe seismic risk (Bilgin 2000).

As in the rest of Istanbul in the 1950s, there were three critical developments in the Kadıköy district. The first was the rapid informal urbanization process emerging from intense migration to cities; the second was the urban development operations initiated by Adnan Menderes; and the third was the industrialization of the Asian part of Istanbul. Although Menderes' operations were mainly implemented in the European part of Istanbul, several new highways also were built. The main boulevard, Bağdat Street, dating back to the Byzantine era, was widened around Kadıköy in the Asian part (Akbulut 1994). Within the scope of these operations in 1958, the expansion of Bağdat Street was realized by the removal of tram lines and the expropriation of gardens on both sides of the street (Eyice 1994). Eventually, Bağdat emerged as the main transportation artery connecting residential areas on the Marmara coast with the urban center of Kadıköy.

Beginning in the 1950s, the low-density and low-rise aspect of the district was replaced by high-rise apartmentalization. The new development plans introduced a new transportation network. The housing production was of two types: cooperative housing and *yapsatçılık* initiated by small-scale contractors (Bilgin 1988). The maximum building height allowance was increased to five stories (Akbulut 1994; Bilgin 2000), which accelerated the apartmentalization of the area not only in the planned part of Kadıköy but also in *gecekondu* neighborhoods such as Fikirtepe. After the construction of the first bridge over the Bosporus connecting the European and Asian parts of Istanbul in 1973, Kadıköy and its surroundings became an attractive residential area for the middle class (Figure 4.5).

Yapsatçılık, as a construction practice with its payment schemes, played a fundamental role in the emergence, development, and growth of the urban middle class starting from the 1960s. On the other hand, *gecekondu* urbanization enabled the rural migrants to be part of urban society and politics. Simultaneous with the construction activities of the middle class, *gecekondu* urbanization started to emerge as a self-help housing solution by rural migrants seeking work as unskilled labor in Istanbul.

Figure 4.5: Distribution of buildings showing the number of floors in 2022

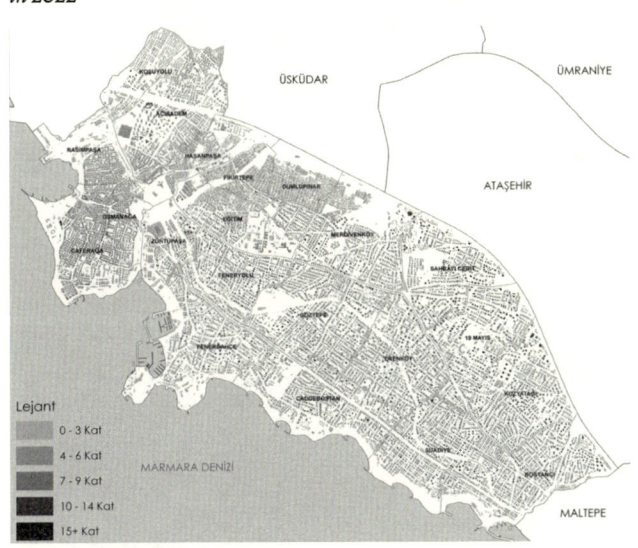

Source: Kadıköy Municipality

4.4 Emerging Informal Urbanization and the gecekondu

In the 1950s, while agriculture in the villages was rapidly mechanizing, especially after receiving Marshall Plan aid[3] following the second world war (Bilgin 2000), the area between Istanbul and Ankara urbanized rapidly. With the private development of Istanbul's industry sector, the city in Ankara's shadow be-

---

3   Between 1948 and 1950, some $164 million was obtained through this aid, 22 percent of which was spent on agriculture, mainly for mechanization (Şenyapılı 1981, 73).

came an urban center where capital was accumulating. When dislocated peasants began to migrate to Istanbul in large numbers, the state's resources for a "planned urbanization" were not enough to provide the housing needed since the state was already occupied in replanning the inner city through demolitions and factory development close to the main arteries. The rural migrants built their squatter dwellings on state-owned land, located close to the factories in Istanbul (Figure 4.6). The dwellings were named after the way they were constructed: *gecekondu* (plural gecekondus), which means "placed (built) overnight". As the city expanded its borders, some neighborhoods found themselves close to the city center, bordered by middle-class housing projects (Candan and Kolluoğlu 2008).

Figure 4.6: Gecekondus in the Mecidiyeköy neighborhood of Istanbul (1959)

Source: German Archeology Institute Archive

Focusing mainly on its national industry and ignoring its responsibility to provide housing, the Turkish state failed to commodify the state-owned land that formerly belonged to the Ottoman Empire (Erman and Eken 2004). The state tolerated the self-help construction activities of migrant workers. However, the urban elite condemned these building's rural style as not being suitable for urban society's modernist ideals (Keyder and Öncü 1994). The informal and illegal means of *gecekondu* construction structured the commodification of land and the integration of the rural into the urban population. Between the modern and the traditional norms, *gecekondu* urbanization was a transitional phenomenon that functioned as a societal and economic buffer mechanism (Kıray 1964). *Gecekondu* was viewed as a transitional urban space that was supposed to vanish as modernization and urbanization became increasingly advanced.

As each new squatter neighborhood sprang up, new urban centers appeared on the city's network (Keyder and Öncü 1994). In March 1949, in Istanbul, there were nearly 5,000 *gecekondus*. In 1950, there were 8,239; in 1959, 61,400; and in 1963, 120,000 (Duyar-Kienast 2005). At that time, 35% of the population, more or less 660,000 inhabitants, dwelled in these settlements (Pérouse 2004). Owing to their increasing political power due to their increased population, the legitimization process of these neighborhoods did not take long; within two decades, the rural-to-city migrants were able to ask local authorities for infrastructure and services (Balaban 2011). Their voting power was a bargaining advantage in populist politics. Additionally, they supplied cheap labor to the private sector. The agency of informality allowed them to create solidarity networks through relatives and village fellowship.

Until the mid-1980s, the government was legislating acts and amnesty laws that incorporated the benefits of *gecekondu*. For instance, the famous Law No. 775 in 1966 supported the improvement of squatter areas by providing long term loans for renovations and improving physical infrastructure and municipal services, the creation of public funds for *gecekondu* upgrading, the construction of apartments for low-income households, the land allocation for homeless migrants, the removal of *gecekondu* housing in geographically inappropriate areas and the restriction of new land occupation (Turkish Parliment (TBMM) 1966). To incorporate the benefits of *gecekondu* housing and favor the increase of urban growth as part of the national development strategy, the act aimed to integrate the benefits of this kind of housing when public resources were limited. In any case, the threat of demolition was constantly at their doorstep since the poor were always at the mercy of state authorities (Erman 2011).

New rural arrivals used whatever materials they could find to make their shelters (Duyar-Kienast 2005). The leftover building materials from Ottoman summer houses were sold by *çıkmacıs* to *gecekondu* builders (see also Ch. 7.3.3).

4.4.1 Construction Methods and Architectural Properties

At first sight, the *gecekondu* houses resemble make-shift, hovel-like, and scrappy rural houses, yet they contain essential utilities that support2 the complex livelihoods of migrants. Their architectural style originated in Anatolian villages and generally consisted of a small house, garden, and trees. They were often described with the discriminating term: 'non-urban' (Pérouse 2004). Tansı Şenyapılı's description of the building process reveals how this affordable and unique mode of construction had traces of vernacular architecture from rural parts of Turkey:

> The first *gecekondus* covered a 25–35 m2 area consisting of entrance space, one room, and a garden. The height of the house did not exceed 2.4 meters. At first, they dug the foundation and placed stones as a base for the surrounding walls. After placing the foundation, they buried it to hide it from the authorities. In the following stage, they placed the walls made of mud bricks [*kerpiç*] or used a wood-framed wall filled with rubble. Once the walls were constructed, they were covered with mud. Mud bricks were a mixture of earth and water with dry straw added as a connecting fiber. This mix was poured into a rectangular mold. The mud bricks were laid on top of each other over the stone foundation, leaving spaces for windows and doors bought from the demolishers. The roof was assembled with tin plates salvaged from factory leftovers or reclaimed wood beams from older houses. It was then covered with plastic coating insulated with tar, or the house was covered with tin plates collected from the industrial waste of neighboring factories. Sometimes the wood frame walls were prefabricated and placed on the site with the help of *gecekondu* dwellers. Occasionally for laying stone walls, old Byzantine graveyards were knocked down, and stone pavements were stolen. (Şenyapılı 1981, 181; my translation)

Their make-shift construction methods were a fast, easy, and affordable way for the *gecekondu* builders to make their shelters; their buildings were also expandable despite the fact that there was the ever-present danger of demolition by municipality officials. According to *gecekondu* Law No. 486 issued in 1924, a squatter house could only be demolished during the construction process; and if it was occupied, a decision from the court was necessary (ibid 2004). Struggling with authorities continuously made these builders fast, persistent and cooperative. To avoid demolition, they used tactics such as bribing the demolishing team, displaying the same political views as the team, stopping the bulldozers with barricades, and organizing neighborhood resistance groups (Şentürk 2016). Since the government barely tolerated them, the relationship with the municipal officials was a constant negotiation:

> If gecekondu dwellers realized that the demolition teams would certainly destroy their houses, they politely asked them to do the job with the minimum harm to the materials because they wanted to reuse the materials of their houses to rebuild them. Sometimes they dismantled the doors and the windows by themselves before the demolition. This last-minute bargain would reduce the cost of rebuilding. (Ibid 2016, 275)

Until they got some deeds for their occupied land, the *gecekondu* construction was continued with the help of local craftsmen and relatives:

> Ali, his brother-in-law, and Ibrahim kalfa [a skilled craftsman] began digging foundation ditches. These were completed after midnight and were packed with stones before dawn. Before the site was left, dirt raked over the level surface of the foundation to camouflage the activity. One week later, they assembled again, with two other men from the village and one fellow worker. Under Ibrahim's direction, they labored through the night, only managing to hang the door at dawn. Part of the roof remained incomplete, but Ali did not want to be late for work. The police had raided the site during the day, and two walls had been toppled to the ground. Ibrahim recommended rebuilding at once and sent a neighbor to ardiye [supply yard] for more bricks. This time they managed to complete the roof, and Fatma (Ali's wife) was brought to the house before Ali left for work. A week later, police notified Ali those legal proceedings had been lodged against him; Years later, he won the case. (Sewell 1966, 120)

Once the household's financial situation got better and the house was safe from demolition, they started to remodel the exterior walls and add rooms to the house (Figure 4.7). They replaced the mud walls by laying concrete bricks from the inside of the house and then removing the old mud wall (ibid). The assemblage of *gecekondu* construction brought together reclaimed materials, social relations, and interest groups. The network of social relations was the major component in this assemblage. Kinship, village fellowship[4] bonds and the support of the neighbors actively supported the process. Later, those networks de-

---

4   Hemşehrilik in Turkish.

veloped into private associations that facilitated and influenced formal urbanization processes. Furthermore, *ardiyes*[5], that, discussed in the next chapter, became the primary resource in providing materials, granting installment payments, and giving credits.

Figure 4.7: Incremental expansion of a gecekondu in Tuzluçayır-Ankara

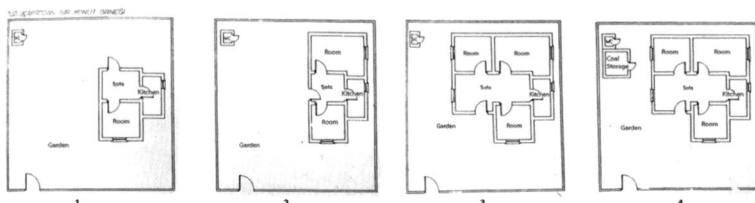

Source: (Şenyapılı 1981)

4.4.2 Role of Ardiyes as Supply Yards and Credit Providers

Ardiye supply yards, which were the origin of *çıkmacı* yards, provided affordable materials to *gecekondu* dwellers since the beginning of Istanbul's rapid urbanization in the early 1950s (Figure 4.8). These yards stored cheap construction materials and reclaimed construction elements from old buildings during urban rehabilitation and infrastructure projects (Şenyapılı 1981; Payne 1982; Duyar-Kienast 2005). Among many other informal solutions invented to account for the absence of certain necessities, *ardiyes* were established by rural migrants who had the financial means to start a business. In the very beginning, they were selling second-hand building materials in the city center; as Payne has stated:

> The ardiyes were an incredibly imaginative institution; faced with the great demand for cheap building components for the gecekondus and noticing the redevelopment projects starting in the city's commercial center, enterprising merchants salvaged the materials from buildings being redeveloped and resold them to self-help housebuilders. This recycling process soon becomes so extensive that architects involved in redevelopment schemes com-

---

5   In Turkish, *ardiye* means 'storage', 'warehouse', or 'depot'.

monly had their fees paid in the form of the scrap value of materials from the building to be replaced, whilst those needing components such as windows to install quickly into a new house could, if they were lucky, get them complete with glazing and even curtain rails. (Payne 1982,121)

Scrap from old buildings was valuable and profitable and the builders were bartering their services with reclaimed materials because of the supply scarcity and the speed of construction processes. Firstly, the *gecekondu* market demanded cheap construction because of limited financial resources and the immediate necessity of dwellings for newcomers. The quality of construction in terms of durability and aesthetics could be improved when a job with a steady income was found. Secondly, the mass production of industrial materials was scarce and expensive. After further development in the informal market, *ardiyes* supplied second-hand and industrially manufactured materials according to their financial income (Payne 1982). The accessibility to materials was as crucial as its affordability; thus, *ardiyes* were widely spreading in new *gecekondu* neighborhoods; meanwhile, the old urban center had already overloaded its capacity for new *gecekondus*.

As the *gecekondu* neighborhoods expanded in the periphery, new *ardiyes* appeared in the new *gecekondu* settlements (ibid). The available material supply from the original yards in the city center was getting harder to transport. Eventually, the supply was not enough; the peripheral yards started to manufacture cheap wall blocks from reprocessed industrial waste and local material; window and door frames; or roofing trusses (ibid). The architectural properties of *gecekondus* were based on the materials and components bought by credits from the *ardiyes*. Occasionally, the materials purchased were not enough to finalize the house, so the *gecekondu* builders had to finish it with whatever materials they could find (Şenyapılı 1981). Because of that, some parts of the facades could differ: one part of the wall might be mud and the other brick. The components such as doors and windows might also not match.

Since the entrepreneurial model was based on cooperation in the earlier stages of *gecekondu* urbanization, *ardiyes* were flexible with their payment schedules. Due to the limited financial resources of the newcomers, *ardiyes* were selling materials to them in monthly installments (Şenyapılı 1981; Şentürk 2016). Installment agreements between the *ardiye* owners and *gecekondu* builders needed a financial guarantor who was part of the solidarity network, e.g., a friend, relative, or fellow craftsmen (Duyar-Kienast 2005). Nevertheless, if some builders could not pay their installments, it did not cause a financial problem for the owner of the *ardiyes* because there was always an increasing demand (Şentürk 2013). The non-monetary logic of earlier *ardiye* transactions began to shift due to the profit-seeking activities of some of these entrepreneurial migrants who were getting wealthier and wealthier.

Figure 4.8: A remaining ardiye in Alibeyköy-Istanbul in 2017. In the background on the left, a new group of residential blocks can be seen

Source: Author's own

Despite the self-help and other non-profit cooperatives, the nature of *gecekondus*, they were also already commodified by *ardiye* owners who got rich by supplying materials to *gecekondus* and construction mafia in the 1960s (Erman 2004). Because new migrants densely occupied the city, there were fewer empty spots on the central state land for squatting. As a result, *gecekondus* had to be built on private land, which was not free like the state land had been. Due to increasing demand, land speculation was escalating, and the cost of construction materials and skilled labor was rising (Özdemir 1999). In addition to the unavailability of land, labor, and materials, the emergence of organized interest groups like *ardiye* owners or local political strongmen also influenced informal urbanization dynamics.

Most *ardiye* owners were transformed into speculative contractors by squatting or buying land in their neighborhoods or by trading *gecekondus*; they also became financers by offering loans to newcomers who did not have steady income (Payne 1982). By getting hold of the scarce material resources for their constructions and purchasing land, the monopoly of *ardiyes* enabled them to regulate the cost of *gecekondus*. Payne indicated that:

> [L]ike traditional agas or feudal chiefs... they were able to dictate the availability of credit and buy-up land on which to erect speculative houses, thereby inflating the prices of adjacent land and houses. (Ibid, 129)

Due to the lack of state authority, some local political strongmen started a 'land mafia' who controlled the land rights and decided who could occupy them (Şenyapılı 2004). Moreover, the squatted land is frequently prey to obscure real estate mafias, who grant themselves false titles of ownership or claim false rights in order to exert pressure on an already fragile population, and claim rents or other taxes by force (Pérouse 2004). As a result, new rural migrants had fewer opportunities to build their *gecekondus*. Solidarity between them were disappearing while the informal market was imposing a harsh capitalist system

As a result of the 1955 and 1966 Industrial Zone Plan, the Maltepe, Pendik, Kartal, and Tuzla districts were established as industrial zones in the Asian part, and a significant portion of the people who work in these areas settled around Bağdat Street and Fikirtepe (Yazıcıoğlu Halu 2010). The first squatter neighborhoods emerged around the Fikirtepe neighborhood close to the urban center of Kadıköy (Türk, Tarakçi, and Gürsoy 2020).

4.5 Economic Liberalization in the 1980s

The 1980s marked the end of the nationalist developmentalism era, and the Turkish economy opened up international capital and commodity flows. The political and economic choices of the developmentalist state were not enough for Istanbul to compete in the global market. However, Istanbul was able to distinguish itself through the rise of its private sector and restructuring attempts. Unlike the previous one, this regime did not function with authoritarian military principles. On the contrary, it adopted conventional policies recommended by the IMF (Keyder and Öncü 1994).

During this time, inner-city demolitions intensified in order to further expand the freeway network so as to solve the traffic problems arising with the ever-expanding population of Istanbul. In this economically liberal scene, *yap-satçılık* loans expanded into gecekondu neighborhoods that had finally received their land deeds after so many years of squatting. *Gecekondu* houses gave way to *apartkondus* (low quality apartment buildings) which lacked sufficient materials to withstand an earthquake.

4.5.1 Phase 2: *Gecekondu* Apartmentalization

In 1983, after a 3-year-long coup in Turkey, the Motherland Party (ANAP), led by Turgut Özal, won the elections as part of a right-wing coalition to fulfill the pursuit of liberalization and deregulation. Despite the previous restructuring attempts, their reforms resulted in lowered income distribution, subsidy limitations, and declining social expenditures (Boratav, Yeldan, and Köse 2001). Their political support came primarily from the rising populations of rapidly urbanizing major cities such as Istanbul; this was due to ANAP's invention of an urban populist strategy, which was primarily focused on the rural migrants in *gecekondu* neighborhoods (Öncü 1988). This urban populism promised prosperity for these low-income dwellers. They bought the dream of pushing their economic stratum upwards through a free-market system independent from former state controls. To accomplish this promise, ANAP took organized steps to legalize *gecekondus* (Dündar 2001; Balaban 2011). The squatted land functioned as a privatized asset that created economic opportunities. Landlords, once squatters, illegally demanded extra 'key money' from new rural migrants to profit from the high housing demand. The prices of housing increased due to profit-seeking activities from urban rent:

> By the mid-1960s, squatting in the traditional sense of the term had disappeared in Istanbul. Settlers had to pay local strongmen for the right to occupy even public land. In the mid-1970s, entrepreneurs with underground connections started controlling public lands in certain districts of Istanbul, selling land and monopolizing all construction activity. (Yönder 1998, 62)

Tahire Erman criticized the populist politics of ANAP for their taking advantage of the social and economic problems of low-income rural migrants:

> Populist politics opened wide the doors to the commercialization of *gecekondus*, which could be interpreted again as the government 'bribing' those who suffered the most from their liberal policies, thus silencing them

by giving them the hope of becoming rich. When its legal approval backed up the tendency of the 1970s to regard *gecekondu* land as a commodity in the 1980s, the 'apartmentalization' of *gecekondus* became a widespread phenomenon. Thus, the once-owner-occupied/owner-built *gecekondus* were being replaced by high-rise apartment buildings. The owner of the *gecekondu* land owned several apartments ('the undeserving rich Other'). In brief, pessimism was felt deeply by some *gecekondu* people who experienced increasing deprivation, while other *gecekondu* people became economically better-off in a short period. (Erman 2001, 987)

After the passing of several land amnesty laws during the ANAP administration, *gecekondu* dwellers were permitted to upgrade their houses to multi-story apartment buildings (up to 4 floors) (Keyder 1999; Pérouse 2014). This allowed them to be the owners of several apartments that could be rented out to new arrivals from rural areas. This new type of housing was referred to as *apartkondus*. *Müteahhits* [contractors] situated themselves in these emerging neighborhoods which, although in the periphery, were still advantageously located because they were, for example, close to access roads, near residential neighborhoods, or in urban recreational areas (Dündar 2001). These processes resulted in a powerful social change among the squatters who, once disparaged as occupiers, had become suddenly wealthier through urban land rent (Bilgin 2000).

In the 1990s, urbanization in Turkey assumed a different dynamic: forced migration (Keyder 2005; Saraçoğlu 2010). Unlike previous migrants from rural areas, Kurdish villagers, permanently displaced by a decade-long armed conflict between Turkish military and Kurdish rebels, experience forced migration to urban areas. In addition, *gecekondu* districts were polarized by ethnic conflicts. The state's inability to support the arrival of displaced Kurdish people has resulted in social disorders, such as unemployment, overpopulation, health problems, criminality, and social disintegration (Erman 2013).

According to Keyder and Öncü (1994), there were three major policy adjustments adopted by the ANAP government that affected radical urban change in Istanbul. First, they created new financial resources for metropolitan governments by increasing national and local tax revenues and taking foreign credits for infrastructural upgrading and global investment projects. Second, they founded the Mass Housing Fund [Toplu Konut Fonu], which gave state subsidies for low-income housing. Third, and most importantly, they changed the metropolitan governance model into a two-tier system: the greater metropolitan and the district-level municipalities (Candan and Kolluoğlu 2008). Consequently, the greater metropolitan municipality of Istanbul transformed into an entrepreneurial organization opened up to global investments. Urban planning processes assigned to local institutions led to the demolition of desolate neighborhoods and inner-city industrial areas.

These adjustments represented the decentralization of the central government's authority in favor of a more powerful local government. The control of Istanbul's critical governmental agencies, attached to central ministries in Ankara, was given to the metropolitan mayor of the greater municipality. In the two-tier municipality system, one part was responsible for garbage collection, repairs, and road maintenance. At the same time, the other part handled land use planning, building control, and building permits. Their bureaucratic power over issues such as local rent control made them remarkably influential. And yet, these changes, resulting from a series of legal amendments in local governance, did not solve the rapid urbanization problems. Instead of acting in the public interest to solve the housing and traffic problems, the officials accommodated the uncontrolled expansion of the Istanbul metropolitan area.

The metropolitan mayor of Istanbul, Bedrettin Dalan, equipped with new financial resources and administrative power, could have modernized Istanbul like Baron Haussmann did for Paris and Robert Moses did for New York[6]. In the next part, I will discuss the circumstances of Dalan's demolitions.

4.5.2 Mayor Dalan and his Demolitions

In the early 1980s, due to the ever-increasing population and unplanned expansion of *gecekondus*, Istanbul had major industrial pollution problems combined with a lack of housing, public transportation, and physical infrastructure. Instead of focusing attention on those problems, the municipal administration pursued profit-seeking activities for global investment. Bedrettin Dalan, a member of ANAP, initiated large-scale projects that promoted Istanbul as a world city within the context of globalization and liberalization (Keyder and Öncü 1994, 409). Dalan's efforts to renew the city center were based on plans for inserting transit routes to the Eminönü peninsula. Geared to the end goal of an international service center, these plans included new office buildings, hotels, cultural centers, and restaurants. During his service (1984–1989) foreign capital was invested in erecting hotel and bank buildings,

---

6   They both initiated radical urban changes by clearing buildings in the inner-city areas
     and destroying historical cityscapes.

transforming Istanbul's skyline with high-rise development in the post-1983 period.

Dalan, like former city bureaucrats, made his urban renewal plans based on demolitions. Instead of solving long standing traffic problems by adding public transportation, he added more roads. With rapid action that bypassed bureaucratic paperwork and heritage preservation legislation, Dalan ordered 30 thousand condemned buildings and old factories along the Golden Horn to be torn down to 'make it green and clean again' (ibid, 410). In order to open a controversial new Tarlabası Boulevard[7], he used the preceding legal system to clear some parcels a nineteenth-century Ottoman neighborhood in the city center (Figure 4.9). Later, this boulevard turned the area into an inner-city Ghetto.

The *Ardiyes* and *gecekondu* dwellers were once again not left empty-handed by this spate of 1980s demolitions, which produced an incredible number of reclaimed materials. From the informants of the fieldwork, it is proved that *çıkmacıs* were active in this period. With the new legalization processes, the building of *gecekondu* settlements spread to the periphery of Istanbul, under the jurisdiction of district municipalities. As a rule, clientelism and patronage relations with district authorities dominated Istanbul's real estate market, which was also relentless when global players entered the game:

> The rapid articulation of the newly elected district councilmen with vested interests in the construction sector on the one hand, and the-regional networks among their largely immigrant constituencies on the other, initially paved the way for a new wave of legalization and retroactive planning in the older informal settlements. (Ibid, 411)

For small and large entrepreneurs, the most popular option for 'making it big' was this construction sector that dominated the nationwide economy. Local governments began to demolish *gecekondus* to create prosperous neighborhoods where they could collect taxes (Keyder 2011). As a result of these developments, the city's periphery was divided into parts where the legal and the illegal coexisted (Erman and Eken 2004; Ayata 2008).

---

7   Tarlabaşı cuts through one of the oldest Greek neighborhoods. The municipality of Istanbul demolished more than 300 Ottoman apartments in 1987 in order to open a main highway connecting the first Bosphorus Bridge. For further reading of the boulevard construction see (Bilsel 2011).

Figure 4.9: A general view of the demolition and salvage activity in Tarlabaşı. On the right, reclaimed doors are leaning on the buildings. On the left, there is a heap of wood

Source: Bayram Muhittin Archive

During the 1980s, Kadıköy witnessed major motorway infrastructure works. Between 1984–87, the coastal arrangement from Kalamış to Bostancı was applied by land reclamation from the Marmara Sea, and the new coastal road was built to reduce and rearrange the traffic on Bağdat Street (Eyice 1994). Large-scale road transportation projects such as the construction of the second bridge increased the accessibility of the district and allowed its complete integration into the city. As a result, real estate values increased drastically, and urban rent was consolidated in the district.

The liberalization of the economy in the 1980s changed the grounds of *gecekondu*'s informality; it did so by commodifying land through rent-seeking projects that spearheaded inner-city *gecekondu* demolition and replacement. Plus, this also had an impact on *how* reclamation, reuse, and scrap dealing adjusted to the new dynamics. The next section clarifies these new urbanization dynamics.

4.6 Neoliberal Development in the 2000s

In Istanbul, globalization dynamics are most clearly seen in the expansion of the finance center, high-rise constructions, and luxurious real estate projects begun during the liberalization of the economy in the 1990s. The redistribution of land ownership was mainly based on informal land occupation from the 1950s until this dynamic changed in the 2000s with the neoliberal economy. The dwellers of inner-city *gecekondus* were dispossessed by land-grabbing urban renewal projects. After the 1999 Düzce Earthquake[8], seismic risk was perceived as an opportunity to renew the aging and structurally weak building stock. Urban renewal can be rapidly executed when facilitated by policy changes. This subchapter focuses on how urban transformation projects took over the urbanization processes in the early 2000s in Istanbul by utilizing demolitions.

4.6.1 Government Interventions for Urban Renewal Projects

Neoliberal activities in Turkey fall into three categories; 1. political projects that promote privatization, globalization, and the end of welfare; 2. economic philosophies or theories that prioritize private enterprise and capital accumulation on urban land; 3. modes of governmentality that see citizens as self-responsible subjects. (Candan and Kolluoğlu 2008, 46)

In contrast to earlier parcel-based investments in the prestigious central areas, neoliberal urban expansion focused on larger plots in the 2000s. With Kadir Topbaş coming to the metropolitan municipality's office in 2004, a new threshold was reached that redefines urban governance and development. Unlike the 1980s' partial development, top-down planning was tailored to large-scale mega projects like the third Istanbul Airport and the Istanbul Canal.

Since 2002, the AK party controlled government led by Recep Tayyip Erdoğan has ensured the administrative and legal grounds for urban renewal projects spanning over 18 years of governance. The most important change was the transformation of the Turkish Housing Development Administration (TOKI). As an institution that provided loans to housing cooperatives when founded in 1983, TOKI had undergone a radical transformation. With the

---

8   Especially after the Düzce Earthquake, some districts in Istanbul experienced a great deal of demolitions. Istanbul awaits a once-in-a-century earthquake since it sits on the North Anatolian Fault. The earthquake revealed that the buildings which are built were not built to endure a 7.2 seismic magnitude. The corrupt contractors of the time did not make the constructions following the regulations. By bribing the authorities, the projects were approved. In some cases, they did not use sufficient structural materials during the construction. Some buildings were built with sand from the sea. In 2014, while I was documenting a demolition in Fikirtepe, I observed seashells in most of the concrete rubble.

abolition of the social housing fund in 2001, the acquisition of land and properties of the Emlak Bankası [Real Estate Bank] after its closure, TOKI became the largest property owner of state land (Pérouse 2013). Between 2002 and 2008, 14 legal regulations expanded TOKI's fields of activity and increased its resources (Balaban 2011, 26). When TOKI was given the authority to make any alterations, of any scale, on the lands it controlled, the institution became the state's construction administration and social engineering tool (Bilgin 2013). TOKI was authorized by the state as the institution with the highest authority over housing and land production.

Regarding the authorization transferred to municipalities to declare an urban transformation area with Law No. 5366, the demolition of 1 million houses in Istanbul was legitimized (Kuyucu and Ünsal 2010). With the passage of Law No. 6306, historic neighborhoods such as Sulukule, Tarlabaşı, Süleymaniye, Fener, and Balat were included in the scope of urban development (Figure 4.10) (Turkish Parliment (TBMM) 2012). In cooperation with TOKI, municipalities have initiated the 'zero-gecekondu policy' to alter squatter neighborhoods into expensive residential areas (ibid, 6).

The *gecekondu* districts and old factory lands within central inner-city areas have become global investment assets for office buildings and financial centers. The government's plan embodied dislocating the poor, confiscating their land, privatizing public assets, and marketing the land for international investment (Aksoy 2014). The government excluded these neighborhoods—legitimated in previous administrations—by defining them as problematic districts with poor living conditions that were inhabited by marginal groups.

With the 5237 Turkish Penalty Code passed on June 1, 2005, the legal expression of the discourse against *gecekondus* became solidified: it imposed a prison term of one to five years for the construction of illegal houses, which it termed a 'crime against the environment'. *gecekondus* always had a temporary status, and their properties did not gain political autonomy. This situation made it easier for local authorities to clear *gecekondus* from peripheral areas. With the help of the government, the real estate sector was able to develop luxury residences equipped with shopping centers, leisure facilities, and office towers for the wealthier groups in those areas.

Figure 4.10: Inner-city urban renewal projects in Istanbul. White traced areas are historic neighborhoods (Tarlabaşı, Sulukule, and Süleymaniye) mentioned in the text

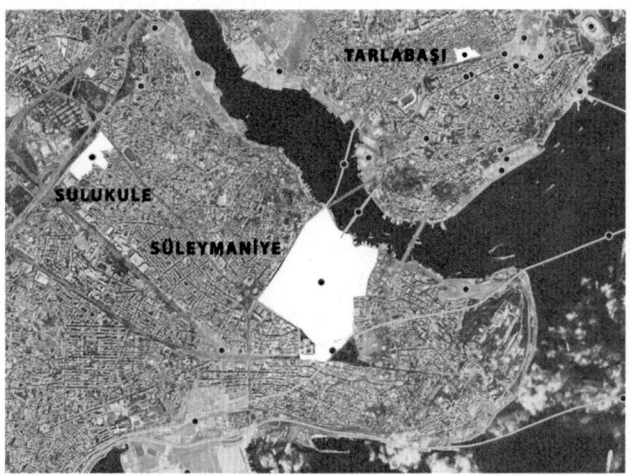

Source: http://megaprojelerIstanbul.com/

Gecekondus, which can be regarded as the city's periphery both socially and geographically, were transformed by forced evacuations and demolitions (Altay 2013). The fact that the government declared forty of these areas 'seismically risky' in Istanbul between July 2012 and December 2013 illustrates the scale of urban renewal at that time (Yalçıntan et al. 2014).

The consequence of urban renewal for the inhabitants of the *gecekondus* has positive and negative results. Those with a limited bargaining capacity with *müteahhits* due to the disadvantageous location of their *gecekondu* land could have an apartment in TOKI houses (Erman 2013). What was more, some lacked a legal title to their property, and these tenants lost access to affordable housing built by TOKI. Urban renewal projects were blamed for removing the urban poor to the periphery and replacing former *gecekondu* settlements with luxurious megaprojects designed for tourism and leisure (Karaman 2008). Briefly, the legal foundations of the neoliberal urban transformation were prepared by the parliament[9]. The most important of all is Law No. 6306 which is also known as Earthquake Law.

4.6.2 Law No. 6306 on Disaster Prevention and Transformation of High-Risk Areas

According to official figures, 18,243 people lost their lives, and 48,901 people were injured in the Izmit earthquake on 17 August 1999 (Figure 4.11) and the Düzce Earthquake on 12 November 1999. In two earthquakes, 377,879 building units were damaged to various degrees (Tan, Kanıpak, and Safer 2016). After this extreme loss, earthquake regulation and building security have become essential aspects of the country's policy. The urban renewal projects specified by Law No. 6306 in 2012 were supposed to create more livable and safe urban spaces (Turkish Parliment (TBMM) 2012). The earthquake showed that the buildings constructed by corrupt *müteahhits* did not withstand an earthquake over seven magnitudes. In the whole region, including Istanbul, the apartment blocks were built with defective materials without official control (see Ch. 4.5.1), and the seismic construction regulations were out of date.

The environment and Urban Planning Ministry announced that half of the country must be demolished and renewed within 20 years when the disaster law was legislated in 2012 (Pérouse 2013). Due to rapid, illegal, and cheap urbanization during the apartmentalization of *gecekondus*, AK Party used a proposed plan of tearing down and rebuilding all 7 million residential buildings as an electoral promise (Balaban 2011). With this necessity based on the seismic risk, the *gecekondu* demolitions, which were infrequent in Istanbul, were accelerated; 11,543 units were demolished in Istanbul from 2004 to 2008, which was an all-time record (Kuyucu and Ünsal 2010, 6). More recently, regarding the damage that will be caused by the next big earthquake, the current metropolitan mayor of Istanbul from the Republican Party (CHP), Ekrem Imamoğlu, stated that;

> Whereas the residential population of Istanbul is 15 million by night and 6 million by day, 255 thousand of the total 1 million 166 thousand buildings in the city were built before 1980, 533 thousand were constructed

---

9   Key legislative changes between 2000–2012 are Law No. 5226 in 2004, Law No. 5327, Law No. 5366 in 2005, Law No. 5293, Law No. 5582 and Law No. 6306 (Angell, Hammond, and Schoon 2014, 651).

between 1990–2000, and 376 thousand between 2000–2019. According to the "Earthquake and Damage Loss Estimation Study" conducted by the IBB Earthquake Analysis Directorate and the University of Boğaziçi in 2018; as a result of a devastating earthquake scenario of 7.5 magnitudes, the number of heavily and severely damaged buildings in Istanbul will be 48,000. The number of medium and higher damaged buildings will be 194,000. According to these figures, 22.6% of the buildings will be demolished. 25 million tons of debris will be generated. 30% of the roads will be closed. There will be a total structural and non-structural economic loss of 120 billion TL. (Imamoğlu 2019; my translation)

Figure 4.11: The destruction caused by Izmit earthquake in 1999

Source: Daily Sabah

Using these statistics, demolition and redevelopment were increasingly promoted by state officials. The Ministry of Environment and Urbanization, TOKI, and metropolitan and district municipalities initiated urban transformation projects by organizing a "destruction feast" (Adanalı 2012). In 2010, the former President of TOKI, Erdogan Bayraktar, stressed the importance of turning vacant lands into lucrative assets and bringing them into the economy (Ünsal 2011, 55). The statistical data above depicts an urban resource that can be reused and recycled; however, the governmental authorities continue to ignore the potential of this resource.

The purpose of Law No. 6306 is to determine the principles and practices of improvement, clearing, and redevelopment for safe buildings and healthy living spaces in accordance with technological and architectural norms and standards in the "high-risk areas". The legislation identified "high-risk zones" that may result in loss of lives and property, and accordingly, "risky buildings" in those zones as "reserve development zones", where new residential buildings could be built. The legislation specified strategies for determining high-risk zones and buildings; processes of evacuation and demolition; and post-demolition development projects. The law also describes the obligations and roles of state bodies.

Figure 4.12: Buildings and areas at seismic risk in Kadıköy

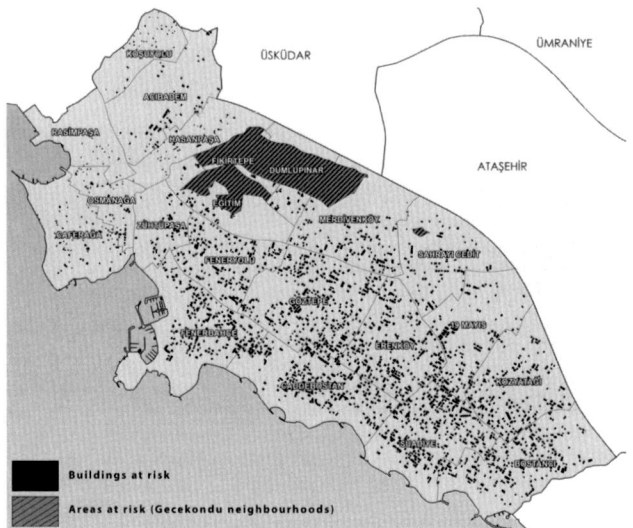

Source: Kadıköy Municipality

This law did not provide an environmental approach to disaster; instead, it mainly had stipulations and loopholes that bypassed NGOs, conservation laws, and questions of human rights violations. It also did not acknowledge disasters other than earthquakes, e.g., climate change. Nor did it have a social policy dimension: it did nothing to address poverty. It only emphasized the regeneration of physical space for redevelopment. Besides giving the appearance of recognizing secondary sectors—such as risky building detection, building control, demolition, and excavation—the policy changes did not prescribe guidelines for the deconstruction of the buildings. Instead, demolitions were accomplished as rapidly as possible to open up space for new construction. In between these rapid processes, scrap collectors also became *çıkmacıs* in Istanbul. The following section addresses the urban transformation process based on seismic risk in Kadıköy (Figure 4.12).

4.6.3 Urban Renewal in Kadıköy due to Earthquake Risk

The second wave of construction in Kadıköy occurred after the Izmit Earthquake in 1999, which was felt strongly in Kadıköy, located along the Marmara coast. While supporting the growth of the construction and real estate sector, 'demolish-redevelop' method in Kadıköy to facilitate urban renewal under the cover of earthquake-proofing. According to the Kadıköy Center - E5 (D100) Motorway Master Plan in 2005, the buildings were once more allowed to be built with additional floors. The legislation of Law No. 6306 provided benefits for the homeowners to renew their dwellings and create lucrative investments for the real estate market (Figure 4.13).

According to law no. 6306, it is the duty of the local municipality to offer rent support to homeowners for 18 months. Additionally, to stay in business, the construction firms offer rent assistance to homeowners. The new zoning code requires the construction firm to have an additional floor that secures construction costs and even profits from selling new units. Usually, after 18 months of construction, the owners move back to their renewed apartments. In most cases, the urban transformation results in increasing the value of the apartments and the neighborhood without any cost to the homeowners, who also receive financial resources that support the costs of moving and rent support throughout the urban transformation process. As a result of these developments, the Kadıköy district turned into a dangerous construction site. Pedestrians were killed in accidents due to dangerous maneuvers of dump trucks in traffic (D. Öztürk 2019). The air pollution increased because of the construction dust. The verdant garden that was Kadiköy lost its glow to the jungle of new apartments as they ate up more and more space.

Figure 4.13: One of the remaining Ottoman Mansions in Kadıköy, Istanbul: Cavit Paşa Villa in Bağdat Street. In front, there is an old Ottoman fountain. At the back, the construction of buildings via Urban Transformation.

Source: Alp Eren Archive

Figure 4.14: Urban renewal in Fikirtepe[10]

Source: Author's own based on 140 Journos Archive (left), Ministry of Environment and Urbanization (right)

---

10   On the left is a house that was previously a gecekondu standing alone after a disagreement with the developer in Fikirtepe. On the right is a 1:1000 scale master plan showing new parcels combining small lots of previous buildings in Fikirtepe.

This transformation process is experienced differently in other neighborhoods, especially in Fikirtepe, which used to be a *gecekondu* neighborhood. Fikirtepe is located on the Anatolian side of Istanbul within the Kadıköy district. The main transportation link, the D-100 (E 5) State Highway, passes through the northern section of the area. The neighborhood emerged as one of the first *gecekondu* districts since the 1950s, and was legalized in the 1990s with state-given land deeds. Its small workshops, sweatshops, and scrap depots served as a multi-functional site combining small-scale production and housing use.

In order to improve its physical, social, and living standards, the Fikirtepe district was declared a 'special project area' as a part of the 1/5000 master plan (Istanbul Metropolitan Municipality (IBB) 2005). In order to provide urban improvements to the district, urban consolidation incentives for land assembly were initiated by turning small, divided joint-owned buildings into larger units. To accelerate the process, the government declared the district a risky area in 2013 under Law No. 6306. However, without the regulatory presence of local authorities and the state, the whole planning process failed by resulting in unresolved agreements between homeowners and developers and unfinished constructions after massive demolitions due to bankrupt developers (Türk, Tarakçi, and Gürsoy 2020). Some homeowners who disagreed with urban transformation measures became a symbol of victimization due to the confiscation of their land rights (Figure 4.14). In addition, some of the small-scale production and service sectors, including scrap collector warehouses, had to move to peripheral locations or change to different temporary locations.

The number of construction licenses issued by Kadıköy Municipality in 2010 was 185; this value approached 521 in 2014, 612 in 2015, 826 in 2016, and 1000 in 2017 (Berkmen and Sırma 2019). This exponential increase also represented the number of demolitions becoming resources for building salvage. Local scrap collectors took over salvaging from demolishers and started material reclamation to sell discarded materials to recycling factories and trade second-hand components. Due to this surplus, depots that already existed in the Asian part extended their capacity and number. However, inner-city depots in Fikirtepe were relocated to peripheral sites. Eventually, they moved closer to the official industrial zone.

4.7 Conclusion

This chapter gave an overview of Istanbul's urbanization process. During the shifts from state-led to globalized to neoliberal economy, the city has been repeatedly demolished and redeveloped. *gecekondu* squatters provide a prime example of how state land is distributed to the rural migrant population. Illegal land occupation was allowed by the populist regime because the governments did not have a housing plan and sufficient economic resources. The history of land commodification describes how current multi-story dwellings are built in formal and informal neighborhoods. Apartmentalization occurred in two main phases: the creation of middle-class housing estates in the 1950s and the upgrade of *gecekondu* dwellings in the 1980s.

Within an environment lacking any official deconstruction guideline, the *çıkmacıs* have adapted to the wide array of historical transformations. The reclaimed materials were often used in the *gecekondus*. Such informal housing expanded the borders of the city where we live now. The *ardiyes* provided resources to the overnight squatter constructions while pragmatically profiting from them. They became one of the major infrastructures supporting 'right to housing' for new rural arrivals.

Today, *gecekondu* construction is no longer allowed by the state. The customers for second-hand materials have changed. The material cycle has shifted. That's why it is critical for the scope of this study to understand how these small *çıkmacı* businesses adjusted to the new market dynamics while neoliberal dynamics shaped by earthquake regulations and the demolitions continue on a mass scale. For instance, Kadıköy went through major development of individual apartments.

5. The Role of Unrecognized Labor

5.1 Introduction

This chapter, based on empirical ethnographic data, examines the building salvage and farming labor activities of *çıkmacıs*. The family members work at demolition for most of the year in Istanbul. They adjust to neoliberal urbanization dynamics to generate income from street scrap collecting and material reclamation. Furthermore, they work seasonally on their farmland in Yazıhüyük. I will argue that, in regard to work insecurity and irregular income, they can be identified as precarious labor. Also, based on their dual lives, I will show that a family's activities can be understood as a bridge between rural and urban.

Rural migration and marginalized minorities are often associated with scrap collecting, waste picking, and building salvage—all of these are activities unregulated by the local authorities in Turkey as well as the Global South in general. They find their own below-the-radar survival strategies for overcoming poverty and unemployment (Bayat 2013). When there is a lack of urban structures and facilities, their solidarity and social networks become relational infrastructures (Simone 2015).

In the first part of this chapter, official and unrecognized actors in Istanbul's waste recycling will be identified. My aim is to highlight their heterogeneous structure and informal means (Gidwani 2015; Tuçaltan 2018); as part of that process, I will describe the activities of *çıkmacıs*. In the second part, I will describe building materials' demolition and reclamation processes. The sections to follow give a detailed description and analysis of the salvage work and the urban life of scrap collectors.

Because of global, political, and economic reasons, the state has neglected family farming in Turkey. Industrial agriculture controlled by corporations took over small-scale local farming activities in the 2000s (M. Öztürk et al. 2018). However, the farmland is a *vibrant object* that strongly influences the two-fold livelihood of *çıkmacıs* (Bennett 2010). It can be regarded as a nonhuman actant that impacts human life through *trans-corporeal* associations (Alaimo 2010) via day-to-day bodily engagement with the soil. Their farmland's agency and its *cosmopolitical* capacities are beyond economic factors (Blok and Farias 2016). In a post agricultural era, their return movements depend on the climate, vegetation and many other nonhuman actors. In the last part of this chapter, I reflect upon their other work life in farmland and agricultural production. Even though they migrated to the city, they are bound to their village.

5.2 Heterogenous Waste Management in Istanbul

Waste has been an income resource throughout the urbanization history of Istanbul. Among the many street vendors and artisans in the city, some professions deal with discarded objects, waste, and their reuse processes. For instance, people called *lodosçu* (beachcombers) were salvaging items and materials after the Southwestern tides changed on the shores of the Bosporus (Aktaş 2010). During the 17th century, the waste collector guild[1] separated waste into reusable objects and materials (Ayşe 2008). Back when Ottoman guilds were representatives of particular professions, the wall masons and demolishers named *yıkıcılar* were responsible for demolishing and salvaging buildings (Çelik 2007). Even after the modernization of waste management systems, unrecognized recycling workers, scrap collectors[2], and waste pickers[3] continue to collect and segregate waste and scrap.

When urban demolitions intensified in Istanbul, the informal waste workers took advantage of infrastructural absences (Ceritoglu and Altay 2016). The overall management of waste flow is heterogeneous because formal and informal actors coexist in managing and recycling the discarded items (Gidwani 2015; Tuçaltan 2018). In the following section, which is based on empirical data, I will first discuss the municipality facilities and the private recycling industry, then move on to the laborers whose participation is unrecognized and unregulated.

---

1   Arayıcı esnafı in Turkish.
2   Eskici in Turkish.
3   Kağıt toplayıcısı in Turkish.

Figure 5.1: Building elements recovered from an apartment

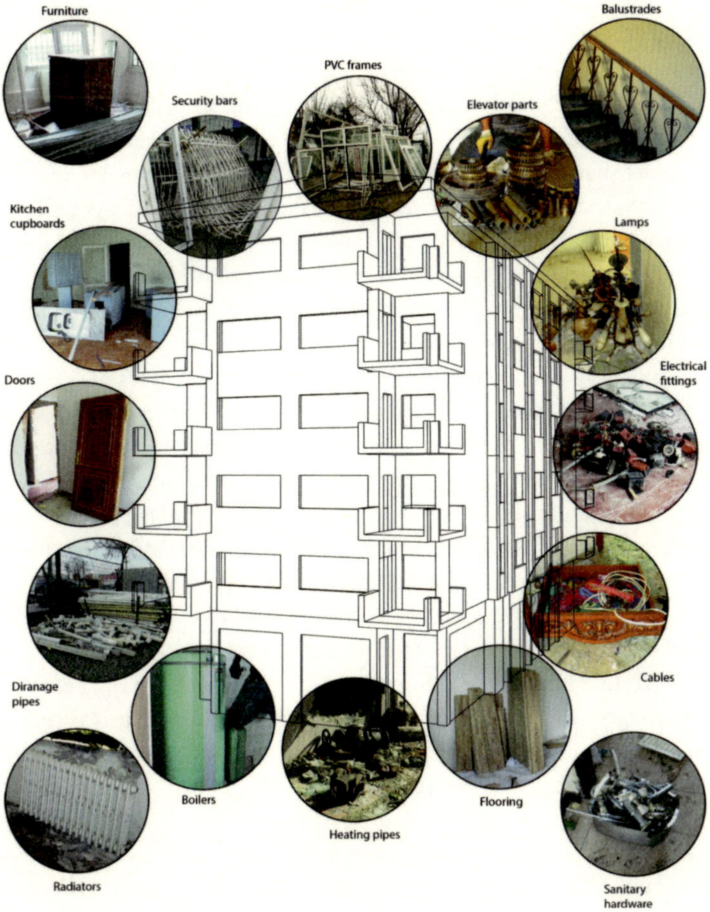

Source: Author's own

5.2.1 Formal Actors: Municipalities and Licensed Waste Collection Companies

Turkey recovered 38 percent of its overall waste in 2020[4] officially (Turkish Statistical Institute (TÜIK) 2020). The collection and separation of domestic waste, that is not sorted out in households, are the responsibility of the district municipalities. Above that level, the metropolitan municipality is assigned to recycle domestic, industrial, construction, and medical waste in the most populated cities in Turkey; however, their collection system lacks the appropriate infrastructure and labor force (Kanat 2010). In Istanbul, some district municipalities funded companies with a waste separation facility to modernize their facility and hire waste pickers and scrap collectors.

The Istanbul Environmental Protection and Waste-Processing Corporation (ISTAÇ) is the main waste management entity in the metropolitan municipality of Istanbul. They select, design, and construct sanitary landfills and function as technical consultants to local administrations. ISTAÇ coordinates industrial and medical waste disposal and has facilities that produce electricity from landfill gas and compost from organic waste. They are responsible for recycling packaging material and the extraction of solid waste from sea vessels. They clean the main arterial roads and squares, coasts, and beaches of Istanbul. Finally, they are in charge of managing excavation and demolition debris dumps. In addition, the company runs a specialized recycling facility with a capacity of two hundred tons per hour. Utilizing that debris surplus, the company assists in the rehabilitation of former mining sites and supplies material for land reclamation projects.

In 2016, at the beginning of my fieldwork, I visited a municipal recycling facility in the Esenler district in Istanbul; it was a sizable warehouse where 70 employees worked. This facility was selling separated waste as raw materials to recycling factories. In the warehouse, they had two different departments: transportation and sorting. In the sorting department, the workers used a conveyor belt to pick out unwanted objects from the bulk waste. There were machines for compressing and strapping among the heaps of paper and plastic. The workers, who earned minimum wage, had 8-hour daily work shifts. Primarily, they were Kurdish and originated from eastern Turkey. They used to

---

4   In European Union, it is 60 percent in 2020 (EUROSTAT 2022).

be farmers or livestock[5] breeders. One of them explained that he migrated to Istanbul in the 1980s to seek a better livelihood because of unemployment in his village. With the help of a relative, he started working as a waste picker and scrap collector when he migrated to Istanbul. He stated: "I found this job through a contact at the municipality. I am lucky to find this job; however, we have a short contract. Our job security is weak, but it is better than to go around all day scavenging waste". By and large, the informal pickers were hired by facilities like Esenler or licensed private companies to collect and recycle waste.

Figure 5.2: A recycling worker is collecting paper boxes on the street in Istanbul. They rummage through Istanbul with their pushcarts called "çekçek".

Source: Ali Saltan Archive

Close to the Esenler municipal recycling facility, there were several private plastic recycling depots in Topkapı industrial zone, among other small industrial production establishments. They granulate plastic waste and sell it to large-scale factories. One of the depots' owners stated that he was buying PVC window frames from scrap collectors who salvaged demolition sites. Some self-employed workers were working with him regularly. The owner was buying these frames by the kilogram and then separated the metal profiles and

---

5   The livestock was killed by the Turkish Military in the 1980s and breeding is banned in the pastures located in south-east Turkey (Zeybek 2020).

sold them to another metal recycling depot in the area. In the depot, the plastic granulating machine was breaking the frames into small pieces. After being traded as raw material, he explained: "PVC window frames become drainage pipes in a factory". After analyzing the exchange at this kind of depot, one realizes that a scrap collector is no different than a waste recycling worker (Figure 5.2) who, as a self-employed individual, sells waste as a commodity; by means of collecting, dismantling, salvaging, or "putting the waste into the carrier, segregating and classifying, all constitute both physical and social labor spent to make waste ready for recycling" (Dinler 2016, 38).

Figure 5.3: Salvaging an apartment building in Kadıköy[6]

Source: Author's own

The municipalities and their privatized companies *want to* adhere to EU recycling standards. In the absence of succeeding that, waste pickers, scrap collectors, and *çıkmacıs* (Figure 5.3) continue to recycle and repurpose waste. The

---

6   At this instant, Engin, Jabir, and Hayatullah are taking down a window frame that faces the Marmara Sea. Engin is hanging out the window (dangerously) to retrieve one last piece. The room is full of debris such as the long PVC profiles lying on the floor. Walking inside the large living room is almost impossible because of all the broken things, especially the broken glass. At the back, the edge of Kınalı Island can be seen, which is an expensive view and reveals this as an expensive neighborhood.

functioning of waste management systems depends on the symbiosis between formal and informal actors. Here, informality should be defined as a heuristic device that helps us think about the blurry border between formal and informal (Roy 2011, 223). It should not be regarded as an economic or social problem but rather as a social existence that can help us understand adaptation, practicality and negotiation practices of street labor (Bayat 2004). Because of this, 'unrecognized' rather than 'informal' is a more fitting definition of their legal and social status.

5.2.2 Unrecognized Actors: Çıkmacıs

Unrecognized laborers in the recycling sector are mostly rural migrants who were able to move to Istanbul in the 1970s and, more recently, refugees. There are two prominent actors in street collection work: waste pickers and scrap collectors. Prior to the daily collection of the municipal waste, which ends up in separation facilities or landfills, the waste bins are visited by the waste pickers who separate and collect recyclable materials and objects. As unregistered and unlicensed laborers in the recycling industry, they sell their waste to metal and plastic warehouses (Dinler 2016; Tuçaltan 2018). Day and night, they roam around the city with their pull carts from one garbage bin to another.

Unlike waste pickers, scrap collectors do not sort out solid waste. They roam around the neighborhoods collecting metal scrap, unused or damaged electronic equipment, old furniture, and household objects of any kind. While shouting "*eskici*" (ragman) from behind their pushcarts, they call out for old stuff and discards to buy from residents. Either they get the objects for free or haggle down to a very low amount of money. Later, they sell collected household items from their stall, pushcarts or flea markets. Sometimes they deal with second-hand shops where second-hand furniture and electronic appliances are sold. Additionally, they trade metal scraps to recycling warehouses or factories. Scrap collectors operate in a zone between street refuse and building salvage because of their mobility and adaptability to second-hand commodities.

Waste pickers are perceived as competitors by the private sector and municipalities. Such competition by the latter is unfair because state-supported bodies have the legislative power to marginalize waste pickers. Unfortunately, waste pickers have limited resources to organize themselves against this competition or related conflicts. Because they are self-employed, they are not represented by any recognized professional body. In South America, waste picker organizations and cooperatives (e.g, OPDS in Argentina and Coopcent ABC in Brazil) contribute to making policy frameworks (Gutberlet et al. 2017). It also shows that the circular economy is not only bound to technical modernization and formal governance issues.

Figure 5.4: Moving salvaged building components[7]

Source: Author's own

Architectural salvage relates to the restoration and conservation of old building parts with historical and aesthetic significance (Addis 2006). During the fieldwork, I encountered a few architectural salvagers who sell second-hand parts of buildings because of their antique or vintage value. In contrast to this, the *çıkmacıs* mainly dismantle modern concrete apartment buildings from the 1960s that were renovated or remodeled with new building parts. Being in good condition, those parts have the potential to become part of the circular economy.

---

7   A scrap collector is bringing a window frame of a gecekondu to a supply yard. The frame weighs between 30 and 40 kilos, depending on the metal profiles inside. The gecekondu was demolished a few hours before. Other items (a washing machine and a satellite TV antenna) in the truck are taken to another second-hand shop. This is a typical size and type of truck for Çıkmacıs.

The *çıkmacıs* are the main actors in building salvage. The city is repaired and renewed by such labor, "continuously re-creating the conditions of possibility for urban life and capitalist enterprise" (Gidwani 2015, 576). When urban renewal via demolitions accelerated in all districts of Istanbul, the workload created job opportunities for the recycling market. Abandoned buildings became a resource (Figure 5.4) and demolition contractors, scrap collectors, and other entrepreneurs were able to benefit. After the intensification of demolitions, the scrap collectors expanded their business with their family-oriented workforce. They brought their relatives from their home villages. If the number of workers was insufficient, they employed Syrian and Afghan refugee workers for cheap labor. Through these strategies, they have adapted to the dynamics of neoliberal urbanization.

Figure 5.5: Transporting salvaged materials[8]

Source: Author's own

---

8   The truck belongs to Engin. They load the metal pieces of the roof before they bring down window frames. The pieces are stacked nicely to organize the load's volume. They will take them to a scrap dealer in the industrial zone. The fences of the demolition site are poorly placed and without a proper door. They have to sleep on the premises to protect their reclaimed materials.

Çıkmacıs generate income from two areas: the recycling sector and the second-hand market. First, they sell recyclable materials to municipality depots or private recycling factories. In this sort of exchange, they are like paper collectors: they act as middlemen between waste and recycling factories, sell their labor, and trade sorted waste as a commodity. For example, the recycled metal prices depend on global exchange prices (Corwin 2018; Dinler 2016). Second, they are part of an unregulated second-hand network of component reuse. Often, they reclaim, collect and repair second-hand building elements in their depots which are visited by a range of customers or whole-sellers locally or from afar (Figure 5.5). Their prices are regulated according to the cost of new products and labor expenses.

Through kinship and village fellowship relations, recycling labor and construction work are distributed among migrants dispossessed from their rural livelihoods (Erman 2001). For instance, most waste pickers come from Kurdish towns; scrap collectors are usually from Nevşehir; scrap dealers come from Niğde; Malatya is the origin city of most building demolishers; the workers who dismantle come from Bingöl; and so forth. After migrating to highly populated cities, the people who take these informal professions use their entrepreneurial abilities and relational strategies to survive and adapt (Simone 2015). More importantly, these relational mechanisms enable *çıkmacıs* to find different jobs via subcontracting and customer referrals.

As described above, their supply yards, warehouses and depots are established in former *gecekondu* neighborhoods. Although stationed at a fixed base, their labor system is very flexible and mobile: they can move their business from one neighborhood to another, from one demolition to the next.

5.3 Building Demolition in Istanbul

Three actors take part in building demolition and recycle-reuse processes in Istanbul: the construction company, the building demolisher, and the *çıkmacıs*. The company is responsible for financing and coordinating the demolition of the old building and the construction of a new building. First, they hire demolishers and sometimes *çıkmacıs* to clear the property. Second, the demolishers tear down the building and discard the concrete rubble at official debris dumping sites. Third, the *çıkmacıs* dismantle the salvageable and recyclable components and materials, which they will store and trade on the second-hand market. Before the intensification of the urban transformation projects, all material reclamation was carried out by demolishers with their own salvage yards. Currently, salvaging of buildings in Istanbul is generally undertaken by *çıkmacıs* with scrap collector backgrounds but, in the other parts of Turkey, demolishers still handle the reclamation part.

These demolitions demand cheap manual labor with official and unofficial subcontracting agreements between actors. Most of the contracts are off-the-record and the labor conditions precarious. Subcontracting without job security allows the demolition and construction companies to end agreements at any time and cut payments. A *çıkmacı* commented on this situation:

> The company hires me as day labor, but they do not pay it daily. If we are lucky, we get the whole amount at the end of the month. But sometimes, they give less. Also, sometimes they pay for our health insurance, sometimes they don't.

In urban transformation projects, the demolition process starts with the property owners applying to state institutions for a seismic risk inspection. If the inspectors deem that the structure is insufficient to withstand a strong earthquake, the building is declared uninhabitable. The owners then arrange with a construction company to begin the renewal process. At that point, the condemned building, including all its materials and components, belongs to the contractor at no cost. After the municipality grants a demolition permit, the contractor hires a demolition company that, in turn, signs an official contract with the contractor. Generally, the demolisher estimates the service costs according to the height of the building. The total cost of demolition is calculated by summing up the costs or wages of equipment rental, machine operators, day laborers, and debris removal.

The workers start the demolition by placing a small excavator on the roof level. Then, they identify columns and beams and make holes in the floor. These holes channel the falling rubble to lower levels. To make the premises secure, they build a construction safety slide that internally lets down the debris to the lower floors. The wooden roof structure is generally reused to make this net (Figure 5.6).

In a large-scale demolition, for example, a housing project with several blocks, the contractor sells the building wreckage to the demolition company who then sells the salvageable building parts to the *çıkmacıs*, who then reclaim the materials. Retrieved from concrete by an excavator, reinforcement bars are sold to scrap metal dealers or recycling factories. *Çıkmacıs* reclaim plastic window frames, doors, radiators, kitchen counters and sanitary equipment. They also pull out lighting hardware, plumbing fixtures, copper electrical cables, taps, and metal pipes; dismantle elevators and central heating systems for metal recycling; and break oversized window frames for plastic recycling. They even reclaim furniture and household items (books, pictures, chairs, sofas, and antique objects) from the previous tenants to sell at flea markets.

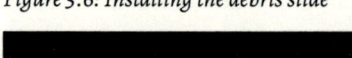

Figure 5.6: Installing the debris slide[9]

Source: Author's own

---

9   The workers create a debris slide to control the rubble falling from the upper floors. The beams holding the surface go through the floor slab. If they don't have enough wood, they sometimes use parts of wooden cupboards left by the old tenants. The man without work clothes climbs over to nail down one last piece of wood while others watch him to see if he needs help. Since the apartment is on a busy narrow street, they have to tear most of it down by hand.

5.3.1 Reclamation Processes

After visiting çıkmacıs in Altınşehir, where there are many of them, I started observing the construction sites around my neighborhood in Kadıköy. The urban
transformation and never ending construction trend, which intensified since
the 2012 law changes, was at my doorstep. I first met Engin, the youngest brother
of the Coruk family, in an abandoned apartment building behind where I lived.
The façade of the building facing my room was ten meters away from me. After all the tenants moved out, I started to observe the demolition site. Sometimes working alone, Engin appeared through the adjacent windows. Sometimes others were helping him. The building was eroding more each day by his
salvaging actions. At various parts of the building, he was dismantling and removing things as if they were special treasures. After days of observation, I decided to visit the site for documentation and meet him. When I passed the metal
security barrier surrounding the demolition site, I realized the apartment building was named Uzay Apartmanı [Space Apartments].
    The entrance and main stairs were filled with furniture that looked a little
warped. There were also some potted plants there. Later I realized that they
were the objects left by the tenants when they moved. As I wandered around
the building, the first thing I noticed was that the front doors of the flats were
removed. Their interiors were severely broken up by salvagers. Bits and pieces
of small rubble were lying on the floor. The stair railing had been removed with
a blowtorch (Figure 5.7). I shouted out to see if somebody was there. A response
in an eastern dialect came a little later from an upper flat. Hesitantly I walked
up towards the construction sounds coming from upstairs. As I stepped on glass
shards, I realized the vertical air circulation felt larger because all the entrance
doors were removed. I found Engin dismantling a window frame. He kept working while talking to me. He was looking for the bolts connecting the window
frames to the concrete by making test holes. Then he removed them by pulling
the frame out of the window gap like a dentist pulls a tooth. He was in kind of a
hurry, almost as if he was running out of time. He was loudly smashing the frame
he had just removed, the glass particles were spreading around the frames and
lifting dust up from the ground.
                                    —from my fieldnotes, entry on 08.10.2016.

With three to four workers, it takes a week to dismantle an 8-floor apartment block. The reclaimed materials and components are relatively new and

high-quality because most owners replaced old ones with the latest components when remodeling their flats. However, there was more glue, spray foam sealant, and other adhesives used in construction as well, which makes it more challenging to take down new buildings. Because the fieldwork was held in middle-class neighborhoods, apartment interiors are in good condition. Modern facades equipped with PVC window frames and shutters are particularly sought after. The window frames, which have narrow dimensions (between 1 and 3 meters) are carefully dismantled to be sold secondhand. When I asked why small sizes are preferred, Engin explained:

> The customers demand narrow window frames. In the villages where we sell the most components, they prefer small dimensions. The houses are smaller, and the climate is cold. Also, they are lighter to carry and transport. We can fit many in the truck since we sell every piece.

Figure 5.7: Cutting metal pipes[10]

Source: Author's own

---

10   A blowtorch is efficient for cutting old pipes although it creates an industrial smell at the site and leaves burn marks on the wall. The buildings in the area were built in the 1970s and have central heating systems made of metal parts. After dismantling, the çıkmacıs will send these parts to a metal depot and sell them by the kilo.

Since Istanbul apartments have wide openings due to the warm climate, the rest of the frames are broken up for recycling. *Çıkmacıs* can sell the reclaimed materials at the spot where the demolition is located; otherwise, they transport the materials to their yards. During our conversation about storage, he said:

> Sometimes a man who sees us working comes in [to our demolition workplace] and asks for the price of the components. We immediately bargain and sell them. In this way, we do not have to transport them to our depots.

The demolition site is not a safe place for *çıkmacıs* (Figure 5.8). It is extremely dangerous, and they have to work in precarious conditions; however, they do not wear proper work clothes. Ali, brother of Engin, protested about this safety issue: "The [heavy] work clothes do not allow me to move freely to do my job. So, I often do not wear them. If you are scared of accidents, you should not work at construction sites." Dismantling activities take place without any labor safety include hammering, torching, breaking, and crushing. They are also all activities that produce dust emissions. When *çıkmacıs* work on roofs or boiler rooms where asbestos has commonly been used, they potentially breathe the hazardous air, but they do not consider this to be a danger to their health. As I mentioned the harms of asbestos and asked his opinion, Engin answered:

> They say asbestos is dangerous, but who listens? Demolishers do not pay attention. They just spray water over the dust. And I have not seen anyone controlling it. We encounter some of these materials in the basements. I know it is a fibrous element. We treat it like any other element. Invisible to the eye, invisible to the attention.

The municipal authorities barely inform the workers about the dangers of asbestos. They also never inspect the demolition sites for safety. The neighborhood itself is even at risk due to the asbestos dust spreading from unsealed buildings (Odman 2019). The dangerous aspects of these materials may affect the health of the workers in the future (See Ch. 7.2).

As self-employed workers, *çıkmacıs* are supposed to pay for their own social security and health insurance. These payments were not very regularly paid by the workers since their incomes were not regular. Ali complained about such precarity: "I could not pay my health insurance last month because I could not work. During the construction, I had a hand injury. A loose metal profile fell while I was pulling out a window frame. When such injuries happen, we cannot continue working so, there is no income".

Figure 5.8: Dismantling PVC frames[11]

Source: Author's own

Engin was earning slightly more from PVC recycling of window frames than his second-hand trade. However, he declared: "There is a big demand for cheap frames. Everything is getting expensive. Especially for those who build summer and village houses". They could quickly sell them at the construction site. That's why a supply yard was unnecessary. They sold salvaged parts to Anatolian traders who in turn distributed the same components to Anatolian cities: Sivas, Tokat, Erbağ, Kayseri, Nevşehir, Niğde and Balıkesir. Once, trom one 5-floor apartment in Kadıköy-Moda, Engin sold 40 pieces of window frames, ten metal entrance doors, 200 m2 parquet flooring, ten interior doors, and five kitchen cupboards to a contractor from Kayseri. They were regularly working with a wholesaler from the Black Sea who was running a warehouse in

---

11   The work requires a lot of strength because the frames are attached to the gap with many screws. First, the glass is broken since it does not have any use. Then the profiles are pulled out, sometimes with a crowbar. After this process, the joint marks on the walls become revealed. Mishaps may release asbestos from the insulation layer.

Fikirtepe. According to Engin, this wholesaler, whose name was Ali, had legal and illegal business connections. He owned a truck and transported goods of all sorts. Ali's connections were expanding to Batumi in Georgia.

In the next section, I will focus on Engin's family, who make their livelihood by scrap collecting and building salvage. Such informal jobs are called 'arrival occupations' (Michael, Deshpande, and Ziervogel 2019, 667). The highlight of the encounter with this family was its valuable empirical contribution that shed light on processes and dynamics observed during the fieldwork.

5.3.2 A *Çıkmacı* Family

The Coruk family originates from a village called Yazıhüyük in Nevşehir. The region is famous for its geographic wonders: the underground cities of the Cappadocians, its fairy chimneys, and its volcanic valleys. The village is named after a 'prehistoric tell', an archeological mound or artificial hill created by the remains of many generations living and rebuilding on the same spot. The tells are made of ancient debris and discarded items. It is interesting that this hill has ancient conceptual connections to the Coruk's present livelihood in Istanbul, where they earn their living from building salvage.

This family is a patriarchal family consisting of three brothers and their parents, wives, and children of 'Yörük' origin—Turkmen nomad ancestors from the Taurus mountains in the same region. Their nomadic story continues: Their dual lives are split between Istanbul and Yazıhüyük. Their migration started when the elder brother escaped to Istanbul at the age of 18. Ali did not want to work on the farm and help his father. 25 years ago, he ran to Istanbul and lived with a former fellow from the village. He left without the consent of his father. Bored of village life, he was a young misfit. Firstly, he worked in a supermarket as a bagger who helped pack groceries. Later with the help of another friend from his village, he started scrap collecting with his pushcart, traveling from street to street. For him, his job gives him a sense of freedom: "Collecting scrap means being free; one can wander around the neighborhoods of Istanbul". The family has been farming for at least two generations, and the father disapproved of his son's choice at first. Later though, after seeing his son maintain a steady income from scrap dealing, and because he was living on the edge of poverty, he decided to send his two other sons to Istanbul. This did not stop them from farming, and

> they also didn't stop salvaging and scrap collecting. During planting and harvest,
> the brothers travel back and forth.
>
> —from my fieldnotes, entry on 27.05.2018.

The youngest of the family, Engin, aged 35, has been a scrap collector for the
last 15 years. As more and more apartment buildings became discarded commodities, he adjusted by hunting for abandoned buildings and traveling from
one neighborhood to another. At his first job, he was getting paid with building
scrap in exchange for a cash debt. They buy the scrap material from the contractor. Their status at the construction site is relatively ambiguous, he explained:

> We are not providing a service for the contractor. We work for ourselves. We
> are self-employed individuals that mine materials from buildings. When
> the municipality comes for inspection, we say that we work for the construc-
> tion company. It's easier. If we explain we are scrap collectors, they ask for
> safety permits and insurance. We try to avoid that.

During my visit to their village in 2018, he said that building salvage tripled
last year since there was high demand for rebuilding apartments in the area
because of seismic risk. I asked him if the buildings that he salvaged really
needed to be demolished because of this risk and he responded: "Some seem
strong enough to survive an earthquake. I would say sixty percent of the buildings were fine. But demolition is good for vitalizing our economy". He further explained that construction quality was better in a middle-class district
like Kadıköy. He added that the buildings should be abandoned immediately
in Fikirtepe since they were poorly upgraded from *gecekondus* in the 1990s (See
Ch. 4.5.1). He made this observation when he was working in Fikirtepe, which
was a former squatter district. Moreover, he observed that the buildings were
built using wet sea sand that caused corrosion in the reinforcement bars in the
concrete.

They rotated their tasks in the buildings where they worked. Dismantling
continued in different stages, but their tasks remained the same. At the first
deconstruction location, one dismantled the window frames. In the second location, the other retrieved the copper electric wires. At the third place, another
cut out the metal parts of the building. Meanwhile, Ali, the older brother, was
hunting for demolitions: scouting in Kadıköy and giving offers to contractors.

To secure the abandoned building and its scrap, they had to guard it day
and night during their operation. Otherwise, the material to be reclaimed

would all be taken by other waste collectors or other individuals (Figure 5.9). As a result, Engin had to sleep on the ground floor of apartments to protect the building from others. Like the zoning hierarchy between waste collectors (Altay and Altay 2008), he said that fights sometimes broke out over discarded material and territorial competition between salvagers. Because of these reasons, cooperation seemed impossible.

Engin and his family were not inspected for labor safety. However, sometimes they were being reported to the municipality because of noise and the complaints from the neighbors. They threw weighty materials out of the upper floors. For that reason, their activities were very loud for a densely populated residential area. When they were dismantling façade elements, it was dangerous for all the workers on the ground floor. Sometimes these materials fall outside the security barriers surrounding the site. It was even threatening to passersby. At the Uzay apartment block, they had to stop for a few days after a complaint. Then, it turned out that demolition permission had not yet been approved by the municipality. They had to stop until the contractor got the permit. For good reason, they generally try not avoid damage the surroundings of the demolition:

> If we do not destroy any surrounding assets like cars or other neighboring buildings, I count ourselves successful. Otherwise, the contractor will not work with us if we are not careful. If there is an accident, we have to pay for our damage. We cannot afford to buy insurance that can cover the damage done by work accidents.

When the construction sector was thriving, Engin and his family members were competing with other salvagers to increase their income from the demolition market. They also increased their income capacity by working on multiple demolition sites at the same time. In July 2018, their team had twelve workers and were simultaneously salvaging six buildings in Kadıköy. These locations were in Caferağa (Moda), Acıbadem, Kozyatağı, Maltepe and Bostancı. Engin complained about how the state did not recognize them as a profession. Without an official tax registration for salvage and scrap collection, they had to pay their own social security insurance as self-employed workers.

Figure 5.9: Guarding reclaimed materials[12]

Source: Author's own

***

12   Çıkmacıs permanently live in empty apartments because they have to guard the reclaimed materials there. They make a temporary environment using the items they
find during the salvage process. Above, we see an electric heater converted into a tea
cooker. The writings on the wall were made by the seismic structural inspectors.

At the demolition site, they dismantled elevator parts, security bars, old boilers, and handrails to be sold to the metal recycling factory. They pulled out copper and brass electric wiring, which were precious elements for trading. Generally, it took one week to salvage a building. There was not a single nail left after they finished their work. They also collected kitchen cupboards, radiators, conduit boxes, electrical sockets and left-behind furniture. Sometimes, if they were lucky, they found antique objects in the basements. On Fridays, they sold whatever was appropriate to a flea market[13] in the Historic Tuesday Bazaar in Kadıköy.

The flea market duty was given to Engin's elder brother, Murat. He inspected the evicted buildings for left-behind objects while others were busy dismantling the building parts. He used the ground floor of the empty building to store the furniture and household items: chairs, tables, mirrors, carpets, books, framed pictures, household ornaments, knickknacks, toys, stereos, shoes, flags, sports equipment, and etc. Every Friday, he went to sell things at the flea market. The flea market was a small part of the large bazaar where all sorts of things could be found, from food to clothing. The flea market in Kadıköy was central and very popular. That makes it an exception to those in Seale's analysis that are socially and geographically peripheral (2015).

5.3.3 Engin's Depot, a Family Business

When the fieldwork started, Engin and his brothers were running a metal and plastic scrap collection depot on the ground floor of a three-floor building in the Fikirtepe neighborhood of Kadıköy. The depot looked like a garage: it had a ramp at the entrance that enabled pushcarts to enter and exit easily. It had been made into one large room by demolishing the inner non-load bearing walls. It was a relatively small space with a low ceiling, which was a bit unexpected for what was primarily a storage space. The walls were stained because of their salvaged materials' dusty, greasy, and rusty content.

There was a small office for one person made from leftover material. In one corner, they piled electric cables; in the other, they put metal bars. There were

---

13   Dinler (2016, 59) makes reference to the economy of gift-exchange (Mauss 2002) when she observes the way waste paper collectors sell the valuable objects that they find in waste bins at the flea market. See also Chris Birkbeck who makes a similar case for garbage pickers in Cali, Columbia, who sell valuable objects to second-hand dealers (Birkbeck 1979).

all sorts of junk lying around everywhere. All over the interior space, there were signs of overuse and damage. There was a sizable digital scale in the middle of the room used for weighing and pricing their recyclable materials. For smaller materials, they were still using an old rusted balance scale. They did not store components here long term.

Figure 5.10: Engin's first depot in Fikirtepe[14]

Source: Author's own

In the morning, they met with other family members before going to the demolitions in their truck. In the daytime, the depot was not busy; however, in the evening, when they all returned to the depot, it became occupied by members of the family bringing the day's scrap collection (Figure 5.10). The ones who worked at the demolitions were unloading the materials like cables and metal parts from the truck. Some of the family members with the pushcarts were carrying the scrap collected during a day's work in the streets of Kadıköy. Sometimes there were others there: refugees, waste pickers, or co-villagers selling scrap to them. Most of the members who worked through kinship relations

---

14   Family members are gathered to weigh their scrap. On the left side of the picture, a scrap collector pushcart is parked. It is a typical three-wheeled barrow that one can often spot in the streets. They are either used by scrap collectors or street vendors.

were getting paid a daily salary; other outsiders were paid for the quantity of materials they brought.

The area functioned as the backbone of small-scale industrial workshops and waste collection in Kadıköy. Because a recent urban redevelopment project resulted in an eviction report in 2016 (See Ch. 4.6.3), Their depot was demolished, after which they moved to another store in the same district. Engin described the situation:

> Since the beginning of the development in Fikirtepe, all the businesses have been forced to leave. We might have to move again in five years. The transformation follows us in the way the demolitions do. So far, we have survived in Fikirtepe. If there is no work here, we will go to Avcılar on the Asian side where urban transformation is progressing faster.

The new depot was larger than the previous one. It had two floors: the ground floor was used as a workshop for dismantling and storing the scrap; the second floor was used as a dormitory. Engin explained how they used the space:

> We are sleeping upstairs. It is very convenient. We reduced our cost of living. Plus, someone should be watching the depot; we have to protect our materials. They are like gold to us; otherwise, the Gypsies could steal them.

While he was breaking an elevator cogwheel for its brass composite, he explained the exchange value of the materials:

> The most expensive one is the yellow (brass) inside the elevator parts. The prices are indexed to dollar currency in the market. Yellow is very valuable: copper comes next. PVC is not comparable. It is the cheapest but there's more of it. (Figure 5.11)

They no longer accepted materials from outside sources. They were only trading their scrap to recycling warehouses and factories because the building salvage was supplying enough resources.

They managed to survive Fikirtepe's gentrification even though they had to move their small depot twice. Like most rural migrants in general, they were part of the precariat. However, by staying mobile through the salvaging of several buildings in several different parts of Istanbul, they remained adaptable. Their activities were not costly, and they could adjust their labor power. Since their field was proceeding along with unregulated, uncontrolled, undocumented, and unregistered mechanisms, refugees were able to find job opportunities in this sector.

Figure 5.11: Dismantling elevator parts[15]

Source: Author's own

5.3.4 Working with Refugees

According to the European Social Policy Network work report, only roughly 21 thousand Turkish work permits were issued in all of 2017 while, at the same time, 1.5 million Syrians were engaged in informal work there (Adaman and Erus 2019). Two refugee workers, Hayatullah and Jabir, used to work with Engin (without a permit) between 2016 and 2018. Our conversations were limited to a primitive level, however, because we could not understand each other without

---

15   In Engin's second depot, all the family members are dismantling the brass parts of an elevator. The two young kids are his nephews. At the back, the boy's father, Ali (Engin's brother), is smoking a cigarette. Ali wants his children to learn their profession instead of going to high school. Ali was not keen on returning back to their village. He likes Istanbul.

the help of Engin, who knew Arabic. They lived in Fikirtepe in a bachelor room[16] with eight other workers, who were either in construction or some other kind of labor-intensive job. The older worker, Jabir, came to Turkey as a refugee from Afghanistan in 2016. After three years of fighting against the Taliban, he escaped from war and joined his relatives in Istanbul. Back in Afghanistan, he used to live in a village and work as a shepherd. Due to the shortage of full-time jobs, he mainly worked in construction, which needed intensive manual labor. With his thin and short features, he could very quickly climb the façade of the buildings from the outside. I learned that his physical skills came from his military training.

Due to the challenging work conditions and Turkey's economy, he clarified that salvaging was only a temporary job for him. His goal was to go to France where some relatives had been relocated to a refugee center. His relatives received money as support from the French government. Plus, he claimed that there were better-paid illicit jobs there. Then, he clarified that his relatives reached France with the help of human traffickers. He was saving money to pay for this dangerous trip. Unfortunately, he was getting paid less than a Turkish worker. Engin paid the refugees a fair wage and took care of them when they were sick. Since having a work permit was complicated and required waiting time, Jabir could only find an unregistered job in the recycling and construction sector. In Turkey, a foreigner under temporary protection can apply for a temporary work permit that takes six months to obtain. Although there were opportunities for seasonal agricultural work in the east of Turkey (Kavak 2016), he preferred to look for temporary work in Istanbul.

Another refugee worker called Hayatullah, aged 18, worked with Engin for almost a year. During the Syrian Civil War, his home was destroyed in Kobane. Later, he fled from Syria with his family in 2016. Before the war, he was a high school student. After his arrival, he lived in a refugee camp on the Syria-Turkey border. The remaining family members were scattered around Anatolia trying to find seasonal work, but he came to Istanbul because it has more possibilities and opportunities. He worked as a waste picker for a while. It was very difficult for him, not so much because of the long hours of walking and carting of material, but rather due to the territorial conflicts with Kurdish pickers and some racist attacks. Six months after the interview with them, Engin informed me that they left Istanbul permanently to find refuge in France. These outcasts

---

16   Bachelor rooms (Bekar odası in Turkish) are shared dormitories for seasonal workers and refugees.

were once again forced to leave in the hope of finding better living conditions (Bauman, 2011). Nevertheless, Engin would not employ them on a regular basis because the number of demolitions had decreased due to recessions in the construction sector. Because of these recessions, Engin was more often in his native village taking care of their family farm. In the following section, I will report on these nomadic circular transitions and dual lives and introduce Engin's farming activities in Yazıhüyük.

5.4 The Circular Mobility of the *Çıkmacıs*

Istanbul is connected to its hinterland via the economic and social mobility of its dwellers who migrated from villages in search of better living conditions and work opportunities. Within an extended network of relationships, informal laborers retain their ties between village and city through their engagement with farming activities, a sense of home and social attachments. Mainly, they live a dual life in order to cope with their limited access to decent incomes in urban centers. Villages accommodate the second part of the migrant's livelihood and become retirement places in Turkey (Öztürk et al. 2018, 513). Transportation and communication infrastructure enables the commuter labor to navigate both zones (Echanove and Srivastava 2014). This is the case even despite the corporatization of the agriculture sector. For instance, forty percent of industrial labor in China comes from rural parts of the country; the workers are firmly attached to the countryside because it provides land to plant and homes to inhabit (Standing 2014).

To better observe the *çıkmacıs*' dual lives, I visited the village of Yazıhüyük in Nevşehir province, where Engin and his family live and engage in the agricultural activities on their family-owned land. As an economic reserve or backup that remains unpossessed by industrial agriculture, their land provides their primary livelihood and safety ground; even still, their financial and social resources there were not enough. In the end, the story of this family is a unique example of a substantial workforce divided between informal waste work and farming: "youngsters are not needed on the farm and, rather than act as a drain on the family resources, are better off going away to support themselves—and, indeed, contribute to the family budget where possible to help maintain the farm" (Öztürk et al. 2018, 522).

Figure 5.12: The house belongs to Engin's father. The washbasin was salvaged from a flat in Istanbul. On summer nights, they live on the terrace.

Source: Author's own

5.4.1 Village Livelihood in Yazıhüyük

After waiting for the public bus, which only ran very seldomly, I arrived at Yazıhüyük village in the Derinkuyu district of Nevşehir city to meet with Engin in late May, 2018. Derinkuyu is famous for its underground city from Ancient Cappadocia that is carved out from the soft volcanic rock of the region, which is also evidence of the fertile earth for agriculture. For generations, the fields surrounded by the mountains were very generous to the people. On the way, I saw a small hill in the middle of the flat plane, which was the archeological tell from which the village took its name. I found Engin in a coffee shop close to the village square, decorated with Justice AK Party flags. The coffee shop is a shelter for the village's male population, where they play card games and kill time. Although there was rampant unemployment there, the village seemed wealthy since the houses were fairly large and well-built and had farm fields in front.
—from my fieldnotes, entry on 27.05.2018.

Before Engin showed me his house and land (Figure 5.12), we sat a while at the coffee shop. He was with a relative whose name was Mehmet. Mehmet related that, after 30 years of doing it, he finally retired from scrap collecting in Istanbul. He explained that most people from the region who migrated to Istanbul in the 1970s found jobs almost exclusively as scrap collectors because the scrap was easy to access as a resource for income generation. The job did not need education or special qualifications. The village solidarity networks in the city provided particular forms of manual labor opportunities through their connection to earlier generations of the same kind of workers. For instance, Engin told me that in the neighboring village, most of the men worked as construction plasterers in Istanbul.

Mehmet chose to move back to the village after his retirement. He explained that after the marriage of his children, there was no reason to stay in the city. In addition, he could not work any longer because of back pain caused by having to carry heavy things in the salvage work. After he sold his *gecekondu* in Fikirtepe to a real estate developer[17], he started to live in a flat far away from the city center in the peripheral neighborhoods.

Mehmet and Engin were curious about my interest in scrap dealing that brought me to their village. They believed that the public image of scrap dealing was associated with dirt and not pleasant, and the village was a peripheral place of seclusion. They explained that the recycling work represented unhygienic conditions. I told them that their unrecognized participation in construction and recycling sectors created an inspirational model that should be supported. All in all, they were sustainably creating value from scrap. However, Mehmet was pessimistic about the future of their profession in Istanbul because of its privatized recycling sector and street collection. Since then, he has wanted to return to the village because he could not obtain better living conditions. Nevertheless, Engin had a different opinion because he found an opportunity in an urban center close to their village. He believed that building salvage work could keep their farm running for a little longer until an economic crisis created unemployment in the cities. He commented on this unpredictable situation:

> The village is a stronghold for me. In Istanbul, I am far from my homeland. The land is home for me. Demolitions could slow down. That is why our scale is small. And we are mobile. But there will always be scrap to collect and deal with in the city. For example, recently, I took my crew to Konya [close to Nevsehir] for salvaging materials and demolition.

---

17   The *gecekondus* were replaced by high-rise residential blocks and their owners had to move to the peripheral areas.

Engin worked for a construction contractor in Konya. He and his team demolished and reclaimed materials from a condemned hospital. He was content with the location and scale of the project in central Anatolia. The work took them 25 days with ten other workers. For technical reasons, the old state hospital had to be demolished by hand. There were eight Afghan workers, also Jabir, without proper permission to work and travel inside Turkey. These refugee workers traveled to Istanbul from Konya in the back of a truck and slept at the construction site. Inside the hospital, there used to be a publishing department in which Engin found 15 thousand books. Later, he sold them to a paper recycling warehouse in Konya.

From the deconstruction, they reclaimed five hundred building pieces which he traded to a local second-hand wholesaler. Then, Engin sold the rest of the scrap salvaged from the hospital to a local recycling factory. When I asked him how he got the job, he explained that it would be impossible for him to get the job if he did not already know the people who hired them in Konya. Otherwise, a local person would have taken the job. He knew the contractor from Istanbul, whom he worked with on several projects. Meanwhile, the rest of the family started working in the European part of Istanbul because the demolitions had nearly stopped in their district. After all, the construction companies went bankrupt after the coup attempt in 2016. Simultaneously they were working in two blocks with 50 flats in Büyükçekmece and one block with 20 apartments in Bakırköy.

The labor network of Engin's family proved that urban transformation via demolitions was spreading to different parts of Turkey, and their business that started as a local reclamation was expanding its limits as well. Their mobility enables them to keep the connection to their village and also to find demolition-related jobs in cities across Turkey.

5.4.2 Agricultural Activities

Engin's family land encompassed nearly 1.5 hectares. There were four small single-floor houses in the four corners of the land. The one-story houses, made of stone bricks, were self-built and had flat roofs. Most of the original components of the houses had been replaced by reclaimed materials from Istanbul. His father and three brothers and their families were living individually in those houses. There was a ramshackle barn at the farm entrance where they kept all the animals: a watchdog, cow, ten chickens, quails used as bait for hunting, and fighting cocks. They owned a tractor with several attachments, but it looked old. According to Engin, farming demanded more attention, special skills, and knowledge than salvage work:

> I learned everything from my father. First of all, you have to know what to plant when. He showed me how to plow the field before spreading the seeds. Then I apply the pesticides. And then, I do the harvest. Apart from that, I have to take care of the animals, like milking the cows. Making cheese from the cow's milk.

Figure 5.13: Engin's inherited farmland[18]

Source: Author's own

Occasionally he came back every two months to check their crops, but in the planting season, which was mid-October for barley, he had to stay for two to three weeks at least. Engin explained to me that the barley crop had to be rotated. If it were planted too often, the soil would lose its quality. So, after barley harvesting, he had to plant vegetables to ventilate the soil. When he was away, his father and his wife looked after their fields, but he was getting too old to do it. In 2017, he harvested nearly two tons of green beans, barley, potatoes,

---

18   Engin's land stands in the middle of their houses. It waits for harvesting after a long fallow period. They planted some fruit trees next to his brother's house in the background. On the edge of the land, they have planted poplar trees, which can be seen at the back.

and zucchini (Figure 5.13). He sold these to a wholesale market in Mersin, a hub for the distribution of agricultural products in the area. The farm and its fields are fertile living entities that have a crucial effect on the human actors. Such multiple agency lies in the aliveness of the more-than-human world (Bennet 2010).

Engin never fully migrated to Istanbul, but his older brothers did. He was the only one who left his wife and two kids behind to help their mother. Unlike his brothers, Engin seemed very fond of village life and appreciated nature, and loved working with the earth. After a very intense day of work in the farm, he liked to go hunting, participating in cockfights with his own birds, or spending time with his wife and kids. His fondness for his village was substantial:

> Farming is a better occupation than salvaging. It is a lot cheaper in the village. We have our vegetables and animals. I feel freer and happier away from the construction dust. The time in the village feels like a holiday even though I have to work harder. However, we do not earn much from agriculture.

It was impossible for Engin to purchase a house with a garden in Istanbul. He decided to build a new larger house in the village with materials he salvaged from demolition sites. It was also a way of investing in his retirement; he did not want to live in Istanbul anymore, which he saw as getting very expensive and harder to live in. He was expecting that the backbreaking manual labor would lead him to retire early. He saw his village property as providing an economic safety net because the construction and recycling industry was unstable in Istanbul. For example, sometimes they did not work for months, especially during a financial crisis that shrank the construction sector.

In sum, his farmland has given them a feeling of social, cultural, and economic stability. The village is their primary home where they left their family and Istanbul seems like a temporary place. Since they are attached to their land and agriculture, they have work opportunities with limited income. Since some of the older brothers are doing the scrap collection and building salvage in the city all year long, the younger brother can keep the farm running. Eventually, it will become a place for retirement, and they prefer to invest and upgrade their homes in the village.

5.5 Conclusion

In order to join the EU, Turkey intends to formalize its waste and scrap collecting according to European waste management standards (Izci 2016). Without taking into consideration the livelihoods of waste pickers, they attempt to adopt management models from industrially developed countries. However, such a transition is problematic since there is already an existing heterogeneous structure. Regrettably, the contribution of informal labor is overlooked by the state, which prioritizes building formal business models based on a circular economy in the recycling industry. Local governments denounce waste collectors as illegal workers, attempt to eliminate them from the street, and try to impose a privatized system. In this new system, the local government supports household sorting, develops waste processing facilities, and supports private recycling companies.

Çıkmacıs can stay out of these conflicts, for the time being at least, because they buy the building scrap from private owners and contractors. In the future, if the municipalities or companies take over demolition salvage, their sector may become privatized. Additionally, they suffer from precarious work conditions similar to those of waste collectors. Workplace safety is often bypassed and ignored in the construction sector (Kolektif 2018). The same is true of material reclamation. A lack of occupational safety and the presence of asbestos threatens their lives (Odman, 2019) but the state apparatus does not inform salvagers about the health danger or do anything to create safe workplace conditions.

Çıkmacıs relationship to economic markets are twofold: recycling industry and second-hand trade. On the one hand, the recycling industry depends on the prices determined by the London Metal Exchange (Corwin 2018; Dinler 2016), on the other hand, second-hand trade is a field free from market regulations.

Adaptation to formal markets and solidarity networks is an important feature of relational infrastructures (Simone 2015). *Çıkmacıs* use the opportunity to extend their field of operation and secure their livelihood within neoliberal urbanization. With the recent developments in the construction sector, demolitions generate an excess of scrap materials and other leftovers that the private owners and contractors undervalue. The *çıkmacıs* anticipated this situation and adapted to changing situations. For instance, they hired new family members and refugee workers. They are flexible in sharing work responsibilities in the family. By establishing a second market, they became suppliers of affordable components. Using their know-how in the street collection, they use their contacts to trade sorted refuse to recycling companies. Yet, they did not entirely cut their relationship with their homeland. Such long-distance commuter urbanity identified as circulatory urbanism creates a continuum between rural and urban areas (Echanove and Srivastava 2014). What is more, the agency of their farmland impacts their movement because it creates reciprocal relationships based on time in terms of seasonal plantation.

By following in the footsteps of others, scrap salvaging becomes an inherited profession. And this relationality provides substantial networking opportunities. Plus, their farmland gives them security if they cannot maintain building salvage and scrap collecting. It provides a place for family members while the others are temporarily in the city. In the village, they can have breaks from precarious labor even though they have to take care of the farm. Plus, it is a safe retirement destination.

6. Second-hand Trade Network

6.1 Introduction

The construction industry in Istanbul has several kinds of formal and informal businesses that facilitate the urbanization process. With the recently intensifying urban renewal projects focused on creating newer safer housing, some of the infrastructural needs gave birth to small entrepreneurs. Such infrastructural 'reuse and repair' economies are always intertwined with the formal sector in emerging countries (Corwin 2018). For instance, because of urban renewal, the number of excavation companies that transport demolition rubble and excavated earth have increased in Istanbul over the last decade (D. Öztürk 2019). As discussed in the context chapter, *çıkmacıs* have been one of the essential suppliers of construction material and informal credit for *gecekondu* squatters. In the face of the municipal authorities' failure to manage CDW, the *çıkmacıs* provide a functioning socio-economic network that can actually fulfill the demand for affordable materials. Their second-hand trade infrastructure, with its relational attributes, acts as part of an assemblage-network.

Their trade infrastructure consists of flea markets, scrap yards, roads, and online marketplaces. These function as stopgaps where the second-life of an object is determined based on its 'residual value' (Hetherington 2004, 157). Their supply yards are filled with all kinds of reclaimed construction materials and components: plastic window frames, sanitation equipment, metal doors, wooden interior doors, old heating systems, parquet flooring, window security bars, wrought-iron railings, garden fences, garage doors, and kitchen cupboards. Originating mainly from the supply yards in Istanbul, these materials flow to Anatolian cities and neighboring Georgia by road transport (Figure 6.1). In major cities like Ankara and Kayseri, where urban renewal projects are intensively progressing, structured demolisher cooperatives have opened second-hand supply yards. To emphasize the role of worker collectives, demolition cooperatives enhance working conditions and create recognition while serving as policy interfaces that acknowledge informal waste management contributions (Dias 2016; Gutberlet et al. 2017).

Figure 6.1: The trade flow of second-hand components[1]

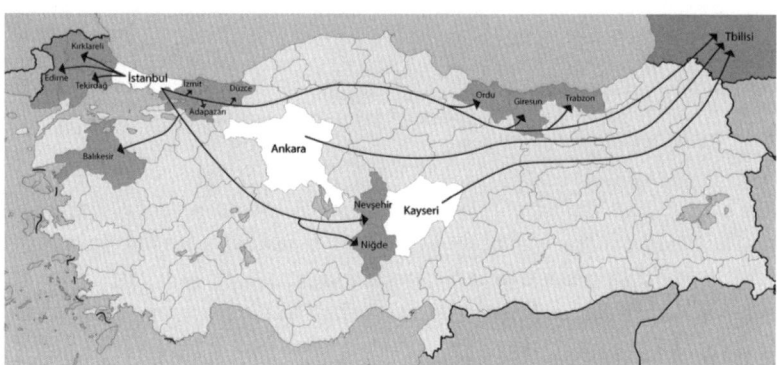

Source: Author's own

Çıkmacıs trade activities and their supply yards function as links between center and periphery, urban and rural, local and international. First, I will describe supply yards where reclaimed materials are accumulated in the peripheral urban areas close to the industrial areas in Istanbul, Ankara, Kayseri, Nevşehir, and Niğde. Because of its importance in terms of international trade, I will also describe a supply yard in Tbilisi, Georgia. I will use field notes, mappings, and satellite images to analyze where these places are located in the periphery of cities.

6.2   Places of Accumulation: *Çıkmacı* Supply Yards in Istanbul

Çıkmacı supply yards are located in former *gecekondu* neighborhoods, mainly peripheral to the center and close to organized industrial zones and recycling

---

1   Istanbul, Ankara and Kayseri (marked red) are the main cities where building materials are reclaimed. Other cities marked in green indicate the places where retailers bring second-hand materials.

warehouses in Istanbul. Since Istanbul is divided by the Bosporus, each side functions independently from the other. Further, Istanbul is growing linearly towards the east and west axis. As a result, the east and west borders (peripheries) of the city are not only geographically but also infrastructurally separated from each other. That's why the empirical findings regarding supply yards are grouped into two parts: the European and Asian[2] Sides of Istanbul (Figure 6.2). The fieldwork shows that some supply yards and depots are clustered together in specific neighborhoods. Independent of these clusters, some of the yards are distributed randomly within urban areas.

Figure 6.2: Map of the Çıkmacıs in Istanbul: White pins indicate places of çıkmacıs

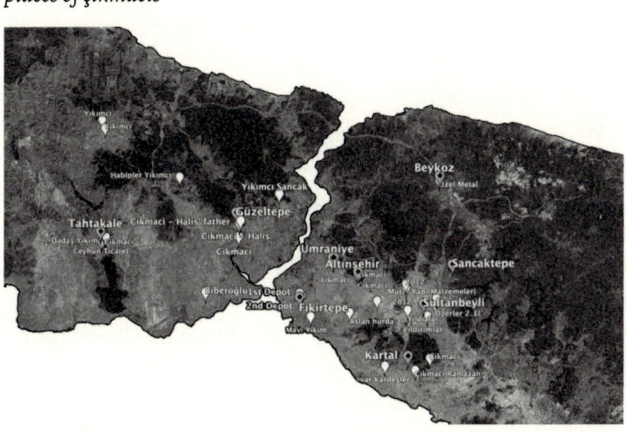

Source: Author's own based on Google Earth

6.2.1 Asian Side

The *çıkmacıs* are located in the Umraniye, Sancaktepe, Sultanbeyli, and Beykoz districts in the Asian part of Istanbul. *Gecekondu* dwellers urbanized these districts with their own resources. During the apartmentalization of housing stock, the single- floor *gecekondus* became apartment blocks with four to five

---

2   Geographically, Istanbul is divided by the Bosphorus strait: One part lies on the Asian continent, the other one on the European continent.

floors. Some of the yards remained in between these buildings. In the following, each section is dedicated to the descriptions of second-hand supply yards.

Ümraniye: Alemdağ Street (Ataşehir) – A Supplier Hub for the Second-hand

Some supply yards, warehouses, and retail outlets are located in the Ümraniye[3] district close to the Istanbul Dudullu Organized Industrial Zone on the Asian side. Among the other types of construction material suppliers, one can easily spot the *çıkmacı* outlets accumulated around the Altınşehir metro station[4] and along Alemdağ Street, which goes towards the industrial zone. Like many other shops, they display their second-hand goods on the sidewalk. Due to their proximity to the industrial zone, the yards form part of a larger supply area in the Asian part. In this area, building demolition contractors were the suppliers of cheap construction components for decades in Istanbul. Each business was demolishing nearly 80 to 100 residential buildings per year when the first interviews were conducted in 2016.

Second-hand elements are stacked and put on display in a makeshift style. Customers are going around the yards with tape measures to find the right window frame or a radiator that matches the dimensions of their home. The old frames are processed and reframed to standard sizes in some supply yards that have production workshops. Aside from selling, these places are affiliated with a demolition practice. In their logos, there is generally some kind of construction machinery: an excavator or a dump truck (Figure 6.3).

Supply yards and retail outlets are concentrated on Alemdağ street, forming a supplier hub for those who want to access second-hand goods for construction (Figure 6.4). Close to this area in the neighboring Sancaktepe and Sultanbeyli districts, the yards are distributed randomly and individually. When I first visited the area in March 2016, there were eight businesses. In 2019, there were ten. Some owners have retained their businesses, some have handed them over, some got bigger, and some went out of business due to instability in the construction sector. Well-established *çıkmacıs* in the market like Rıfat maintained their positions because they are experienced and have a large clientele in the construction sector. After migrating to Istanbul at an

---

3   For the urban development of Ümraniye as a gecekondu neighborhood, please see (Erder 1996).
4   The stop is on the M5 Üsküdar-Çekmeköy Metro line.

early age, Rıfat started working in construction and eventually became a well-known demolisher. His story takes place between the informal housing of the past and the current neoliberal urbanization dynamics.

Figure 6.3: Business cards of çıkmacıs

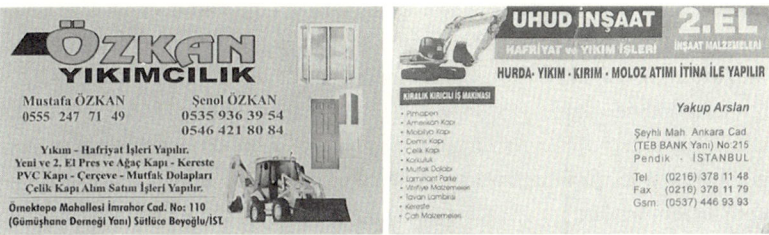

Source: Author's own

Figure 6.4: Çıkmacıs in Altınşehir

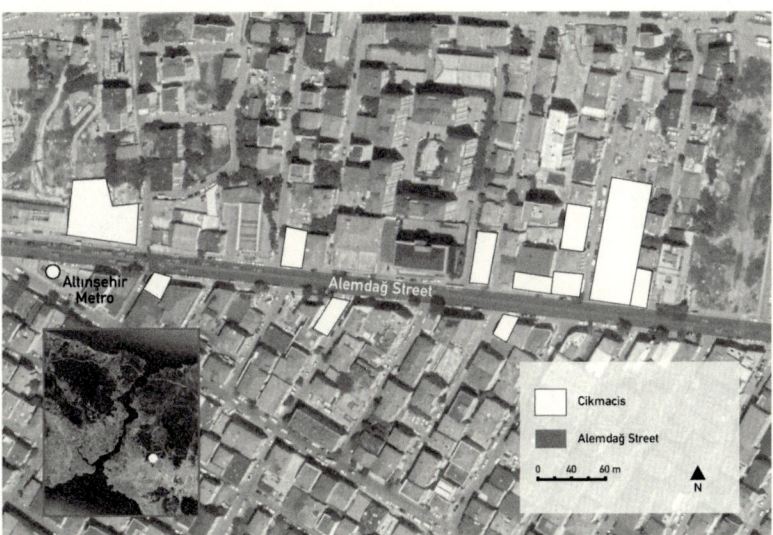

Source: Author's own based on Google Earth

Rıfat, the Master of Demolition

When I first met him in April of 2016, Rıfat's office was located in a makeshift structure assembled with salvaged metal bars that were probably part of an old warehouse. Below his office, there was a yard where building parts were stored and repaired in a workshop (Figure 6.5). In the corner of the stairs leading me to the office, a pickaxe and a shovel reminded me that they were ready to be used in a demolition or excavation. Hesitantly I entered an office decorated with 1990s furniture. There was a painting of a landscape depicting rural Turkey. It was difficult to get an appointment with Rıfat; his secretary did not understand why an interview request would be coming from a university student like myself. It was unusual for them to be interviewed because their work dealt with unwanted things. Due to unregulated market dynamics in the demolition market, I was aware of the illegal power relationships within the fields of waste collection, scrap dealing, and *gecekondu* construction (Beyond Istanbul 2017).

Figure 6.5: Spatial diagram of Rıfat's supply yard

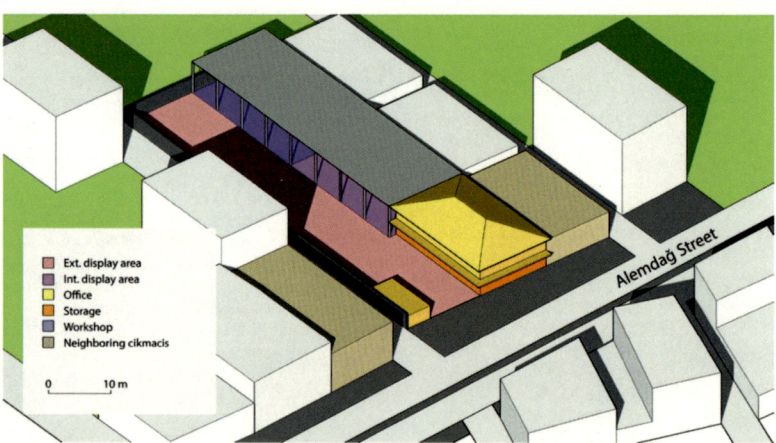

Source: Author's own

Rıfat, 62 years old, sat at his desk, dressed in a suit and sporting a typical mustache. In this setting, he looked like a kingpin, like a lord of demolition. He migrated years ago from his village, Arapgir, in Malatya. Like many construction and service-related professions, he proudly stated that, since the

Ottoman period, the most successful demolishers in Anatolia were from his village. According to him, the modern demolishers inherited their discipline from "a Bozuculuk" [a 'breaker'] in the Ottoman period. He said he had worked in the construction sector for 40 years. Since he began, he has taught his profession to more than 200 professionals. He complained that everyone involved in construction, from unskilled workers to scrap collectors, has begun doing demolitions nowadays because of the renewal of housing stock intensifying since 2013.

Figure 6.6: The entrance of the Rıfat's supply yard

Source: Author's own

In the 1970s, he demolished municipal buildings, road infrastructures, cinemas, factories. Additionally, they tore down Ottoman mansions and traditional houses during apartmentalization. In the 1980s, he worked on the Tarlabaşı boulevard demolitions (see Ch. 4.5.2). Back then, he was trading reclaimed materials from the old buildings to squatters; wood floor beams, wooden roof structures, clay bricks, masonry blocks, window frames, doors, and parquets. The materials he traded were traditional when he started but, as time went on, they got industrialized. From the concrete factories that he demolished in the late 1990s, he cleared reinforcement bars out of the rubble. Using a machine that straightened twisted or bent bars, he was selling the bars to squatters. Such materials were scarce for cheap constructions. Once they got affordable, he got rid of the straightening machine. More recently, he took part in clearing the wreckage of buildings after the 1999 Düzce (see Ch. 4.6.2) and 2011 Van earthquakes. It is significant to observe that the peak points in his business success were paralleled with the turning points in the urbanization developments in Istanbul. Those experiences made him the most experienced demolisher of all in the area.

At the current time, like the rest of the shops in Altınşehir, he confirmed that they were selling second-hand components to suppliers who ordered them in advance and then resold the items in Anatolian cities in the Marmara, Black Sea, and Aegean regions. In contrast to the *gecekondu* period, they were now selling to people living in rural parts of Turkey. Each shipment to Anatolia with a truck transported 600 to 700 hundred component pieces. He handed over the second-hand trade of the business to an old employee. Since there was a high demand for demolitions, he focused more on managing them than the supply yard (Figure 6.6). In the following quote, he describes the demolition process in detail:

> The contractor is responsible for getting a demolition permit from the municipality. For that, there should be an earthquake damage report from the experts. All the utilities like water and electricity should be cut. There needs to be an inspection that confirms that nobody is living in the building, and finally, a controlled asbestos removal should be conducted. But that is not generally taken care of by the authorities. We do not have the proper asbestos protection gear. For years, we did not control it. As a first step, I make an agreement with the contractor who manages the overall rebuilding process. In this contract, I agree to a subcontractor fee determined by my expenditures. The rent of the demolition machines, gasoline, labor wages, and debris damping are the major costs. After determining the fee, the scrap value of the materials that I buy from the contractor is deducted from the overall cost of the operation. Then I start hiring construction workers depending on the scale of the building. I generally hire workers from Bingöl to remove the components. They have been doing a similar line of work on the construction sites since they migrated. The workers who sledgehammer the walls are less experienced and qualified. I do not prefer Syrian and Afghans because their work is lousy. We put a small compact excavator on the top of the building, which is 3 tons, that demolishes the floors to a certain level. We use a small one for buildings that are higher than five floors. Then, an excavator with a jackhammer continues the demolition from the

ground level. During this process, we water the broken concrete to control the dust.

In 2016, they were demolishing four or six buildings on average per month. The month I visited them in March 2016, they demolished 18 buildings. And, on average, they removed 1800 building parts from each building. They chose standard dimensions of PVC window frames for reclamation: between 150x150 and 100x100. The larger frames were broken and sold to plastic recycling collectors. He was concerned about the wasting of double-glazing glass, but there was no way to recycle them. They removed the rebar steel from the concrete with excavators, making them into massive and heavy metal balls. They sold the balls to a metal scrap dealer who would then sell them to a metal factory. He complained that scrap steel prices decreased because the factories imported cheaper metal scrap from Russia. After all, the rates of recycling materials were dependent on international exchange rates, but second-hand components have their own independent valuation based on labor and infrastructural costs.

Rıfat represents an experienced actor in the market. Due to his long history in the demolisher profession rooted in his family and village, his business actively adapted to decades of urbanization processes. When industrial construction materials were scarce during informal urbanization, he supplied reclaimed materials to *gecekondus*. These types of supply yards were previously known as ardiyes (Duyar-Kienast 2005; Payne 1982; Şenyapılı 1981). More recently, he has been selling salvaged materials to entities outside Istanbul. Besides him, there were other new actors in the market such as Serhat, a recently established entrepreneur who I will focus on in the next section.

Serhat, the Entrepreneur

Serhat, age 56, is a demolisher and a second-hand trader of Kurdish origin that I met in 2016 at his shop. In 1975, at the age of 16, he migrated to Istanbul from Ağrı, an eastern region in Anatolia. He immediately began working on apartment construction projects as an unregistered and unskilled laborer. He and his partner opened their demolition business three years ago at a time when the demolitions were increasing.

Their business had three divisions: demolition, material reclamation, and trade. He started his outlet in the Altindağ district six months ago because that district was known for its second-hand markets. Serhat said that the market in Altınşehir was very competitive, and the relationship of sellers was not organized enough to form a uniform institutional identity that could represent their rights. The cluster of 10 shops was well known in the area since the beginning of informal development in the area. His business partner mainly organizes the demolitions, while he manages the shop and deals with customers. They sometimes host workshops on repairing and resizing old PVC frames, and sometimes they produce new frames through a manufacturer in Habibler in the European part of Istanbul (Figure 6.7).

Figure 6.7: The pop-up workshop area inside Serhat's shop

Source: Author's own

In the last three years, they demolished nearly 80 apartment blocks along Bağdat Street, which is the busiest transportation axis that cuts through the Asian districts along the Marmara shore: Kadıköy, Kartal, and Ümraniye. Beyond that, they worked in neighboring districts: Ümraniye, Dudullu, and Çekmeköy. From each demolition of an average apartment block with four floors, they reclaimed 120–140 component pieces; this added up to 960–1120 pieces on a monthly basis.

Individual customers, primarily from Istanbul, were buying second-hand components for small-scale remodeling projects. They sold in bulk to customers from the Black Sea region, especially ones from cities like Düzce, İzmit, Balıkesir, Giresun, Ordu, and Trabzon. These customers filled their trucks with large shipments while visiting several shops. Most of them owned shops back in their cities. Serhat stated that most of the components sold to the Black Sea were used to repair summer or village houses. The transactions were in cash and some earnings remained unregistered. He also mentioned that some Romanian traders came and bought many second-hand goods five years ago.

Before starting, they hired unskilled construction workers from an informal day labor hiring site [amele pazarı]. He mentioned the neighborhood Küçüksu[5] as a place for hiring Afghan workers. For a demolition, he hired 4 to 5 workers. He also rented two demolition excavators with an operator. The size and cost of demolition excavators change according to the size of the building. They demolish a 6-floor apartment block within five workdays if there are no delays due to an accident or complaint.

When I last revisited the area in 2018, Serhat had moved to a larger space across from his old shop, where he had an open yard and an enclosed shop area. His partner left, but he kept the business going with his family members. He retained the second-hand items and began trading new cheap components because the demolitions had slowed down and material reclamation was at a minimal level. However, he clarified that the situation was temporary because there was still a high amount of housing stock in Istanbul that had to be renewed.

Serhat worked as a construction worker for a long time. Having a lot of experience as a construction worker, he could adapt his entrepreneurial skills and sector relationships to new dynamics in the market. As a result of managing fewer demolitions after the decreasing demand, second-hand components remained in short supply. However, the other shops were not as flourishing as Serhat's outlet. For example, Mazlum, discussed in the next subchapter, could not keep his business.

---

5   Küçüksu is a neighborhood in the Beykoz district on the Asian side of Istanbul. It is a hiring hub for Afghan workers who live in crowded circumstances in neighboring Yenimahalle. Early in the morning, hundreds of Afghans gather on the main street, expecting to be employed as a day laborer by Turkish foremen like Serhat. After agreements for a 'day rate', the foremen loads them in their vehicles and brings them to construction sites, production stores, sweatshops, gardening, and waste collecting sites (Karadag 2021).

Mazlum's Bankruptcy

I interviewed Mazlum in March 2016 (before the coup attempt). He was displaying his reclaimed components on the sidewalk. He was 42 years old and had migrated from Tunceli. He had worked in the construction sector for over 30 years. Before that he installed electrical and ventilation systems in new buildings in Russia, where international Turkish construction companies were doing large-scale projects. Then, he was leading demolition workers for several businesses in Altışehir. When he first migrated in the 1970s, he used to live in a *gecekondu*. He stated that there were *Çıkmacıs* who were financing the construction of the squatter houses and added; "Rıfat was one of them. They were refurbishing wooden parts of old traditional houses that they demolished".

After gaining enough experience from Rıfat, he decided to develop his own business. He mentioned that the demolition business was at its peak after the earthquake legislation. Seeing this opportunity as a result of urban renewal, he took over the shop from a sanitary appliance wholesaler and started to sell second-hand components from his shops. The rest of reclaimed materials was traded to scrap collectors with pushcarts. In a workshop not far from their retail outlet, they repaired old PVC window frames. As he explained:

> We sell second-hand items at nearly one-third or one-fourth the price of a new one. The price is determined by bargaining. Often, we repair a frame with some other frame's hardware. Cheap frames have to be fixed anyway. The fixtures or the insulation become broken down in time. The average lifespan of a PVC frame is 20 years. In the old times, wood frames could last longer if one looked after them with proper wood treatment. But everyone wants to change them out with a PVC frame because it's cheaper and needs less maintenance. Nowadays, cheap goods are preferred by people who remodel their storage spaces like old coal basements or attics and old *gecekondus* for renting to refugees. These refugees are from Syria, Afghanistan, Kyrgyzstan, Uzbekistan, and Senegal. As a solution to this problem, the government housing agency (TOKİ) should supply dwellings for refugees, especially for Syrians because of the war".

The construction sector, which was already showing signs of decline, was impacted negatively by the failed 2016 coup attempt in Istanbul. As a result, the booming situation changed, and some new actors were not able to avoid bankruptcy. When I visited the area in 2019, Mazlum's retail sign had been removed and replaced by that of another retail seller.

Altınşehir has been a second-hand supplier market since the beginning of informal urbanization. The second-hand market is located near a construction supplier area and industrial zone, unofficially making it a well-known hub for low-budget customers and Anatolian and Georgian wholesalers. It regulates its own dynamics, but the sellers do not have unity and are very competitive with each other. With its long history, the place itself has become a local resource for self-sustainable residents. One of the pioneers, Rıfat, has enabled the existence of such a market locality. Based on my observations, this market survived many fluctuations in a construction sector with frequently changing actors. Apart from this hub, there are other suppliers on the Asian side. These are individually located in newly developed districts that were squatter neighborhoods 30 years ago. In the following subsection, I will examine these supply yards.

Sancaktepe, Kartal, Pendik, Sultanbeyli – Scattered Locations
On the one hand, Sancaktepe and Sultanbeyli districts were developed by informal urbanization, and they became residential areas where working-class residents have dwelled (Işık and Pınarcıoğlu 2001). On the other hand, Kartal and Pendik, which share a shoreline with the Marmara Sea, are industrialized districts that accommodate small and large factories and retail businesses in between residential areas. These districts accommodate several recycling companies, metal and plastic warehouses and *çıkmacıs*.

Ulaş: From Newspaper Work to Demolitions
Ulaş, who is from Çanakkale, is 36 years old. He studied business management at the Eastern Mediterranean University in Cyprus. For the last ten years, he was a construction contractor and is now a demolition expert. In 2016, his supply yard was located on Yakacık Street in Sultanbeyli (Figure 6.8). Before, he worked as an audit manager in a national newspaper and as a sales manager for an energy drink. After having insight from his close friend about the growing demolition sector, he decided to take over the previous shop two years ago to manage demolitions and sell second-hand components. His business was registered as a construction and decoration company.

He preferred customers from Trabzon, Adapazarı, and Malatya that bought wholesale. For instance, he had a client who was a livestock breeder from Malatya. This client traveled to Istanbul once a year with his livestock on his large truck before a religious sacrifice holiday when trade tents were erected in certain parts of Istanbul. Before going back to his village on the last days of the holiday, he visited Ulaş's shop to load his truck with second-hand components next to the remaining animals that he did not sell. He mentioned another truck driver customer: "He does not leave empty-handed from Istanbul after unloading the goods he transported. Taking two to three hundred items from the shop, he sold them back to his hometown in Trabzon. In his home village, he either rents a storage space or an empty field to sell the items. Another regular customer purchased all the interior components to remodel their village house in Rize, located in the Black Sea Region.

Even though he was making more money from wholesaling, he also sold second-hand components to individual consumers on internet marketplaces such as 'Letgo'. In this manner, he increased his internet presence. When I asked him whether he planned to create a website, he replied it wasn't required at the present because he had enough clients and didn't keep the components in his depot for too long. Plus, he had neither the time nor the payroll budget to maintain a website. He did the administration and management work, and his employees were responsible for the physical labor.

In 2016, he employed ten people without a contract: two were foremen; one was a craftsman and master repairer of reclaimed metal and wood components; and one was a shopkeeper. The rest were day laborers from the hiring site. Their business drastically changed after three years. On the second visit to the area in 2019, the shop was unrecognizable; there was a new 3-story building at the back of the old shop. By the side of the depot workshop, there was a yard with some reclaimed items on display. In a brief talk, Ulaş said that the demolitions had slowed down due to substantial competition over the last three years.

In order to adjust to the market, He decided to expand the retail part. Keeping the front, he demolished the back part of the shop, which was an old squatter house. Later, he erected a new building connected to the old part. It was not lucrative to keep up with demolitions, so he began stocking more newly manufactured doors and kitchen cabinets. He was still making demolitions but less of them. For that purpose, he kept the yard where he stored reclaimed components.

Figure 6.8: Ulaş's supply yard

Source: Author's own

Urban renewal projects opened a new path for Ulaş's ambitious plans. Within five years, he accomplished this by opening up a retail part where he sold all sorts of new doors. In contrast, the second-hand retailer in Beykoz that I will refer to in the next subchapter was determined to maintain affordable second-hand components. He invested in repairing components rather than selling new manufactured goods.

Beykoz: Distribution Center to the Istanbul's Black Sea Villages

Beykoz district is at the northern end of the Bosporus on the Anatolian side. Having borders with the Black Sea, it is the least populated district and is covered with forests, small villages, and gated communities. Currently, urban development projects cannot access Beykoz because the forests and natural habitat are being protected by law. However, the third bridge and its highways constructed in 2016 by the AK Party administration pass through the area. Urban expansion is planned to expand to the North of Istanbul.

Demir is a 40-year-old scrap collector from Niğde. When he migrated to Istanbul 25 years ago, he began his career with the help of a fellow villager. He wandered in the residential districts with his pushcart and called for used household items. Like the rest of his village, Keçikalesi, he was professionally involved in collecting and selling scrap and second-hand items. 13 years ago, he expanded his scrap business by purchasing 4 acres of land and turning it into a retail yard (Figure 6.9) in Beykoz Cumhuriyet village, a district in the Black Sea Region of Istanbul. It is located 50 kilometers from the urban center. I first encountered Demir's yard during an excursion to the construction of the Northern Highway that goes over the third Bosphorus bridge in 2016. He was a very ambitious businessman and had a strong entrepreneurial vision:

> I am a well-known trader all over the country, from Giresun to Van, from Konya to Elazığ. My secret is customer satisfaction through word-of-mouth recommendations. Three generations of customers find us and buy materials. Since our business got successful, customers from outside the village are visiting. Although wholesale is more profitable, I want to stay local.

He was pleased with the number of customers representing a potential for other producers in the village, especially farmers: "I am introducing my customers to my fellow villagers who produce dairy products and local fresh vegetables. I am making our village known to outsiders". By taking a superior position and believing that he brought wealth to the village, he saw himself as a successful entrepreneur.

The source of his construction materials derived from his visits to demolitions in 2013. He bought reclaimed materials that he dismantled with his team; sometimes he also bought them from the contractor. He had a well-equipped workshop to repair the existing window frames. Plus, he has large storage facilities in the village. His team consisted of his relatives from his village. He was frequently sending materials to Niğde.

Because of the quality of his products and low price, low income and middle-class families preferred to visit his yard (Figure 6.10). Due to his accomplishments, he was once interviewed by a local newspaper. He even opened another shop.

Demir's second-hand depot supplies cheap components for rural parts of Istanbul. Villagers in the area often visit his establishment for repair and construction projects. As long as the building stock is renewed by demolitions, his model can survive within neoliberal dynamics, especially in a national economy dependent on the construction sector. However, such entrepreneurial approaches and accumulation of second-hand materials is no different on the European Side. There is a similar distribution of *çıkmacıs*: they are located separately in the Eyüpsultan district and there is an agglomeration of depots and supply yards in Tahtakale, which is situated in Avcılar.

Figure 6.9: Spatial diagram of Demir's supply yard

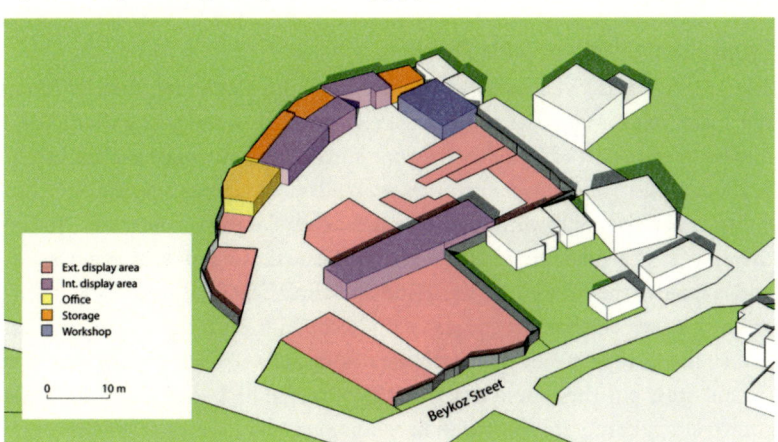

Source: Author's own

Figure 6.10: Demir's PVC frame displays

Source: Uzel Metal

6.2.2 European Side

Eyüpsultan: Güzeltepe - Old Çıkmacıs

The area is located between Eyüpsultan and the Kağıthane district along the main road, Mareşal Fevzi Çakmak Caddesi. Formerly, Kağıthane[6] and Alibeyköy were part of an industrial zone surrounded by working-class neighborhoods. The workers were living in *gecekondus* and later *apartkondus* (see Ch. 4.5.1), which they built with their own resources close to the factories. Today, the area has become one of Istanbul's largest real estate development zones and is close to the city center. The deindustrialization of the area enabled gentrification, which changed the social and economic structure of the district. Unlike the European side, a few *çıkmacıs* from the *gecekondu* period remained in this area, but they could not participate in the high-end transformation controlled by corporate construction companies.

From Father to Son, Halis' Supply Yard

Halis, from Sivas, was 33 years old and running a supply yard near the old industrial valley along the Alibeyköy Creek on Mareşal Fevzi Çakmak Street. He had studied tourism at the university and his father was a retired demolisher. He took the business over from his father in 2014. For nearly 30 years, his father ran their previous supply yard that was situated on the same street. The area experienced the usual deindustrializing factory demolitions and massive development described elsewhere. The municipality confiscated the property of Hilas' father's old supply yard on which they had been squatting since the 1990s. They could not stay because their land deed was temporary. The spot became a municipal depot for road maintenance, and a new metro station was built next to it.

After his father's retirement, they rented a smaller property where there used to be two *gecekondus* with a garden (Figure 6.11). The gardens became their storage yard; the houses were transformed into offices and enclosed storage spaces . The salvaged plastic window frames leaning over a triangular stand were displayed in the yard surrounded by ramshackle garden walls. At my visit

---

6   The area was a large demolition site: concrete debris, rusted metal parts, corrugated roof material and structural remains in 2011. On this land today exist government offices, a university campus, shopping malls, offices, and high-end residential blocks. For further reading on Kağıthane's urban transformation please see (Özçevik and Tan 2013).

in 2014, they were not doing demolitions anymore, and Halis was only selling second-hand components that he bought from scrap collectors and demolishers. He expressed his frustration about corporate firms:

> They used to demolish factories along the Alibeyköy Creek, Golden Horn, and Marmara Shore. When corporate companies took control over the market, demolishers like my father could not compete with them. We were a small business. We hired ten laborers, and my dad did not invest in machinery. I could continue the demolition business, but I was not interested because it demanded heavy labor and the work conditions were dangerous.

Figure 6.11: Spatial diagram of Halis' supply yard

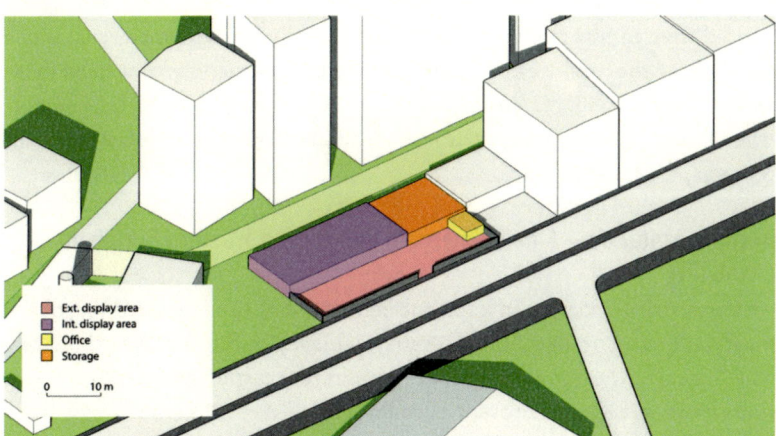

Source: Author's own

Eventually, Halis made an agreement with some scrap collectors to remove reusable components from demolitions. In his supply yard, he charged double what he paid the scrap collectors. During the interview with Halis, scrap collectors came with their truck and unloaded some leftovers from a condemned squatter house: an interior door, a metal exterior door, a PVC frame, a window security bar, and a marble kitchen counter. One of them from Niğde, where scrap collectors usually come from, stated that they did not have a shop to sell their components. Still, they wanted to launch a website to sell their stuff, not only giving them to scrap yards or second-hand shops but also putting them in an online marketplace like gittigidiyor.com, a site for second hand goods in Turkey supported by eBay.

The building components are affordable for villagers living close to the periphery of Istanbul. Halis mentioned that there used to be more customers from the neighborhood because the demand for cheap products in the informal settlements was higher. When most of the *gecekondus* were transformed into apartment blocks and later large residential projects, Halis mentioned that fewer customers were interested.

Halis complained that the second-hand market was unstable, had a low profit margin, and lacked experienced demolishers. Instead of individual customers, he had more wholesalers from the Black Sea and Central Anatolian region visiting his yard.

Halis' supply yard sets an example of how second-hand businesses are inherited from family members. The demand for inexpensive materials comes mostly from the rural areas, where incremental constructions continued in Istanbul Black Sea villages. In contrast, the next part highlights that the demolishers' businesses increased their second-hand stock in their yards near urban renewal projects in Avcılar.

Avcılar: Tahtakale – A New Emerging Hub for the Western Periphery of the City

Avcılar district is located in a seismic zone that has been declared one of the most dangerous. In 1999, it was severely damaged by the Düzce earthquake[7], which occurred 190 km away. According to a recent earthquake damage projection report, an earthquake over 7.0 magnitude will destroy 233 buildings, cause severe damage to 1,261 buildings, and create moderate damage to 5,545 buildings (Sesetyan et al. 2020). In the same area, the developments of the Başakşehir district and the Olympic stadium have attracted government investments that fuel the construction sector. There were metal and plastic recycling warehouses along 0–3 Kuzey Yanyolu Road in the Tahtakale neighborhood of Avcılar

---

7   After the Düzce earthquake in 1999, the Avcılar district was the most devastated area in Istanbul. The main factors for this were the building's poor foundations and structural systems, and that 90 percent of the buildings were constructed with weak concrete using marine sands with shells (Dalgıç 2004). Even though the replacement or reinforcement of the buildings are urgent, the rehabilitation projects are moving very slowly.

(Figure 6.12). I spotted four second-hand supply yards along Istanbul Street in 2019.

Figure 6.12: Distribution of çıkmacıs and recycling warehouses in Tahtakale

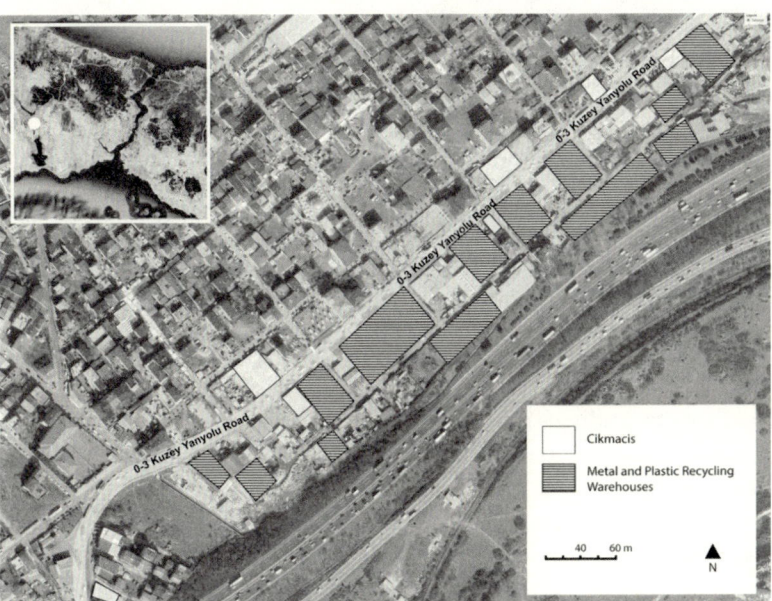

Source: Author's own based on Google Earth

Tezel Brothers: Experience is a Way to Success

While passing through Istanbul Street in the Tahtakale district, I spotted the Tezel brothers' banners on both sides of the street: "Demolition and Remodel Works." It was impossible not to notice the supply yard while driving up the road because there were second-hand components overflowing onto the pavement. On one side, they owned their depot, and on the other side, they were squatting in an abandoned supply yard (Figure 6.13). They covered the façade of the warehouse with images of heavy construction equipment and a photo from a demolition where a water cannon was spraying water at the rubble. Outside, they were displaying the PVC frames since they were durable in various weather conditions, and inside, they had metal and wood components, which were more expensive.

Figure 6.13: Spatial diagram of Tezel Yıkım

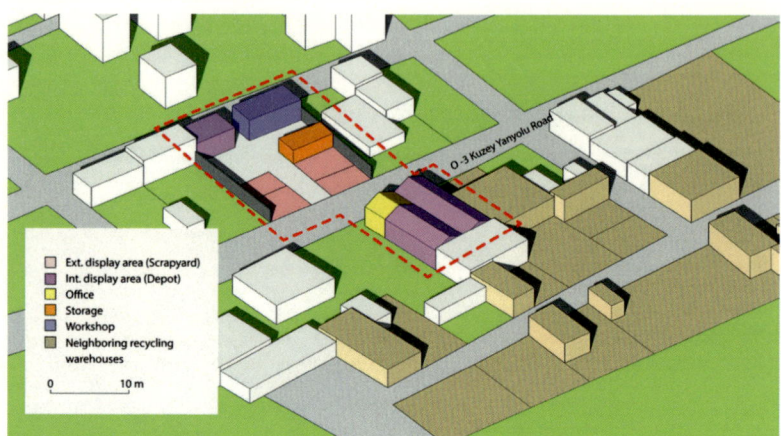

Source: Author's own

They were trading second-hand components to customers from peripheral districts of Istanbul and neighboring cities: Kırklareli, Edirne, and Tekirdağ. After the Syrian conflict, there was a considerable demand for cheap construction items from *gecekondu* owners who remodeled their houses in the area. Using these components, these owners transformed their gardens, attics, sheds, former barns, and other spaces in order to rent to Syrian refugees in the Tahtakale and Şahintepe neighborhoods. For nearly a decade, these peripheral low-income districts became densely populated by refugees. One can easily spot Arabic graffiti while taking a walk in the neighborhood.

Süleyman and Gürbüz first migrated to Istanbul in the 1970s from Arapgir village in Malatya. They knew their fellow villager Rıfat whose business was located at Altınşehir on the Asian side (see Ch. 6.2.1). Establishing their family business in 1987, they squatted a field in the Zeytinburnu district on the European side. Here the first *gecekondu* neighborhoods emerged among the factories. At the time, they worked on the deindustrialization demolitions along the Golden Horn. They were selling the materials and components they recovered from factory demolitions to *Gecekondu* dwellers and sometimes offered informal credit to dwellers for building their houses. Süleyman commented on their role:

New arrivals squatted the state land, and we supplied them with construction materials. It was a time when there were no rules, and the mafia was strong in the *gecekondu* market. After informal houses were seen as a problem for city development by the government, we started demolishing them. First, we helped, later we destroyed.

Their second-hand trade declined after the *gecekondus* were targeted by the government for investment projects. Contradicting their first constructive relations with *gecekondus*, they were hired by the municipality to demolish squatter houses in the 2000s. For instance, in 2007, they conducted *gecekondu* demolitions in Ayazma and Tepeüstü[8] . Forgetting that they were also once migrants, the brothers commented: "It was sad to see people homeless. The state promised to place them in newly built TOKİ housing with affordable credits. Somebody has to do the work for the good of our country".

They relocated their supply yard to Tahtakale after selling their yard in Zeytinburnu, for which they obtained the land deeds in the 1990s. With that money, they expanded their business by investing in demolition machinery: three excavators with hydraulic breaker and digger attachments, one long-reach demolition excavator with jaw cutter, two mini excavators with bucket attachment, and two jackhammers with air compressors. He explained their entrepreneurial reasons for this business expansion:

We used to do demolition all by hand using sledgehammers and pickaxes. For a more professional business we had to keep up with the competition, so we bought heavy construction equipment. Corporate customers or governments expect to deal with an established business.

In 1999, after clearing earthquake debris from several sites in the Avcılar district, they saw the potential of moving their depot to the Tahtakale area located close to Avcılar. Süleyman described this potential: "It was an ideal location where recycling warehouses were established. We were selling the reinforcement bars to metal recycling warehouses. There were not many materials to be reclaimed from damaged buildings, only steel". With other demolishers from

---

8   The urban renewal projects in Ayazma and Tepeüstü neighborhoods was the first large-scale transformation project in Istanbul between 2004 and 2007. The residents, mostly from the urban poor, were forcibly evicted and displaced from their decades-old settlements as the neighborhoods were "cleansed" for redevelopment and offered to developers for prestigious projects (Uzuncarsili Baysal, 2013).

different parts of Istanbul, it took them months to remove the severely damaged and totally destroyed buildings in Avcılar. What is more, it was an arduous task because the earthquake destroyed the buildings and people died in them.

Overall, the brothers were confident that they were doing a crucial job that enabled reconstruction processes after the 1999 earthquake and urban renewal projects. Plus, they were still supplying cheap material to the poor and refugees. Since they were located on the western border, they had customers from other cities. Their location among other recycling depots supported their visibility in the district. Since they were the oldest and most experienced, there was a dense circulation of materials in their depot. They said that there were less construction projects in Avcılar than Kadıköy because it had low-income households. Still, there was work potential since the municipality was giving financial support to the families in high-risk buildings.

6.2.3 Overview of Supply Yards in Istanbul

The infrastructure of the *çıkmacı* supply yards spreads out over both sides of Istanbul. Their workplaces appear in grouped or singular depots on lands they squatted During the rapid urbanization in the 1970s. The supply yards on each end of the city, Altınşehir and Tahtakale, are located close to the peripheral recycling warehouses and construction retail markets. The diagrams of the supply yards show that yards have storage, display and repair workshop spaces.

In the past, some *çıkmacıs* on the European Side demolished factories during the deindustrialization of the city center. Later, they participated in the clearance of squatters. Currently, they reclaim materials from urban renewal projects. For instance, Rıfat and Tezel Brothers have been part of this historical transition. Some of the *çıkmacıs* are wholesalers buying materials from demolishers or scrap collectors. Old and established ones also demolish buildings. Further, they use online marketplaces to sell second-hand items to individual customers. Georgian second-hand traders also do business with them.

Their mobility is an essential factor in maintaining their livelihood. Their flexibility can be observed in their labor structure also: they hire family members and refugees. This informal model is beneficial for the unstable market. In 2012, the number of reclaimed components increased. However, after the coup attempt in 2016, the numbers were declining due to economic instability. Due to these fluctuations in the construction market, *çıkmacıs'* operations are either shrinking or expanding.

Each actor has a role in spreading the magnitude of the informal practice (Simone 2009). Rıfat shared his knowledge and experience to other salvagers and reterritorialized the *çıkmacı* network by transferring his knowledge to others. According to sectoral and individual changes, supply yards may appear and disappear but the network continues to survive and expand its borders. Similar knowledge transfer occurs when the profession passes from father to son (see Ch. 6).

In the following subchapter, material reclamation processes outside of Istanbul are discussed since the urban transformation is not only associated with Istanbul.

6.3 Demolisher Supply Yards in Anatolia

Based on what I learned from Istanbul's *çıkmacıs* and following the path of the second-hand components being distributed out of Istanbul, I visited Ankara, Kayseri, Nevşehir, and Niğde. These cities were also awash in demolition waste excess because of urban renewal. Some *çıkmacıs* in these cities were operating in eastern regions where military conflict had destroyed the urban environment. Some of them worked in removing earthquake debris. And some of them, in Ankara, formed a demolition cooperative on the periphery of the city.

6.3.1 Ankara: A Demolisher Cooperative

Ankara, Turkey's second-largest city after Istanbul, is located in central Anatolia. The capital has a population of approximately 4.5 million in the urban core and 5.6 million within its provincial borders. Ankara has grown through rapid urbanization since the 1980s (Şenyapılı 2004). Half the population used to live in *gecekondus* (Özdemir 1999). The central government initiated urban renewal projects through a series of legislation in those areas, and they were executed by large and small development firms and TOKİ (Güzey 2009).

In Turkey, demolition is an 'unsystematic' deconstruction process. It seems to function arbitrarily and spontaneously by frugal efforts of individuals who barely make ends meet. These efforts, which echo the early industrial era when goods were frequently broken and had to be fixed and reused, are very sustainable. (Thompson 1979). For over a decade, the local demolishers have operated as a cooperative, which is located in the Tatlar area, also known as Karpürçek, part of the Altındağ district (Figure 6.14). Being 30 km from the city center, it is a rural area at the city's edge. Together, they are responsible for the clearance and dismantling processes of buildings in the city.

Figure 6.14: Location of Ankara Demolishers' Cooperative

Source: Author's own based on Google Earth

Mehmet, Debris of Earthquake and War

Before the cooperative formed, the demolishers were located in the city center. The municipality of Altındağ sold them public land for affordable prices. During this transition to the periphery of Ankara, they became a cooperative. Now, the cooperative consists of 34 individual businesses forming a cluster of supply yards and warehouses.

The structure of the site looks improvised and ramshackle but, at the same time, sorted out and functional. The cooperative is 10 km away from the closest Ankara neighborhood. In between there are empty fields and the steppe. Its closest neighbor is an abandoned wrestling arena. In the yards, five-meter-long beams leaning over the surfaces created a splintered wooden façade. The warehouses themselves were hidden behind these surfaces (Figure 6.15).

Mehmet, aged 62, said that, for him, demolishing was an inherited profession. When he was young, he worked with his father and grandfather on demolition jobs. Due to a lack of professional training in this field, the workers had to learn from kin or fellow villagers. Mehmet said that he was expecting his grandson to someday be an excavator operator. The grandson, Ali, was already at work, taking out nails from an old wooden beam.

Generally, they used their heavy machinery and operators. If theirs were not available, they rented excavators and other equipment. During their work, Mehmet provided daily insurance, which covered health and employment benefits for his temporary workers. Yet, since it was temporary, the workers were employed in precarious conditions. He said that the Turkish workers did not like working in heavy labor. It was sometimes hard for him to find day laborers. In those cases, he employed experienced Iraqi workers. On rare occasions, he hired Syrian refugees, but he did not prefer working with them.

Mehmet pointed out that their business doubled after launching their website. In addition, he made some strong connections with the local government and subsequently received an invitation to tender meetings for governmental building deals. He was also a strong supporter of the AK Party. For large-scale projects, the members of the cooperative came together. Besides Ankara, they also had many projects in other cities: in Bursa, they were dismantling a hospital; in Gerede, they were demolishing a private rest area of a bus company; and, in Bolu, they were bringing down the old municipality building. For jobs outside Ankara, they were renting a flat where all the workers could live. Either they brought the reclaimed components back to Ankara, or they sold them to a wholesaler in the same location. Since their base was in Ankara, the trade was controlled from the cooperative site in Tatlar.

They had customers from neighboring villages and cities and even as far away as Georgia. There were many hobby gardens with small-sheds and country cottages around the area. For instance, he sold 500–600 pieces to a farmer from Konya. Furthermore, he made clear that construction permissions were not checked very strictly in the rural regions:

It is forbidden to make new construction in 2/B lands[9] without permission. However, no villager follows the rules because they know there will be a

---

9   Based on the Forest Law No. 6831, 2/B lands are places that lost their forest quality (for instance after a fire) (Turkish Parliment (TBMM) 1956). After being given land deeds based on properties such as private property or state treasure, they could be used for agriculture, animal husbandry and dwelling.

zoning and construction amnesty sooner or later. They even bribe the municipality or pay fines in small amounts.

Figure 6.15: Mehmet's depot with a Turkish flag

Source: Author's own

For Mehmet, urban renewal was not the only reason for demolishing buildings. Earthquakes and war were also reasons for destruction and reconstruction in the eastern region. In 2016, he worked in Şırnak (Cizre and Silopi) to clear the debris of destroyed buildings as a result of armed conflict.[10] He explained that the quantity of reinforcement bars in some destroyed buildings was three times higher than a typical building. After the destruction, Eastern cities in Turkey, where the Kurdish population was the highest, were immediately registered as risk areas associated with Law No. 6306 for reconstruction processes. In some cities, renewal designated by TOKİ followed the central government's decisions on land expropriation. Mehmet observed that the

---

10   According to a report by the Union of Chambers of Turkish Engineers and Architects, buildings were destroyed by armed forces during 2015–2016 clashes between Turkish Military and Kurdish militant forces. The combat zone was declared as a 'risky area' based on law no. 6306 issued by the Council of Ministers (Union of Turkish Engineers and Architects Chambers (TMMOB) 2019).

building leftovers—wood, brick, and corrugated metal parts—were used by the survivors to make permanent shelters.

The demolishers were forced to move out of the city center by the municipality. During this transition, they stayed together as a worker organization. Furthermore, the cooperative structure enabled them to be recognized as a formal organization. For instance, Mehmet could participate in tendering processes. With the recent tectonic and political dynamics, he became an exclusive actor in the construction sector. Mehmet cleared and reused building remains in parallel to these conditions: earthquake debris, war wreckage, and excesses of urban renewal projects. The following section focuses on a similar cooperative structure in Kayseri.

6.3.2 Kayseri - Local Suppliers

Situated in Central Anatolia, Kayseri is a large industrialized city with a population of over a million. As a result of investments in local industry since the early days of the republic, Kayseri is counted as the first city to be among the Anatolian Tigers[11] of the Turkish economy (Karatepe 2003). In the 1990s, the urban area grew exponentially because of industrialization and domestic migration, which resulted in informal urbanization. Currently, it receives a growing refugee population from Syria because of the work opportunities there (Shakhsari 2014).

Özcan, The School Teacher

Like Ankara, Kayseri demolishers were located on the edge of town (Figure 6.16). I was surprised to find that they also formed a cooperative business structure. Their single-floored, *gecekondu*-style buildings constructed with brick and wood were hidden behind the second-hand building elements. More significantly, long wooden poles and part of a roof structure were leaning against the walls of the buildings. At the foot of Mount Erciyes, the supply yard seemed like a boundless place full of building leftovers: stone and brick piles, doors, iron bars, window frames, heaps of cut wood, metal profiles, roof tiles, and all sorts of junk. This scenery revealed that the repair and maintenance of the city are beyond formal governance and state domination

---

11   Anatolian Tigers is a term that refers to the Anatolia cities (Denizli, Kayseri, Gaziantep, Balıkesir, Konya) that have broken remarkable economic and industrial growth records since the 1980s (Demir, Acar, and Toprak 2004).

(Graham and Thrift 2007). The view also highlights a necessity of organizing material cycles that exists in flux. Not only because infrastructure breaks down constantly, but things decay —waste away—based on time (Viney 2014).

Özcan, aged 45, a math teacher in a high school, was taking care of his family's business after work. His father, Mehmet, who is now retired, started their demolition business in 1976 after several experiences in wholesale trade. In 2003, the family stopped doing demolitions. Instead, Özcan established a wood workshop that made doors and kitchen cupboards. Still, they were part of the demolisher cooperative, consisting of 24 small individual businesses located in the Konaklar neighborhood in the Melikgazi district of Kayseri. In the cooperative, several businesses assumed responsibility for: recycling, salvage, and production; scrap dealing, demolition, excavation, furniture production, and PVC windows; and sanitary equipment trade. Özcan said the cooperative earnings were neither registered nor invoiced but they still all paid a minimum income tax. The cooperative was initiated by Özcan's father, Mehmet, in 2010 by assembling the first group of businesses. Özcan explained his father's intention: "He formed the coop in order to avoid eviction and gain a formal institutional identity. Having a cooperative created a defined professional field which we lacked for decades."

At first, the cooperative was squatting on state land in the center of the city and did not pay rent; the state had them in a court battle and were trying to kick them out. Then, the land got more valuable due to its location. Because of these circumstances, the municipality offered them a newly planned industrial site on the periphery of the city. Last year, they bought 600 m2 of land from the municipality. The municipality promised to develop the new site. They were not so easily convinced to leave their central location since the development of the new site was prolonged due to a lack of resources. However, they did believe they could turn their businesses into small manufacturing workshops at the new site.

Özcan explained that, since they did not have heavy equipment, they used to demolish old country houses by hand in the 1980s and 1990s. That was when migrants from the villages in eastern Turkey were coming to Kayseri. Apartment blocks replaced the traditional buildings. After agreeing with the developer, they bought the overall house as scrap material. Reclaiming bricks, stone lintels, roof tiles, and roof beams, they sold these vernacular components to villagers who constructed houses in their villages and rural migrants from eastern Turkey who built squatter houses.

Figure 6.16: Location of Kayseri Demolishers' Cooperative

Source: Author's own based on Google Earth

After the nation-wide natural disaster risk legislation in 2012, Kayseri also was affected by speculative renewal projects. Despite the fact that Kayseri was not located in a seismic-risk zone, there were demolitions of traditional houses going on there. Additionally, there was a five-year exponential growth in the real estate market. By 2018, the projects slowed down due to the economic crisis. According to Özcan, there was a prominent real estate bubble in Kayseri. Since the 1990s, he was frustrated about how buildings have been replaced by concrete apartments:

> I used to maintain my income by selling massive masonry stones reclaimed from traditional houses. Mostly Armenian. They are extinct now. We sold the stones that were used to build *gecekondus*. Now, we are demolishing them.

There were fewer vernacular materials obtained from buildings. The industrial components like plastic frames or steel doors were easily disassembled from a building. There were many more wooden beams in the cooperative supply yard than in Istanbul (Figure 6.17). Damaged and overly old wood was cut to be sold as firewood. Additionally, there were antique building parts that they sold to hotels in Cappadocia. They purchased rare building parts to use in restoration projects.

Figure 6.17: The beams from old vernacular houses are used for roof structures

Source: Author's own

The customers with low budgets, especially refugees, were visiting their supply yard from neighborhoods like Eskişehirbağları, a *Gecekondu* Prevention Zone[12]. Özcan highlighted that they have had more Syrian customers who rent apartments in the zone during the last five years and he clarified:

> The owners are repairing their old houses to fit several refugee families. They became rich from renting, and as a result, Eskişehirbağları became a refugee neighborhood. Refugees cannot find regular jobs. They survive from waste picking which is supposed to be illegal.

---

12   *Gecekondu* Prevention Zones (Gecekondu Önleme Bölgesi) are serviced plots of land provided for incoming migrants that are released once the infrastructure is put in place; land is parceled out and allocated according to approved housing construction policy, generally accompanied by some technical support from local governments, see also (Ch. 7.3.3).

The second-hand trade of the cooperative was not only local but also international. Özcan mentioned a trader called Bego from Batumi, Georgia, who bought second-hand components from the cooperative:

> He drives to Istanbul, Antalya, Bursa and Eskişehir. He fills his truck with cheap materials and sells them in Georgia. Depending on the demand, he also buys furniture and retail goods. The border is flexible since Georgians can travel without a visa, and there is a free trade agreement between the Turkey and Georgia.

The regular visits of Georgian traders prove that the demand for second-hand components goes beyond international borders. However, their visits did not follow a regular pattern. Local visitors from low-income neighborhoods and Cappadocian hotels regularly buy materials.

6.3.3 Nevşehir and Niğde – The Motherland of the *Çıkmacıs*

Nevşehir and Niğde are two small central Anatolian cities founded on the west of Kayseri. Compared to the rest of Turkey, urban renewal projects were not as intense in these two cities. People from both cities began migrating to Istanbul in the 1970s. Generally, they found jobs in scrap collecting through kinship relations and village fellowship. At the time of my visit, there were three supply yards in different parts of Nevşehir that had similar spatial layouts to the ones in Istanbul. Two of them were located in the industrial zone and one in Karapınar village. The owners of these places used to work in Istanbul as scrap collectors with pushcarts. In 2012, they began salvaging buildings in Istanbul. Maintaining their village relations, they arranged to ship items from Istanbul every three to four months. Concerning the decline of demolitions in 2018, they remarked that there were fewer second-hand components reclaimed in Istanbul. They mostly traded the items to villagers who had farms and vineyards in the area. These people were building small huts and cottages to watch their crops.

One of the owners of the yards (Figure 6.18), Mehmet used to be a truck driver and later a scrap collector in Istanbul. Coincidentally, he was a relative of Demir, whose supply yard was located in Istanbul (see Ch. 6.2.1). Every month, he transported 200 items from his brother-in-law Demir's supply yard in the Beykoz district. From demolitions of traditional houses, he was getting roof components, wood beams, and roof tiles. Like the *çıkmacıs* in the region, he was selling second-hand items reclaimed in Istanbul and new pieces produced in Gaziantep. He said that budget customers preferred second-hand. What's more, he was actively using online second-hand markets and Facebook's product and service pages to advertise and show his items. Through online marketing, he sold several components to a truck driver from Ordu in the Black Sea Region, and he sent window frames to İzmir.

Figure 6.18: Mehmet's supply yard in Niğde

Source: Author's own

Nevşehir and Niğde supply yards were strongly connected to Istanbul because of the rural migration in the 1980s. They brought most of the second-hand materials from Istanbul and distributed them to the surrounding villages. Local urban renewal projects were not present as they were in Konya and Kayseri. As a result, the amount of second-hand material excess from local projects was low.

6.3.4 Overview of Supply Yards in Anatolia

The demolisher supply yards in Ankara and Kayseri become cooperatives to gain a formal identity. The municipality removed the demolishers from the city center to the perimeter and sold them land in small installments. Since they are a cooperative, they divided the land equally. They also share building demolition and salvage tasks. They pass information to one another in order to help each other. In contrast, the second-hand supply yards in Nevşehir and Niğde are scattered across the city. Due to the migrative associations of the area, they bring the materials from Istanbul and distribute second-hand components to villages. The business they do with Georgian exporters reveals the international trade routes. Free trade between Turkey and Georgia makes such a material exchange possible. *Çıkmacıs* prefer to sell wholesale because it brings a larger amount of cash at one time.

The second-hand customers are mainly locals, villagers, and farmers who make small-scale constructions in vineyards, country cottages, barns, and hobby garden sheds that are not liable to construction and zoning regulations. This gives a freedom to construct small-scale properties based on their needs and resources. Local authorities do not often control such small-scale constructions that can be categorized as informal self-help construction. The level of informality increases in the rural parts, and the demand for second-hand is substantial. The ownership of the supply yards passes down through kinship relations. However, some did not stay in demolition and reclamation. Their permits allowed them to shift between different sectors. They look for different ways for income. For instance, Özcan is making furniture but he stayed with the cooperative nevertheless. Their entrepreneurial maneuvers relocate them into the formal sector.

In addition to building reclamation, the Ankara cooperative is taking part in clearing condemned buildings caused by an earthquake or military conflict. Their role in clearing destruction is part of a heavy-handed system that erases the urban fabric physically and socially through forced evictions and Turkish-Kurdish military conflict. It is interesting to observe that demolishers are deeply integrated into this system created by the AK Party administration.

6.4 Second-hand Export: Georgia

The research in Georgia began when the *çıkmacıs* informed me about the activities of Georgian wholesalers. Following this information, I found an advertisement entitled 'Used windows from Turkey' on Facebook during a site visit to Tbilisi in 2018[13]. Then, I contacted a Georgian wholesaler for a visit and an

13   I first visited Tbilisi to attend the first edition of the Tbilisi Architecture Biennial in 2018. After completing preliminary research with the help of local architects, my findings

interview. The Georgian capital of Tbilisi, the most populous city, is the final destination for second-hand components from Turkish cities.

In the background of free trade, there is the bureaucratic, emigrational, and economic cooperation of the legal protocols between Turkey and Georgia. Second-hand dealers in Georgia use the advantages of business agreements and customs duty privileges between the two countries. In addition to being a migration destination for Georgian job seekers, Turkey also has mega projects and high-budget investments in Georgia's transportation and tourism infrastructure.

The traders travel with their trucks and visit supply yards in Anatolia to collect and ship second-hand elements back to Tbilisi and Batumi. The demand for cheap construction goods results from poor economic conditions and scarcity of industrial production in Georgia. Additionally, due to financial absences and incremental self-help construction, the repair culture in Georgia is another reason for the demand for second-hand trade.

The supply yard was 15 kilometers away from the city center. The owners also had a storage place in another location in Tbilisi. Most of the items were displayed randomly outside in a yard. There was a small rough stone building in the yard used as a workshop and an office. The owner, whose name was Giga, was 28 years old. He was from the Autonomous Republic of Adjara[14] in the country's southwestern corner bordering Turkey and the Black Sea. Like most Adjara people, he knew Turkish well enough to initiate an interview. His ties with Turkey began at a young age when he traveled to the Black Sea region of Turkey for several jobs: seasonal agricultural worker in tea picking, alcohol and cigarette smuggling, and second-hand car trade. After these experiences, he ended up helping his father, who was bringing construction materials to Batumi from Turkey. After the intensification of urban renewal projects in Turkey, they observed that cheap components were being reclaimed from demolitions. As a result, they decided to import these components.

Once a month, Georgian traders visited several *çıkmacıs* in Turkey. They traveled through Anatolia until their truck was full of building materials. Giga mentioned that one of his relatives in Bursa[15] arranged the demolition of 5-blocks of apartment buildings. He would bring his employees to Bursa to work

---

were first presented in a lecture as a pre-event; later, the documentation of the findings was exhibited in the biennial.

14   Adjara is primarily Muslim and has its own language.
15   Bursa, located in northwest Turkey, is its fourth most populous city.

in the demolition, salvage the blocks and transport them to Tbilisi. He was expecting to get five truck loads that they could sell within two months. According to him, such large-scale demolitions were the most profitable for his operation. If such a large batch of items arrived, he would distribute them to several storage places in different cities in Georgia: Kobuleti, Kutaisi, Batumi, and Kakheti.

In 2018, they brought two trucks full of 700–800 pieces of construction components every two months: wood parquet, windows, doors, heaters, and old natural gas boilers. Each shipment was posted on a Facebook[16] page as videos or photographs. They sold them at 2–3 times the incoming price. The number of second-hand components was insufficient to supply the demand, and they decided to produce new items in their workshop (Figure 6.19).

During a revisit in February 2020, Giga said they were bringing fewer second-hand items from Turkey because there were not as many demolitions last year. They had become more focused on their own new product production. Nevertheless, they were still dependent on Turkey as a source of raw materials. According to him, the cheap construction items were particularly needed by Georgians:

We do not have an established industry since the Soviet period[17]. Russians took away all their factories after independence. Owing to the lack of industry, we are dependent on other countries. Most households are barely making ends meet. We need cheaply produced or second-hand items in the construction sector. After socialism, the Soviet micro-districts were developed by former dwellers and newcomers. Since then, cheap items are necessary.

---

16   In Georgia, Facebook is regularly used as an online marketplace.

17   Georgia was conquered by the Russian Empire in the nineteenth century after a long period of Ottoman and Persian dominance. Georgia had its own independent state from 1918 to 1921 when it became merged into the Soviet Union. Georgia became a constituent (union) republic in 1936 and remained so until the Soviet Union's collapse in 1991. The Georgian economy was modernized and diversified during the Soviet era. Georgia declared sovereignty on November 19, 1989, and independence on April 9, 1991 (Collier and Way 2004).

Figure 6.19: Giga's Supply yard in Tbilisi. The brick building is the workshop area.

Source: Author's own

The need for affordable construction materials that Giga mentioned has its roots back in the housing shortage coming after the end of the Soviet period. The informal urbanization in Georgia that followed the fall of the Soviet Union was concurrent with informal urbanization in Turkey during the 1990s. The self-help construction culture coincided with informal urbanization trends in two different instantiations: *gecekondus* and post-Soviet kamikaze loggias. In both cases, due to accelerated liberalization, industrialization, and urbanization, the state was not able to provide for necessary housing infrastructure. For such self-help construction cultures, affordable construction materials and all sorts of found materials are essential. It creates valuable input to understand how building material reclamation and second-hand trade are embedded in the construction sector as a secondary market.

The fieldwork clearly shows that the considerable demand for cheap materials in Georgia is due to the inability of local industry to provide such demand. Because of the free trade agreement, second-hand components can be imported from Turkey at low cost. Georgian wholesalers visit *çıkmacıs* all over Turkey and have been transporting second-hand building components for the last five years. The excess of the reclaimed materials produced by neoliberal urbanization are unwanted and invaluable items from previous Turkish urbanization processes. The research shows that this excess has a considerable impact on the retail market in Georgia.

6.5 Discussion of Findings

Neoliberal dynamics actively urbanize Istanbul and other densely populated cities in Turkey through national urban politics and legislations. It is essential to observe that urban transformation has the same pattern of creating demolition waste in Istanbul as it does in other highly populated cities in Turkey. Additionally, other catastrophic events like earthquakes and war make buildings unusable. All these dynamics add up to the creation of complex assemblages of building reclamation businesses, groups and cooperatives.

Repair and maintenance do not depend on individuals but a network. The performance of a network is measured by the associations of its parts or the transitiveness of agency from one to the other (Latour 2007). Each part has emergent properties. Such emergence lies in the parts of assemblage in which every constitutive part has an agentic force that can reveal itself to extend the borders of a network and increase its function (Farías & Bender 2011). The assemblage of *çıkmacıs* operates as a trade network that is deterritorialized and reterritorialized by governmental powers, market dynamics and foreign trade. For instance, the Georgian second-hand exporters expand the trade network. This activity breaks down or reshapes the boundaries of assemblage and can be described as a deterritorialization or reterritorialization that influences the level of heterogeneity (DeLanda 2006; Deleuze and Guattari 1987).

Another conceptual reference to assemblage is apparent in the work experience of Rıfat. Recall how he transmitted his know-how to a coworker who later started his own second-hand business. As a result of that, the size of the market network increased. This shows how the labor network is socially and materially constructed (Simone 2015). *Çıkmacıs* learn the profession from each other and their associations multiply the magnitude of the network geographically and socially. There are other nonhuman actants in the network. For instance, the second-hand market expands its borders by utilizing second-hand supply yards as immutable mobiles (Latour 2007) to deliver second-hand commodities. Their purpose is the same in all situations and locations: to store, display and repair.

This chapter examines the spatialization of second-hand trade in different cities that form a network of relations in different ways. In contrast to scattered individually-operating yards in Istanbul, the suppliers in Ankara and Kayseri have formed cooperatives to have legal representation and constitute a professional identity that enables them to bid legally on demolition tendering. In the Global South, it is a common strategy for informal waste workers to create their own organizations in order to gain some political power (Dias 2016; Gutberlet et al. 2017). As a result of such inclusion, the *çıkmacıs'* cooperatives bought their land with low-cost installments from the Municipality. However, they lost their land in the city center. Unlike waste picker depots which are frequently raided by the authorities (Dinler 2016; Tuçaltan 2018), they can survive with their organization and could even switch to a different production model like Özcan's business in Kayseri (see Ch. 6.3.2). The cooperatives store and sell reclaimed materials at their sites where each one has their own space. That cooperative structure does not exist in Istanbul. All that being said, second-hand Istanbul depots group together in the Asian and European parts of the city.

Çıkmacıs' mobility and flexibility are critical to their survival. Their adaptability to different situations is also seen in their labor structure: to maintain a low-cost business, family members are mobilized in order to expand the business; also, refugees and new rural migrants are brought on board. The prices of the second-hand elements are often determined by negotiation. As a result, this second-hand trade is able to stay out and not be controlled by monopolistic dynamics. *Çıkmacıs* can decide on their selling prices daily: If they are in survival mode, they can reduce their prices. Because of these aspects, low-budget customers prefer visiting their yards.

Nonetheless, their working conditions remain unregulated due to insufficient legislation and poor governance. In fact, they use the informal territory of building demolition to their advantage in order to find a way to control their second-hand market dynamics and labor organization. The demolishers have been the main actors in building reclamation for decades in Anatolian cities. Entrepreneurs seeking work from various areas were engaged in this market due to the increasing urban development projects. Scrap collectors, in the way that they can easily enter and exit the second-hand market, remain relatively flexible actors in the scene compared to demolishers.

PVC frames are the common components found in yards in Istanbul. Compared to these, the accumulation of industrial components in demolition cooperatives is less. Old vernacular materials like wood and masonry stone are more common in Anatolian yards because traditional houses in urban centers have already largely been demolished for multi-story apartment blocks. Some rare items having an antique value are preferred for expensive restoration projects in tourist areas. By contrast, second-hand items were used in rural houses or farms. However, most of the worn-out wooden parts are used as firewood.

Kayseri and Ankara demolishers do not bring components from Istanbul. On the contrary, Niğde and Nevşehir *çıkmacıs* import Istanbul's components because of the trade and labor network and kinship relations created since the beginning of urban-rural migration. Additionally, the Anatolian depots are visited by Georgian wholesalers who buy and export a significant number of items to Batumi and Tbilisi, Georgia. The lifespan of waste continues through second-hand accumulation and distribution to different villages and cities. In terms of the Georgian triad, it is critical to see urbanism as a kind of metabolic activity because urbanization creates material flows that influence the production of space and livelihoods in regional geographies (Heynen, Kaika, and Swyngedouw 2006).

7. Nonhuman Agency

7.1 Introduction

> Things are alive and active not because they are possessed of spirit – whether in or of matter – but because the substances which they comprise continue to be swept up in circulations of the surrounding media that alternately portend their dissolution or – characteristically with animate beings – ensure their regeneration. (Ingold 2007, 12)

A host of other micro-practices is subsumed within these broader practices, many of them occurring concurrently. Cutting, ripping, tearing, reducing, shredding, compressing, wrapping, moving, sorting, separating, and so on. And it is through some of these micro practices with materials, which together work to coproduce salvage and remediation, that asbestos is reanimated (Gregson, Watkins, and Calestani 2010, 1081).

Air can be what Ingold terms a "surrounding media" that can change the properties or states of many other materials. The *çıkmacıs'* activities themselves can also be seen as a surrounding medium that results in the emissions of asbestos. In the context of waste's materiality, the empirical part of the research shows that such corporeality and coexistence are manifested between *çıkmacıs* and certain discarded materials, namely PVC and asbestos. To exemplify this conceptual statement, I discuss three topics relating to the unrecognized agency of materials: environmental degradation, workplace safety, and dwelling construction. The empirical precedents are based on participant observations, conversations, and field notes.

In the literature review chapter, I argued that the abundance of PVC, in the form of waste material and second-hand window frames, can be viewed as either a passive resource or a nonhuman actant. The first view requires a focus on the many ways in which waste is retrieved by the formal sector, for example, when it re-enters industrial production cycles (Gutberlet, 2017; Dias 2016). Such a perspective cannot be sidelined because economic factors play a significant role in creating the excess of reclaimed materials from industrial production and urbanization.

In the second view, derived from actor network theory, the materiality of waste is discussed as a viable actant (Bennett 2010; Hawkins 2010; Gregson and Crang 2010). Hawkins explores how a plastic water bottle's association with healthy lives, hydration, and clean water obscures the materiality of plastic waste (Hawkins 2009). The environmental problem of its mass accumulation in nature is put in the spotlight. Like plastic bottles, PVC window frames are overproduced during industrialization.

The functionality, affordability and mass production of PVC window frames result in their over-consumption. The production and recycling process of PVC creates hazardous emissions but the governing bodies often ignore them. Material reclamation of PVC frames is precarious due to poorly regulated demolitions. Interestingly, the motive for these demolitions is an earthquake, one of the most potent nonhuman actants, one that changes the built environment on an even more extensive scale.

The policymakers, city planners, and architects have to consider the earth's tectonics in urbanization and dwelling construction. Configuration of cosmopolitics in the presence of earthquakes represents the importance of recognizing the coexistence of human and inhuman worlds (Blok and Farias 2016). Not to mention that the destructive material agency of an earthquake is 'taken advantage of' in order to finance the construction industry, which is in turn powered by the real estate market in Turkey.

To discuss the agency of matter, I divided the chapter into two parts. The first part is focused on PVC and asbestos as active actants within building reclamation and demolition assemblage. In the second part, I concentrate on examples of dwellings made by incremental construction using reclaimed components. These dwellings were created in the rural parts of Turkey where building code regulations are not as strictly enforced.

7.2   Active Matter Before and After Reclamation

In the social sciences, 'materiality' is often defined in the following way: the concept that a cultural artifact's physical qualities influence how it is utilized. However, because materiality focuses more on consumption and the agency of things, such an object-oriented perspective necessarily leaves out the production process. An actant, whether human or nonhuman, makes an impact, causes a result, or alters the trajectory of events (Latour 2004). The production and dematerializing processes like recycling can be defined by "the flux of materials and their transformations" (Ingold 2007, 9). During the recovery processes of buildings, a wide range of objects and substances become active: PVC frames, doors, glass, concrete, reinforcement bars, electrical cables, doorknobs, sanitary fittings, plumbing fixtures, marble, ceramic tiles, radiators, heating systems, boilers, elevators, kitchen cupboards, roof beams, rails, parquets, roof tiles, security bars, furniture, and asbestos.

7.2.1 The Excess of Second-Hand PVC Window Frames

An excessive amount of white PVC frames can be found in second-hand supply yards all over Turkey. Its roots go back to industrial construction technology and consumer culture advancements. PVC frames with double-glazing are promoted as affordable products that reduce noise and heat loss. Because of cold winters, building density, and traffic, such properties are highly desirable in middle-class households in Istanbul. PVC profiles that carry the double-glazing windows serve as the main body of the frame with the support of metal profiles inside. When such technology was first introduced to the construction market in the early 1980s, the old wooden single pane window frames were replaced with the PVC frames flat by flat.

The wooden window frames were discredited because of maintenance difficulties: they had to be regularly cleaned and sealed and they were not able to hold double-layered glass. Made by carpenters, wooden frame production needed a lot of expertise and craft to process wood profiles. However, the material cost and manufacturing of PVC frames were cheaper and faster, partly because of profile extrusion technology. With this technology, the frames' energy-saving properties were enhanced because the plastic profiles of the frames could be produced with air chambers inside. Technically, these profiles reduced energy loss.

An Istanbul PVC piping manufacturer, Pimapen, first introduced the technology in the 1980s. The PCV factories eventually replaced carpenters, who were expensive and slow because of their manual labor. At first, the frames were called Pimapen but later, other manufacturers in the market called them by different names. In the Turkish retail market, the product is still called

Pimapen but not as its technical name. In 1980, one of the TV advertisements for the double-glazing glass advised:

> (While the banknotes were flying in front of a window on the TV footage) If you are not rich enough to throw your money out of the windows, listen carefully! In a building, most of the heat is lost from the window openings. If you installed the new technology, 20 percent of the heating cost would be in your pocket. When buying a flat, ask for double glazing. Burn less, warm up more. (ISICAM 1980)

In another advertisement from the early 2000s, the main character was a doctor, played by a famous comedian with expertise in 'windowology' (Pimapen 2000). He was shown curing a sick household by prescribing the right type of plastic frame. In addition to the effective promotion strategy within those advertisements, every neighborhood in Istanbul had a PVC frame franchise that exhibited new products.

PVC frames were regarded as a necessary household appliance that was installed or purchased to improve the heating condition of old flats, which needed remodeling and upgrading. However, PVC's animate properties are often ignored. Those properties arise from the recycling process that changes its substance structure and associations with its surroundings. The environmental impacts of PVC in the petrochemical and recycling industry remain invisible to the governing bodies and the public in Turkey. In the following, I reveal the hazardous properties of PVC.

7.2.2   PVC as a Raw Material

The discovery that PVC could be manufactured from a waste product of the petrochemicals industry was the catalyst for its widespread use. According to Heinrich Böll Foundation's report "Plastic Atlas", the industry created a monster: "Although it was increasingly known that PVC production harmed both the environment and human health, the petrochemicals industry took advantage of the new possibilities to turn a waste product into profit" (Fuhr and Franklin 2019, 10). According to the same report, 71 million tons of plastic (16.2 percent of overall production) were used in the construction sector in 2017 (Hazardous materials within CDW have an underestimated impact on the built environment and urban life. 1), and 10 percent of 407 million tons of worldwide plastic production in 2015 consisted of PVC (ibid).

Figure 7.1: The distribution of plastic production per sector in 2017

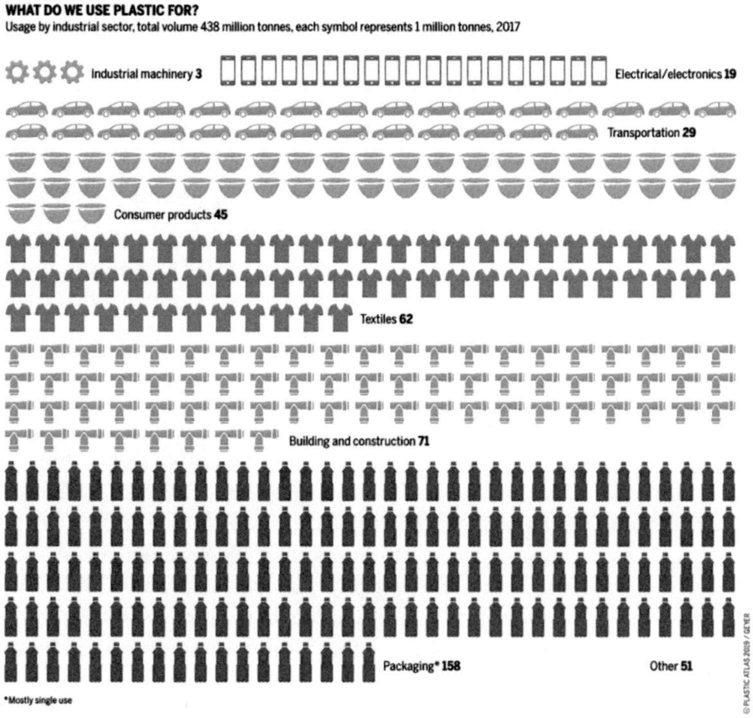

WHAT DO WE USE PLASTIC FOR?
Usage by industrial sector, total volume 438 million tonnes, each symbol represents 1 million tonnes, 2017

*Mostly single use

Source: (Fuhr and Franklin 2019)

Plastics are often blended with toxic chemical additives such as plasticizers, fire retardants, and colors to enhance their qualities. Many of these additions improve the material's flexibility or durability. Although it may be true that all plastics can be recycled, it should be kept in mind that PVC's production causes CO_2 emissions and its melting releases highly toxic dioxins. Plastic recycling workers' lives are hazardous and heavily exploited within the context of global capitalism (Hulme 2015).

Throughout its production history, plastics have damaged the environment and human health (Thornton 2002). When being recycled, the process results in the substance being released into the water or air, and it eventually ends up in the human body. According to the seven plastic recycling codes[1], PVC is rated as 3, which means it is difficult and dangerous to recycle.

In 2017, 71 million tons of plastic were used worldwide in the building and construction sector (Fuhr and Franklin 2019). Referring to this amount of production, its indestructible mass impact on environmental degradation is undeniable. Due to its durability, solidity, and lightweight properties, PVC is widely used in building technologies; however, the average lifespan of a PVC window frame is between 20 and 30 years. In recycling processes, PVC's thermoplastic nature supposedly allows the material to be heated and molded or extruded many times without losing its technical properties. However, according to the report titled "Window of Opportunity" in 2003 by the World Wildlife Fund (WWF), PVC frames have many negative impacts on the environment:

> PVC is a product that uses a non-renewable resource. It cannot be sustainable: oil makes up 43 percent of the raw material required to make PVC; PVC windows generate 43 percent more waste than timber windows: 82 percent of total PVC waste goes to landfills; 15 percent is incinerated. Only 3 percent is recycled; PVC waste will rise to 6.4 million tons by 2020 when the capacity to recycle it will be a fifth of what will be required; it takes eight times more energy to manufacture a PVC window than an equivalent timber frame; throughout the use and disposal of the product, the overall environmental burden is significantly less for timber windows than for PVC windows hazardous chemicals are released into the environment during the incineration process of PVC. (C. Thompson 2005, 10)

These environmental burdens of PVC window frames are often disregarded in the Turkish context where the affordability and functionality of the product are more important considerations than its toxicity. Unfortunately, no report on the amount of PVC frame waste in Turkey exists. On the other hand, they are the most recycled and reclaimed building elements in the yards. *Çıkmacıs* greatly contribute to extending PVC's lifespan. Due to their relational impacts, PVC frames have a considerable weight on the agency of materials. Such arguments based on this kind of agency can introduce new ways of engagement with PVC beyond its economic value.

---

1   Resin Identification Code (RIC) is developed by the American Society for Testing and Materials (ASTM).

7.2.3 Recovering PVC

Çıkmacıs sell oversized windows to recycling companies. They remove the double-glazed glass and break the frames on the demolition sites. Custom-produced large frames cannot be sold second-hand because they are hard to transport and store, and the dimensions are generally unfit for reuse. Instead, the broken profiles containing metal and plastic profiles are sold to the recycling factory based on weight price per kilogram. At recycling factories, the frames are granulated into PVC powder recyclates. This mechanical recycling has four stages: first, the frames are shredded into smaller parts; second, the metal is broken apart from the plastic; third, PVC and rubber are separated; and lastly, the PVC is re-granulated. Unlike European mechanical recycling, the double-glazing glass on the frames is not recycled since it is broken on the demolition site and is mixed with the demolition debris. As a final product of mechanical recycling, the metal and PVC powder are sent to manufacturers. The PVC powder is processed to produce new construction pipes, window profiles, and injection molding products.

The frames with smaller sizes are kept intact to be sold second-hand. Some of them are repaired or reframed with low-level production technology. This kind of production takes place in the supply yards equipped with makeshift plastic framing devices. Based on my observations in Fahri's workshop, a skilled-worker cuts the plastic profiles and inserts recovered metal reinforcement profiles that give rigidity to the plastic frames. For attaching the profiles, he uses a makeshift PVC welding machine and acrylic glue. Sometimes he even processes recovered double-glazed glass without properly sealing air between the two layers. The end product is far from the quality of the newly produced frame; nevertheless, the price is affordable for low-budget customers. Consequently, the second-hand frames are distributed out of Istanbul through trade routes. As a result, the plastic continues its life span in other buildings, and the excess material waste is reassessed as a second-hand product. The prolonged life span of the object has positive impacts on sustainability and environmental change.

7.2.4 Asbestos Exposure

Between 2000 and 2010, 130 thousand tons of asbestos was exported to Turkey from abroad (mainly from Greece and Russia) (Odman 2019). It was used extensively in the construction sector until its ban in 2010 due to its carcinogenic dangers (Union of Turkish Engineers and Architects Chambers (TMMOB) 2017). Building components that contain asbestos are corrugated cement roof plates named after the brand name Eternit[2], wall claddings, vinyl-based flooring, ceiling boards, heat isolation, fire-resistant boards, radiators, boilers, and drain pipes. Its properties in its solid state are very significant: strength, durability, and the ability to withstand high temperatures. However, when its fibers are released into the air by a decomposition process, its hazardous properties are activated. It has to be handled cautiously. Such transformational features of materials enable them to perform. Gregson and Crang (2010) claim that asbestos exerts its effect by establishing connections with human and nonhuman counterparts. For instance, they discuss the non-human agency of asbestos and its material metamorphosis in shipbreaking (Gregson et al. 2010). That is why materials like asbestos must be considered in their transformative states rather than just in their stable ones.

Depending on the date of the construction, building materials containing asbestos were heavily used in some buildings in Kadıköy from the 1950s to the 1990s (Odman 2019). In her study, Odman creates a risk map of Kadıköy (Figure 7.2) based on production statistics, construction dates, and current demolition sites. This map overlaps with the sites and depots I visited in Kadıköy, and it especially overlaps with Fikirtepe, where large-scale demolitions occurred. The demolition sites were places where asbestos fibers were potentially mixing into the air and affecting the health of the workers and neighboring residents. The map also shows public areas (marked in red) that are located close to Asbestos exposure risk. The authorities ignore the dangers revealed by this map.

It is important to conceive of asbestos as an active substance. As Gregson and others remarked:

> This means that material can no longer be consigned to the category of 'dead' matter, positioned as stuff that is, at best, there to be manipulated and, at worst, the irrelevant baggage of unreconstructed materialism. Neither does this mean thinking in terms of categories such as 'hazardous' that work both to separate off human and physical worlds and to prop up constructivist readings of material. Rather, we want to think of asbestos as ma-

---

2   Founded in 1905, Etex company, also known as Eternit, started producing asbestos fiber cement products in Belgium. These products contained 90% cement and 10% asbestos. In 2021, the founders of Etex were sentenced to 16 years for the death of 3000 Italian workers employed by a factory in Turin (Boggio 2013).

terial handled in practice and practices. (Gregson, Watkins, and Calestani 2010, 1067)

Working in old apartment blocks in Kadıköy, *çıkmacıs* often end up working with some components made of asbestos. The workers were not thoroughly informed about asbestos' effects on human health and did not use any protective outfits or masks. When I asked them if the building was checked for asbestos, they did not have any information. In the Turkish demolition regulations, it is stated that asbestos abatement should be done. In any case, the authorities did not inspect the buildings during my field visits.

Figure 7.2: Risk map due to asbestos exposure from demolitions in Kadıköy- Istanbul

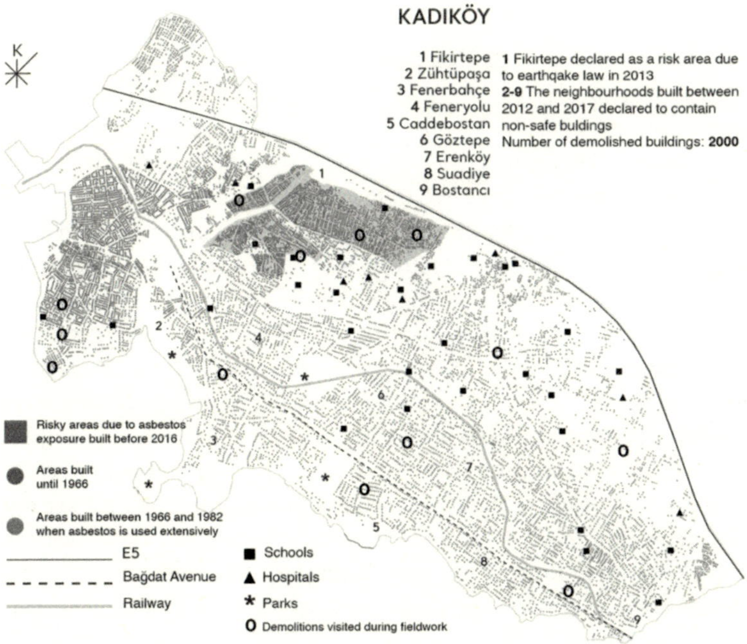

KADIKÖY

1 Fikirtepe	1 Fikirtepe declared as a risk area due
2 Zühtüpaşa	to earthqake law in 2013
3 Fenerbahçe	2-9 The neighbourhoods built between
4 Feneryolu	2012 and 2017 declared to contain
5 Caddebostan	non-safe buldings
6 Göztepe	Number of demolished buildings: 2000
7 Erenköy	
8 Suadiye	
9 Bostancı	

Risky areas due to asbestos exposure built before 2016

Areas built until 1966

Areas built between 1966 and 1982 when asbestos is used extensively

———— E5

– – – – Bağdat Avenue

———— Railway

■ Schools
▲ Hospitals
★ Parks
O Demolitions visited during fieldwork

Source: Author's own based on the asbestos risk map (Odman 2019)

Since the reclamation took place in several parts of the building simultaneously, the workers operating in different parts were under an invisible exposure. For instance, a worker cutting metal parts of the heating system could be a reason for release of Asbestos fibers attached to the heat insulation layer. When suspended in the air, the workers might inhale the matter and damage their lungs. Since exposure may cause cancer after a decade, the effects of asbestos on workers' health remain largely unknown and invisible.

Based on the statement of Engin in Chapter 5, the demolition sites are not inspected regularly, and the workers do not wear work clothes. Taking risks on their own, they do not use masks or other protection against dust and asbestos emissions while dismantling roof structures, heating systems, and heat insulation material. For them, as long as asbestos is not seen, it is not considered to be harmful to their health. However, they are not aware of the long-term effects of substance exposure.

7.2.5   The Agency of Toxic Materials

It is critical to highlight that recycling is aligned with capitalism in that it seeks to increase industrial productivity (Thorton et al., 2002). During the production and recycling processes of PVC frames, some of its hazardous compounds are released by incineration. The effects of these compounds on the environment are often overlooked by the petrochemical and recycling industries. Stepping back for a moment, we can think about trans-corporeality and how it considers all embodied beings as connected to the material world through their reciprocal relationships and transformative interactions (Alaimo 2010). Thus, relationships between demolition workers and these toxic materials can be seen as resulting in trans-corporal associations which these industries do not see.

Çıkmacıs act as unacknowledged people that dismantle, collect, and transport the reclaimed materials. During these activities, they make contact with other materials whose existence remains independent from human control. During demolitions for salvaging components like PVC frames, there is a high possibility of asbestos exposure in old pre-ban buildings. The recycling emulsions of plastics and the interaction of human bodies that deal with the toxic environment could explain that waste is not exterior to humans but a trans-corporal agent with much power to change the course of processes.

The materiality of waste has a positive connotation, but seeing it from the perspective of a circular economy via recycling, reveals the implicit harm of the material to the human and nonhuman world. To some extent, the sustainable development and recycling industry remains a wasteful and dangerous surplus of the capitalist construction industry. In the following, I will discuss the power of reclaimed components and their second lives that are utilized to create dwellings.

7.3 The Utilization of Reclaimed Materials in Buildings

In the context chapter (Ch. 4), I demonstrated that unsorted demolition waste was a crucial resource for low-cost constructions and informal urbanization. Earlier versions of these *gecekondus* resembled one-roomed village houses roofed with clay tiles. At that time, they had stone walls but the ones built later were made of prefabricated components like corrugated sheets, salvaged concrete panels, and found window frames (Pérouse 2014). Rooms were added step by step to extend the makeshift squatter houses:

> Incrementalism, as a labor intensive and historical accretion, is an important form of dwelling as assembly and is common to a whole range of urban processes and forms, from housing and policy to infrastructure and culture. (McFarlane 2011, 659)

Slow-paced construction of gecekondus is banned and criminalized by the state in Turkey. Even now, building salvaging as a gathering process links the cooperation between reclaimed materials and urban incrementalism. The secondary life of building refuse continues to exist through material recovery and trade activities through second-hand valuation. My research reveals how second-hand building components are still utilized in different dwelling constructions in rural parts of Turkey and Tbilisi in Georgia. Even though Tbilisi is different in terms of its urban and urbanization context, it shares a common ground with the rural parts of Turkey, namely, it's a housing problem. *Gecekondus* in Turkey and dwellings in the Gldani microdistrict of Tbilisi were developed incrementally. In Gldani, the *gecekondu*-like dwelling expansions are vertically attached to old Soviet residential blocks.

Generally, second-hand materials are used for an upgrade or repair. The components are used in summer dwellings, village houses, hobby garden huts, seasonal farming shelters, and vineyard cabins that host recreational and farming activities. The openings are modified according to the size of the second-hand frames manufactured for a former building in Istanbul.

The precedent dwellings are not categorized as illegal like *gecekondus*, but I see them as being in a gray zone where state control mechanisms do not apply regulations strictly. Apart from the urbanization context, the arrangement of reclaimed components in incremental examples represents unique socio-material alignments because of things' different relational and processual properties. Referring to Bennett (2010) on the importance of thing-power over specific waste assemblages, McFarlane discusses that such groupings depend on gathering processes in the formation of the incrementally constructed dwellings (McFarlane 2011b). The importance of second-hand components stands out for their necessity in construction, excessive accumulation, and frugality in the rural context. I see the thing-power in how reclaimed components get involved in the design process and become part of the new buildings through incremental constructions.

The agency of PVC frames is fundamental: they are affordable, available in high quantities, and traded outside of Istanbul. During my field research, I observed that the sizes of second-hand frames determine the design of the building openings. During construction, the builders have to adjust the space dimensions and openings according to the available dimensions of the second-hand components. The owner has to frequently coordinate the builders for these adjustments since the search for second-hand components is always going on. Further, the incremental construction follows an intermittent process in which resources are sometimes scarce. Occasionally, the construction stops and waits for components to be found. Such capacity and trajectory of things to animate people for the construction processes and the design of the buildings are further discussed in the next section that is based on empirical findings.

7.3.1 Construction in the High Plateau: Susuz - Kastamonu

Fahri, a 35-year-old man, bought reclaimed materials from a building on his street in Bulgurlu, a former *gecekondu* neighborhood in Üsküdar. On the lot where he bought the materials, in the 1970s, a squatter house used to stand. After zoning amnesty in the 1990s, the gecekondus were modified into three-story apartments. As a result of the urban transformation act in 2012, the zoning regulations were upgraded to five floors in the district. In 2016, the owners demolished this apartment to build a new one. During the demolition process, Fahri closely followed the construction to get cheap used construction components and made a deal with the scrap dealer reclaiming components. Fahri remarked:

> I had a limited budget to rebuild the village house. I had to wait for a good opportunity. Otherwise, it would be even too expensive to buy from a *çıkmacı* yard. Instead, I made a deal with the scrap collectors before selling the components to a second-hand wholesaler. Buying from a yard would be more expensive because they would make profit over the incoming price.

Eventually, he bought kitchen cupboards, a kitchen counter with a sink, four interior doors, six PVC window frames (100x150 cm), two small toilet PVC window frames (40x40 cm), and one PVC balcony door. If he purchased them new, he would have paid 5 to 8 times more, he admitted. He was still looking for a metal door for the entrance and vinyl parquet flooring. Due to his limited financial resources, he was only able to make a few small remodeling repairs to his flat in Istanbul. But here, in his family village in Kastamonu, he was able to entirely rebuild his family house.

Fahri used these materials in his new family house in Susuz, located in the Western Black Sea Mountains. According to Fahri, there were 140 houses in the village. It is not inhabited during the winter. Like many village houses in the Black Sea, the old house, partly burnt, was made out of wood. After a landslide, it was considered uninhabitable. It was no longer legal to build new houses on new land in the village. However, if a house was severely damaged, like Fahri's family's house, they were allowed to repair or build a new one in the same spot. Unlike the old one, the new house has a concrete structure. It stands on concrete beams. However, as he pointed out:

> It is not allowed to be built with concrete anymore in the region. According to new regulations, all the houses should have traditionally built wood structures. Still, you can use PVC frames on the windows.

Like other houses in the village, the house had two stories with 100 square meters of floor space each. After they completed building the first story, his parents started to live there. He was in the middle of completing the ground floor when we met. The plan consisted of three rooms, a kitchen, and a bathroom. There was one less room on the first floor, but the rest of the plan was the same. The dwelling was planned to accommodate two families.

After finishing the load-bearing concrete structure, he sent the dimensions of the windows and door frames to the construction workers so they could make the façade and door openings (Figure 7.3 and 7.4). He said they were lucky that the construction was still going on when he found the components; otherwise, he probably would have had to knock down some walls. In this way, he could fit the frames to the openings. The size of the kitchen is arranged according to the size of the cupboards (Figure 7.5). They completed the roof with old wooden beams salvaged from the former house. The roof was then covered with insulated metal panels. Apart from the concrete structure and clay bricks, most parts of the house came from reclaimed materials. In the following section, I will discuss a different rural dwelling in a different village because the availability of second-hand materials determined the construction development. The frugality of the owners offers an excellent example of the ethical meaning of 'buying second-hand'.

Figure 7.3: West façade of the dwelling with a metal door salvaged from Istanbul

Source: Erdinç Eşref Uslu Archive

Figure 7.4: Second-hand façade elements

Source: Erdinç Eşref Uslu Archive

Figure 7.5: Second-hand kitchen cupboards

Source: Erdinç Eşref Uslu Archive

7.3.2 The Village of Çıkmacıs: Yazıhüyük – Nevşehir

Yazıhüzük village is located in central Anatolia within the city limits of Nevşehir. There are 700 houses in the village, all built around the farming lands (Yazıhüyük Municipality 2021). Additionally, sheds, storage units, and barns are also positioned around the land. construction of buildings up to two stories is allowed in the village. According to the law designated for places with less than 10 thousand population, permission from the local municipality is necessary to make a new addition to a house (Turkish Parliment (TBMM) 1985). In the first stage, the villagers build the ground floor. After several years, due to matrimonial extensions of the family, a second floor will be built.

During my field visit, Engin, the scrap collector who I met in Istanbul (see Ch. 5.3.2), showed me his relative Mehmet's farmhouse (Figure 7.6). Engin said that the traditional construction method used to be stone masonry. However, currently, the villagers built the houses with reinforced concrete structures because it was cheaper and more practical. A local craftsman helped Mehmet with the construction. The new building provided additional space for Mehmet's extended family, which consisted of four brothers, their wives, and their parents. After marriages in the family, they made additions to the existing building. Additionally, a one-story house was built on the farmland. The construction was achieved by incremental process depending on the availability of second-hand materials and financial resources.

The two houses were positioned at the edges of the privately-owned agricultural land. The construction phases were at different stages. The ground floor was occupied in the older one, and a floor was added above the existing roof. The construction of the first floor was still in progress. The new house next to the old one was not occupied yet, and only the rough construction of the ground floor was finished. Even though the people were from the same family, the constructions were financed and managed separately.

The newly built first floor had seven rooms, and the floor plan was 70 meter-square. The ground floor was 45 meter-square. It was planned to be larger than the ground floor to create an open garage space that could also be used for storage. Plus, balconies were added to the second floor. A new exterior staircase was installed to provide vertical access between the two levels. For the façade of the first floor, second-hand window frames were used. The frames used to belong to an apartment in Istanbul. Engin explained that he sold the frames before Mehmet started to put up the exterior walls. Therefore, he could determine the dimensions of the façade openings (Figure 7.7). Engin responded:

"They have to wait for me to deliver the components for a few weeks. I looked for high-quality second-hand [materials]. I brought the window frames with me when I was coming for the harvest". Engin also sold Mehmet kitchen cupboards and heating radiators from a flat in Kadıköy. The radiator was not installed yet because the main structure was only finished recently.

Figure 7.6: Two houses and agricultural land in Yazıhüyük

Source: Author's Own

The building façade shows different histories. The ground floor was constructed 40 years ago and it had smaller window frames and was built with load-bearing stone walls. Mehmet said the ground floor went through a renovation ten years ago. They replaced the old wood frames with PVC frames and added an extension to the entrance made of plastic profiles. The adjacent house with a single floor was also constructed by the same incremental logic.

In the adjacent house, the first stage of the construction, the ground floor, was recently completed. A staircase was constructed for climbing on the flat roof, which would be the first floor for the next generation of the family. However, the owner explained that it would not be completed for at least another five years. Unlike the other house, the façade elements were ordered from a manufacturer because they wanted new windows. After all, the contractor had already built it. They did not want to deal with enlarging the openings in order to install a used window frame. Mehmet explained that when he purchased the kitchen cupboards from Engin, they adjusted the size of the kitchen to accommodate them. They were specifically looking for a second-hand entrance door which they had not yet found. Such situations delayed the construction.

Figure 7.7: PVC window frames from Istanbul in Yazıhüyük

Source: Author's Own

When I asked about the building permissions, Mehmet explained that they did not apply for permission yet. Nonetheless, it was unclear if they would ask for one. These two houses are good examples of the different stages of incremental construction in the village. The incremental way of construction is a slow process dependent on second-hand components, uncontrolled building permissions, and personal relationships with public authorities.

Some of the construction projects in Yazıhüyük are built under the radar of state zoning laws. These projects take place within a network of informal personal relationships with small local governments. Social relations are more valid than bureaucratic mechanisms. Not only is the law loosely applied and controlled in small villages, but also people rely on the construction amnesties and low fines issued by the state. It is crucial to highlight that the amnesty legislation is used as political publicity before local and general elections. Such factors explain the circumstances enabling incremental construction processes determined by the agency of things in terms of the construction period and dwelling design. In the next section, I will examine how incremental construction of a migrant neighborhood is achieved under the provision of the state and how second-hand materials influence the typology of architecture.

7.3.3 Eskişehir Bağları - Kayseri

The district of Eskişehir Bağları is part of Kayseri province in Central Anatolia. The Eskişehir Bağları district was planned as a *Gecekondu* Prevention Zone at the periphery of the city when informal housing was perceived as a problem that conflicted with urban modernization processes. Utilizing these projects, the government tried to solve the housing problem by expropriating state land and supplying affordable home loan credit to low-income individuals. Legislated in 1966, Law No. 775 aimed to prevent new squatter houses, supply shelters for migrants whose homes were demolished because of illegal means, provide new dwellings for rural migrants, and improve urban living conditions in slum areas in migration-receiving cities (Turkish Parliment (TBMM) 1966). According to this legislation, the local governments were made responsible for making zoning plans, managing the developments, and providing the infrastructure.

In 1994, the metropolitan municipality of Kayseri began to expropriate the state-owned land in the district to supply housing for rural migrants and stop them from building *gecekondus* without any infrastructure and planning. The municipality planned 7200 parcels on 3 million square meters of land, and 6000 were reserved as 210 to 250 meter-square plots (Karayel 2019). The municipality leased the plots with long-term affordable installments to the rural migrants. Therefore, the population of the district reached nearly 150 thousand.

At first, Kayseri houses could not be built higher than one story; right before the 1998 local elections, the height limit became two stories; later, prior to the 2002 elections, the height limit was raised first to three stories and then to four (ibid) (Figure 7.8). Within these changing zoning decisions, the residents were responsible for financing and constructing the houses. According to the second-hand supplier, Özcan, the construction took place incrementally; first, the dwellers built the main concrete structure of the ground floor, leaving reinforcement bar sprouts over the roof; later, they put up the walls on the ground floor and started living there, then they completed the other floors. Occasionally, they could not finish the exterior wall plaster because of a lack of financial resources. Currently, the district remains unfinished, and dwellers are trying to lower the construction costs by using inexpensive materials and components.

Figure 7.8: Eskişehir Bağları district in Kayseri

Source: Author's Own

Özcan observed that the district's population increased while refugees from Afghanistan and Syria replaced old dwellers. Old rural migrants who became the owners of the single-family houses moved to better flats close to the city center. The dwellings were modified into small apartments accommodating large refugee families. Even the basements used for storage were transformed into flats. Özcan clarified that, during remodeling constructions, second-hand materials were preferred because the owners did not want to spend their financial resources on constructing the dwellings. Additionally, they wanted to make as much rental profit as possible from the increased real estate demand due to the influx of refugees. Unfortunately, the refugees with low incomes had to live on what they could find. Most of the time, it was hard for them to find a place because of ethnic discrimination in the area (Kuru and Karanfil 2021).

With the demolition of neighborhoods, excessive quantities of construction waste were produced locally. The demolishers reclaimed the materials from traditional stone houses and concrete apartment blocks built in the 1980s. From traditional houses, the demolishers primarily recovered wooden roof beams, roof tiles, and clay bricks. Moreover, they salvaged PVC frames, interior and exterior doors, and flooring elements from the old apartment blocks.

In different parts of rural Kayseri province, locally reclaimed materials were adopted to construct vineyard sheds and farming shelters (Figure 7.9). Özcan explained that wood reclaimed from the roofs of old houses was used chiefly in the vineyards. In the other places visited in the area, I observed that such materials were used for the small-scale construction of sheds and small shelters. The legal status of such small constructions remains ambiguous.

The kinetic city is temporary in nature, dependent upon ephemeral conditions, and often built with recycled materials: plastic sheets, scrap metal, canvas, and waste wood. These materials also enable modification and reinvention. (Mehrotra, Vera, and Mayoral 2017, 18)

Figure 7.9: Makeshift vineyard shed in Ürgüp

Source: Author's own

Rahul Mehrotra attributes 'kinetic' properties to informal urbanization trends distinguished by flux, unpredictability, and indistinctness. Reminiscent of those kinetic qualities, the reclaimed materials in Kayseri have enabled a modifiable, reinventive, and responsive built environment; an environment that leans against the critical conditions and housing problems of the local government's zoning plans. The 'kinetic' aspects of adaptive reclaimed materials and the incremental contribution of the people there can function to accommodate critical livelihood conditions. Second-hand components are smartly translated into functional spaces by innovative reuse, self-organized labor, and trade networks. In the following, I discuss the urbanization of Gldani in Tbilisi, where those attributes of buildings are created with second-hand materials.

7.3.4 Micro-district: Gldani - Tbilisi

As a result of the second-hand trade between Georgia and Turkey, intriguing examples of incremental construction practices with second-hand components from Turkey were found in the Gldani district in Tbilisi, Georgia. Gldani is a micro-district, or micro rayon, located in the northern periphery of Tbilisi. Originating in the Soviet Union, the micro districts are mass housing settlements that cultivated the socialist ideal of rapid urban growth that attempted to solve housing shortages within the borders of the Soviet Union. Gldani micro-district is based on a master plan conceived by the Soviet regime between 1968 and 1972 and then finished in the 1980s (Secchi and Spita 2018). The project-based dimensions, acknowledged by Soviet standards, had the target of providing housing for 147 thousand residents (Elettra and Gurgenidze 2018).

After the dissolution of the Soviet Union in 1991, the district went through a significant change in their housing environment. State-owned apartments were reclaimed by dwellers who turned them into informally privatized dwellings. Such rapid and unrestrained built environment transformation could not be regulated because of limited urban planning and infrastructural resources. The residents were freed from standardized living conditions by the transformed environment that allowed them to modify the former Soviet apartments according to their needs (Assche and Salukvadze 2013).

During the last 20 years leading up to Georgia's independence in 1991, the former Soviet republic experienced severe political, fiscal, and social crises (Bouzarovski, Salukvadze, and Gentile 2011). Due to the already collapsing building industry, housing shortage, and densely overcrowded households, legislation was enacted in 1989 that allowed "balconies, recessed balconies, and verandas" to be attached to individual housing units (Gegidze, Manjavidze, and Opel 2016).

The residents took advantage of the gray zone that opened up after the law was passed to expand their homes. Their spatial alterations involved two architectural interventions: enlarging private spaces to make them communal areas and adding extensions to flats (Figure 7.10). Public spaces were captured and informally privatized for individual gardens, commercial shops, and parking spaces. External 'parasitic architecture' attachments, known as 'Kamikaze Loggias', began springing up all over Tbilisi during the years of political chaos between 1991 and 1995 (Elettra and Gurgenidze 2018; Wainwright 2018).

Figure 7.10: Building extensions: kamikaze loggias and rooftops add-ons in Gldani

Source: Author's own, 2018

These loggias in the form of outdoor platforms connected to existing floors can extend the plan of flats up to 40 square meters (Secchi and Spita 2018). They are built over steel-bar-frame structures installed next to the buildings and weakly connected to their reinforced concrete block walls. The lower floors are sometimes equipped with a private staircase. Alternatively, the extensions function as terraces or are closed by the owners to obtain one or two more rooms. The owners use their own aesthetic criteria to decide the window sizes and other architectural details of each loggia without any worry about zoning restrictions or other limitations. This all results in a fairly impressive display: a complete freedom of architectural style, material, and color. Consequently, an architecture has emerged in Tbilisi that is unique among post-Soviet cities.

With limited financial resources and no state support, the residents recreate their homes in whatever way they want to.

Figure 7.11: Unfinished facade in Gldani

Source: Author's own

For the last 18 years, the alteration of the original architectural plans in Gldani can mainly be detected in the altered façades of the housing blocks. The façades consist of different sizes of modified openings with old and new window frames. They were constructed with various kinds of bricks and plaster. The façade itself reflects the construction history by its combination of original Soviet elements and new second-hand additions.

Although loggia construction is no longer legal in Gldani, informal practices continue there. In order to affordably make so many building alterations, one needs cheap construction materials and components. The second-hand traders of Tbilisi have been providing materials to Gldani for years. Giga, who is a *çıkmacı* with a yard on the city's outskirts, informed me that he still had a few customers who were renewing the facades of their Kamikaze Loggias in Gldani. He said they were buying PVC frames, metal apartment doors, and radiators.

During my visit to Giga's yard, one of the customers explained that he built the walls of a building extension ten years ago but has never had enough money to finish it until now. He was looking for window frames and doors to enclose the extension. When I visited his extension, I observed that the walls were built with lightweight concrete bricks. They were uncovered and had cement mortar patches. The openings for the window frame were intentionally left blank for future repairs and the wall was unfinished (Figure 7.11). The steel columns were visible. It was like a large balcony. The customer was using the extension as a utility space, indoor patio, and a place to store fruits and vegetables. One part of it was built as a sitting area but it was winter when I saw it so it looked more like a shed or depot. He explained that the space in its current form was suitable for warm summers but that they had to cover it in plastic wrap for the winter. He said the construction felt never-ending because collecting inexpensive second-hand materials took a lot of time.

7.3.5 Architectural Reuse

> Houses and limited infrastructure are added onto bit by bit; the mobiliza-
> tion of family labor buys time for a small business to grow; migration is used
> as an instrument to pool together savings in order to start a new economic
> activity; mobile work crews are formed to dig wells, help with construction,
> or deliver goods until they make enough contacts to specialize on one par-
> ticular activity. (Simone 2008)

Non-metropolitan places are changing in such gradual ways in Turkey, while big cities are under the bombardment of privatization and financialization that does not allow such processes. Outside main cities, the agency of salvaged materials remains a critical factor in dwelling construction to this day. The footprint of salvaged materials is visible within the gathering of the components, second-hand trading activities, and its architectural integration into the design of the dwellings. The time required for construction depends on the owner's financial resources, access to second-hand parts, and ability to find inexpensive new materials. The volumes and façades of the resulting buildings are determined by the size and shape of the second-hand materials (Figure 7.12).

I also described how second-hand components are utilized during incremental construction processes in Turkey and Georgia. Such cooperation between urbanization, construction methods and reclaimed components is produced by the agency of the materials, gathering processes, uncontrolled zoning, building obsolescence in the urban areas, and material flows organized by *çıkmacıs*. To the same extent, the agentic role of the reclaimed components has an effect on the rural construction processes in the assemblage of the building.

Figure 7.12: Plan A-Susuz, Plan B-Yazıhüyük, Plan C-Tbilisi

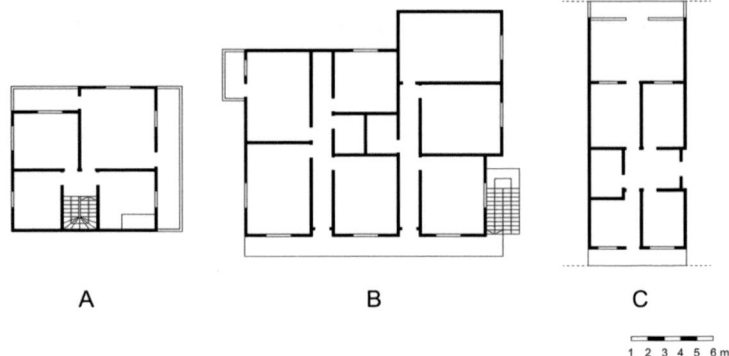

A   B   C

1 2 3 4 5 6 m

Source: Author's own

7.4 Remarks

Ingold suggests that all materials are processual and relational things that exceed a conceptual materiality that only focuses on consumerism and the functionality of artifacts (Ingold 2007). From this perspective, based on empirical findings, the agency of discarded materials was discussed in terms of three different subjects in the chapter: pollution, labor health, and dwelling construction. PVC window frame manufacture and disposal results in a discharge of toxic chemicals that endanger the environment and human health.

Asbestos is another dangerous and invisible agent that becomes active during demolitions. *Çıkmacıs* are not aware of its risk. It remains invisible because, even though there are asbestos handling regulations, the government generally ignores it. Balayannis (2020) argues that the stipulations for how to remove toxic waste are not necessarily what is actually carried out in the field. If legislative and administrative apparatuses recognized the agency of toxic waste, the effects of these materials on living things and the environment could be abated through new control mechanisms. The theoretical framework of 'new materialism' problematizes the materiality of waste pointing out the animative power of substances and their associated assemblages (Bennett 2010; Hawkins 2010). This framework can help us address the ethical dimension of waste in everyday life.

The afterlife of PVC frames creates linkages between different kinds of incremental construction projects such as a village dwelling, farmhouse, state-supported neighborhood building, or a post-Soviet era apartment. The findings show that the legislative framework is loose in these areas. As discussed in the context chapter, these associations could be seen as the result of urbanization processes in Istanbul that determine the ways buildings become trash. The non-human trash acquires a new and unique value through cycles of reuse initiated by human labor.

The agency of second-hand building materials determine their installation know-how, building facades designs, and the overall incremental construction processes. When suitable components are found, the construction project is said to be 'in progress' and when they are missing, it is said to be 'put on hold'. Such timelines set the tempo of Incremental construction.

Reclaimable building materials are not simply a resource for the recycling industry and should not simply be called 'waste'. Their agency is more complex: they open up avenues of exchange and spread into different geographies through informal waste labor, reuse practices and second-hand trade networks. They influence the ways informal architectures are incrementally constructed.

8. Conclusion

The primary goal of this book has been to generate an analysis of the assemblage of *çıkmacı* material reclamation processes through the identification of the human and nonhuman actors involved. In order to address the research questions, the emergence of the *çıkmacıs* during particular historical urbanization periods was delineated (see Ch. 4). By doing so, their role in the 'pop-up homes' *gecekondu* construction was highlighted and this, in turn, revealed the origin of the CDW surplus. At the present time, they are adapting to neoliberal urban transformation in which salvaged materials are currently being circulated outside the major cities.

This book reveals how the *çıkmacıs'* dual livelihood—scrap collecting and farming—allowed them to move between the zones of city and village. The network of supply yards is examined spatially and ethnographically to reveal how second-hand construction elements are distributed. Supply yards are vessels for *çıkmacıs'* relational activities that circulate commodities and create assemblages of materials. In addition, I put an emphasis on the role of PVC and asbestos' agency in order to confront the human-centric approaches. This approach can reveal the impacts of materials on human health and dwelling construction.

This conclusion has three parts. First, it gives a research overview that highlights the conceptual framework; the association of theory and methodology; and the research findings. It explains the cross-disciplinary approach to the concept of waste and material reclamation as well as pointing out gaps in existing research. It covers how political economy and assemblage thinking are utilized to describe the research subject's economic aspects and urban multiplicity. Ethnographic fieldwork strategies are also reviewed. Secondly, the chapter provides practical suggestions for architects, urban planners, and other related bodies governing and planning metropolitan areas. Lastly, I reveal the research challenges and restrictions and conclude the book with proposals for future projects.

8.1   Research Overview

This multi-disciplinary research perspective incorporates different fields: ethnography, architecture, and urbanization. It contributes to an observation of diverse subjects and processes: unrecognized forms of migrant and refugee labor, rural incremental construction, material reclamation, demolition, urban transformation projects, labor mobility, and cartography of second-hand networks. These processes come together not only for economic reasons but also from interaction between the social and the material. Urbanization can be thought of as a gathering process in which materials and human activities merge to form a network of interactions.

My research perspective on the subject involves an acknowledgment of the political economy behind urbanization processes and the integration of assemblage thinking; ultimately this allows one to see urbanization as an alignment of different elements. Assemblage thinking enables us to focus on everyday practices and urban realities which are planned one way but lived differently. Urban renewal projects are planned to replace existing buildings in the city. Second hand building materials that are rejected by these projects are assembled together to form rural dwellings. This process is enacted through slower procedures like incremental construction. The assemblage of *çıkmacıs* multiplies based on absence of state planning, the salvaging interventions and informal networks.

8.1.1   Theoretical Framework

The reuse of construction components has been practiced throughout human history. Due to natural disasters, cities have been destroyed and debris has been reclaimed as a construction material since the beginning of civilization. For instance, the remains of ancient Greek cities are reused in informal settlements or incrementally-constructed rural homes in Turkey. Due to contemporary economic forces, reclamation practices in low-income countries operate in an informal economy. However, dualistic economic models of governing informality tend to ignore or formalize unrecognized practices (Portes, Castells, and Benton 1989). Formalization in waste management creates a homogenous order that leads to privatization (Tuçaltan 2018). The exclusion of waste pickers from formal waste management sidelines informal labor's contribution to urban sustainability.

Each culture's valuation of waste is different. The general theoretical approach to the subject in the West has a tendency to view the question in a binary of waste and humans. This does not allow for a broader comprehension of waste circularity. There is often a presumption that waste is something external to the human body (Douglas 1966; Thompson 1979; Scanlan 2005). In this body of literature, the concept of waste is often viewed with an anthropocentric lens. For example, if some object fulfills its purpose for humanity, it is then discarded out of the human network. Human-centric categorization of waste also downgrades its animate properties.

There is, however, another kind of approach to the subject. Waste has the power to create what Hawkins refers to as transformation networks (Hawkins 2010). Through these networks, the lively and vital 'thing power' of discarded matter has a profound impact on the human sphere (Bennett 2010). For example, CDW affects architectural design practices that focus on deconstruction, reuse, and recycling. Allowing for a distributive agency between the social and the material, this book adopts a more inclusive approach to waste. Everyday practices like reclaiming or salvaging have an intimate relationship with discarded components and prove that the human and non-human world are perpetually intertwined.

Here, the concept of what waste is varies from culture to culture and place to place (Hawkins 2010). In addition to this, waste is a social construct (Gregson and Crang 2010). For those who have limited accessibility to capital and infrastructure, waste is a vital material resource. For example, in places where there is a housing crisis, sustainability is achieved by using what can be salvaged from the surrounding environment (Mehrotra, Vera, and Mayoral 2017). Economically disadvantaged classes tend to be the predominant laborers of gleaning. Within this environment, resilient practices like the çıkmacıs emerge. In short, the lack of urban waste management results in people filling in gaps by addressing these issues as an ad hoc 'relational infrastructure' (Simone 2015).

The Global North has more systematic and formal methods of waste management. However, that does not necessarily mean that reuse and recycling is better there than elsewhere, where reuse practices are very creative. Trying to read the latter through the lens of western circular economy debates would limit the aims of this research because, in Turkey, the recycling industry functions through a synthesis of the formal and informal spheres. To better understand this synthesis, I discuss contributions of Turkish reclamation enterprises within the framework of urban assemblages (Davis 2006; McFarlane 2011; Dovey 2014; Simone 2015).

Rather than focusing on broad worldwide narratives, assemblage thinking calls for a detailed thick description of site-specific urban situations (McFarlane 2011; Blok and Farias 2016). While focusing on the lives of *çıkmacıs*, I have tried to avoid dichotomies and general assumptions that are rooted in the broad categorizations of global politics and economy. However, we cannot avoid the political economic framework because it explains the context of urban renewal. The commodification of land via 'apartmentalization' and urban renewal projects have been addressed as socio-political developments aligned with neoliberal urbanization agendas (Ch. 4).

The dichotomy between formal and informal practices may affect the ways in which governmental legislation intersects with the everyday tactics of the populace. But in fact, the boundaries are unclear. Assemblage thinking provides the potential for investigations of these liminal circumstances. Using this approach, it is possible to avoid seeing things only from the perspective of the overarching frameworks that promote formalization of waste management. While establishing formal rigid systems, these frameworks ignore emerging informal practices and nonhuman agency. Relationships and actor heterogeneity are vitally important for assemblage analysis.

Within such networks, emergence of nonhuman elements causes transformation and unexpected arrangements (Parnet and Deleuze 2002). For instance, CDW is a dynamic agent that participates in the configuration of urban life. Hazardous materials within CDW have an underestimated impact on the built environment and urban life. Additionally, the network of supply yards is composed of spaces with diverse functions where surplus is accumulated, revalued, and traded. They pop up in different locations, and they are part of a larger trade network.

The assemblage of *çıkmacıs* contains very complex associations that can tend to go on forever. For the purposes of this study, I have limited my target to reclaimers (scrap collectors and demolishers), CDW, urban renewal projects, laws, regulations, second-hand markets, supply yards, refugees, migration networks, coops, communication, earthquakes, and other transportation infrastructure. The association of these actors have various impacts on human health and dwelling construction. This assemblage layout—an alternative to the human hegemony over geography point of view—shows how cities are assembled with nonhuman forces.

An earthquake represents what Anders Blok and Ignacio Farias (2016) have reinterpreted as the 'cosmopolitical' capacities of earthly forces to influence urban development strategies. The Düzce Earthquake in Turkey had the effect of changing urban renewal regulations and building codes that, in turn, led to the creation of safer housing. Many NGOs claim that policymakers use the earthquake argument to speed up urban renewal so that the construction sector can generate lucrative assets for capital investments (Adanalı 2012). As a result of this increase in the demolish and rebuild cycle, more second-hand markets are created. This cycle also leads to the activation of other materials such as Asbestos. The governmental authorities and çıkmacıs turn a blind eye to the issue of asbestos as an environmental health hazard but NGOs are warning about its long-term detrimental effects.

To investigate the movement of CDW and its active agency, I employed 'follow the thing' methodology and this led me to 'multi-sited' ethnographic fieldwork. As discussed in assemblage thinking, thick description of place specific narrative of çıkmacıs is the guiding principle of my fieldwork because it creates an understanding of forgotten actors and urban inequalities (McFarlane 2011a). In this study, the inequalities are interpreted as unrecognized and sidelined agencies of both human labor and waste materials.

8.1.2 Following Things on Multi-sites

The infrastructure of cities is organized in such a way as to keep waste's materiality invisible to us. Following the secondary life of salvaged materials can greatly improve the conceptualization of waste. Their material existence takes place in the unforgotten thresholds of the commodity chain. International waste trade deports urban waste to the Global South where end-of-life ships are discarded on recycling beaches in the Indian Ocean (Gregson et al. 2010). The follow-the-thing approach allows for the grouping of multiple sites to show the relationship between second-hand material networks and local reclamation methods. Such multi-sited fieldwork in my geographical research also captures the circular movement of çıkmacıs.

Abduction is a term used to refer to the inferential creative process of developing new hypotheses through "the processes of revisiting, defamiliarization, and alternative casing [case analysis] in response to unexpected research results" (Timmermans and Tavory 2012, 167). It is a way of recalibrating the hypothesis or theory obtained from the empirical data. Employing the abductive framework, I assembled empirical information based on observations and conversations with the informants. Then, I instantly updated my hypothesis grounded on pre-existing theoretical input. Revisiting demolition sites and supply yards after data analysis enabled me to broaden the perimeters of fieldwork and rephrase research questions. For instance, the initial research was geographically located in Istanbul. At first, I assumed that the second-hand supply yards would only be located in major cities like Istanbul because of rapid urban transformation. Later, I learned from my informants that materials were being traded outside Istanbul. In light of this finding, the field research expanded to Ankara, Kayseri, Nevşehir and Niğde, and the neighboring Tbilisi. I acquired from my informants an empirical knowledge of *ardiyes* (supply yards for *gecekondu* builders during informal urbanization in the 1970s). Only after that did I find some research evidence from earlier literature that they actually existed. As a whole, abductive reasoning led me to reveal the uncharted geography of discarded construction elements.

The use of photography functions as a unique tool for constructing relational bridges between researcher and informant. During the fieldwork, the publication of an online photo essay allowed me to clearly establish my researcher identity. In addition, they were pleased with the article because it provided an alternative narrative to the usual one of their salvaging being perceived as 'dirty work'. That publication became central in allowing me to meet new informants throughout the remainder of my research. The detailed captions accompanying the photos present a more lucid understanding of the everyday labor since they act as short vignettes. They connect the main text and images. The non-linear logic of montage (Marcus 1990), which I used to construct the visual narrative, offers an alternative path for the reader to follow.

The interdisciplinary merging of ethnographic and architectural research provides a useful methodological variation for taking fieldwork notes with spatial analysis. For instance, in order to make comparisons, I created volumetric diagrams of supply yards which are produced from surveys and mappings. They accompany the descriptive ethnographic text to provide a deeper impression of the supply yards. Secondly, architectural analysis of dwellings allows for a comparison of spatial variations. The architectural plans display how incremental practices result in rural building designs that differ dramatically from urban ones.

8.2 Empirical Overview

Previous research on Turkey's informal waste management focused on waste pickers who collect and sort household trash (Altay and Altay 2008; Şen and Artıkişler Kolektifi 2014; Dinler 2016; Tuçaltan 2018). *Çıkmacıs* and their impact on waste management and urbanization has not previously been researched. Moreover, the transformation of CDW to second-hand building materials has not been systematically investigated in a Turkish context.

The research reveals *çıkmacıs'* pathways of emergence from rapid urbanization and their adaptation to neoliberal urbanization (Ch. 4). I focus on them because of their role in affordable building production. They have existed since the *gecekondu* neighborhoods began being developed in Istanbul back in the 1960s. The squatters built their dwellings with reused materials that they purchased from *çıkmacıs* or whatever they could find. For example, one of them was selling second-hand components that he recovered from inner-city demolitions during the 1980s. After several decades, the *çıkmacıs* have organized their own deconstruction processes to create a second-hand market.

The current state administration mobilizes its resources to replace the seismically weak housing stock. In their search to create construction investment assets, the Turkish AK Party has adopted the demolish-and-rebuild dynamics since 2012. As a result, urban renewal projects have created a substantial amount of CDW. Since then, demolition and material reclamation have become part of a secondary construction sector as has, for example, excavation works (D. Öztürk 2019). As discussed in chapter 4, Kadıköy is one of the major residential areas where such urban renewal creating CDW via demolitions is at its peak.

In chapter 5, I focused on labor activities: the demolition and reclamation processes, work conditions, the organization of labor, and the circular movements between urban and rural 'homes'. In recently modernized cities, waste management systems, built upon the coexistence of diverse participants, have informality ingrained into them (Gidwani 2015; Tuçaltan 2018). Istanbul's CDW management is also diversified into official, private, and informal actors. Recycling factories and municipality facilities recycle construction materials gathered by *çıkmacıs*. The dynamics between informal and formal practices is volatile in such contingent socio-material networks (Simone 2015; McFarlane 2011a). Because of such interwoven formation, economic evaluations based on dual models are not instructive for a relational approach. That is why informality should be a 'heuristic device' that aids the analysis of the two spheres (Roy 2011).

Çıkmacıs develop tacit knowledge and practices that enable them to be resourceful despite their lack of access to the official labor market. Their resilient and relational strategies exist somewhere between the local and global level. On the one hand, they feed reclaimed construction components into a second-hand market regulated by themselves, on the other, they sell scrap materials to a recycling industry directly intertwined with the global stock exchange. As a result of this two-way adaptation, social and economic relationships create a diverse system where informal and formal actors co-function together. However, the possible future formalization and modernization of waste management could someday eliminate their participation. Street collectors are already facing such expulsion.

Çıkmacıs' mobility is a very important part of their flexible labor structure. For example, they sometimes work outside their territory. Based on the number of sites and amount of jobs, they expand their workforce to include family members or villagers. In order to maintain their low-cost operation, they also hire refugees, especially from Afghanistan and Syria. Such a labor force often finds work in this informal sector as soon as they arrive in cities. These jobs are easy to get because there is no legal or bureaucratic process. Through networking, they follow in the footsteps of previous arrivals who have created a kind of loose infrastructure.

Social alliances are an essential aspect of relational human networks (Simone 2015). *Çıkmacıs* find jobs through networking. They generally work with a construction contractor, possibly a relative. Sometimes they simply scan streets to find demolition sites. Apart from positive sides of their self-organized dynamics, it should be noted that their dangerous work conditions, low income and lack of government benefits reveal the *çıkmacıs* as being part of the precariat (Standing 2014).

The demolition regulations in place for the reclamation and demolition operations lack expertise and technical knowledge. Salvageable materials are mentioned but the removal standards and technical methods are not identified. In addition to such legal vagueness, the authorities do not appropriately inspect the sites. They only come to the demolition site to fine them if there is a noise complaint by a neighbor or physical damage to the neighboring properties. That's the only way they are officially recognized.

Çıkmacıs are not recognized as an official profession. Lacking formal attention, they are not adequately informed about workplace safety. Particularly, they are not aware of asbestos' impact on health. They usually have work-place accident insurance, but this does not cover the long-term effects of heavy labor. They cannot afford the high costs of self-employment benefits. They do the dirty work of a circular economy yet remain unrecognized and invisible. In this competitive and unruly threshold where *çıkmacıs* stand, territorial and sometimes fights often occur between them.

Çıkmacıs transition between Istanbul and their home villages. The family members or workers from the same village, whose employment status is uncertain, come for a short time from the village to the city as seasonal workers. Officially categorized as unskilled workers in the city, they are capable farmers. To emphasize their dual livelihood, I focused on a scrap collector family that practices material reclamation and farming (Ch. 5). The members of this family occasionally travel between Yazıhüyük village and Istanbul. Their farmland creates a stable ground for them in relation to the fluctuating economic and social conditions of the urban sphere. Hence, they did not migrate to Istanbul entirely because of their nomadic occupation. Additionally, their farmland socio-ecologically impacts their livelihood through various types of vegetation that need to be attended to at different times of the year. This farmland is a *vibrant object* that incarnates multiple agencies (Bennett 2010). The liveliness of this farmland embodies manifold agencies of human and nonhuman actants and their symbiosis.

Their constant movement back and forth between their village and the city shows that their migration to the city never really happens completely. For instance, they only ever come to Istanbul temporarily, leaving behind their families in the village because it is too expensive to bring them along. Their main concern is upgrading their village houses to live in with their families and retire. To sum up, nomadic labor that depends on agriculture and building salvaging, creates a different kind of 'circular urbanism' (Echanove and Srivastava 2014).

With the emergent capacities of the assemblage, new types of relationships and activities can be created through second-hand trade (Farias and Bender 2011). The network of *çıkmacıs*, through their supply yards, distributes components to rural dwelling constructions in Turkey and neighboring Georgia (Ch. 6.4 and Ch. 7.3.4). Flea markets, scrap yards and digital marketplaces all feed into their system of distribution. The yards serve as connections between the center and the periphery, the urban and rural, and the domestic and foreign. From these supply yards, the reclaimed materials are distributed to villages. The fieldwork findings associated with supply yards are discussed in terms of their temporality. Supply yards appear and disappear due to the periodic shifts of the mobility and sector dynamics. The network of trade is deterritorialized and reterritorialized while relational aspects between actors redraw the physical borders of distribution (DeLanda 2016); this occurs, for example, because of their circular movement and economic fluctuations in the sector.

The distribution of yards in Istanbul shows two patterns: scattered single yards and second-hand hubs on the Asian and European sides of Istanbul. The hubs are located near industrial zones, recycling depots, and sites closer to urban renewal. Others are situated randomly in former *gecekondu* neighborhoods. The status of the yards change depending on the populist politics before an election. At first, the yards were illegally occupied but later they gained temporary legal status. After a time, they faced eviction because their land had acquired real estate value. Such politically oppressive state tactics make the *cikmacis'* assemblage less flexible, which results in lessening the diversity of its actors (Delanda 2006).

The yards are networked through an extensive word-of-mouth network rather than through commercial advertising. The demand for second-hand building components comes from neighboring cities, Anatolian towns, and other rural villages outside Istanbul. The exchange is not only domestic but also international. Second-hand traders from bordering Georgia visit the yards regularly. From a larger social perspective, market spaces in the Global South function through a set of relationships in which people jointly use spaces, chances, moments, uncertainties, possibilities, and conflicts (Simone 2011). Similarly, the network of yards in this study shares these same social processes that, in turn, constitute an interactive surface of the social and material spheres. Despite its messy and disorderly appearance, the supply yard functions as a threshold and a transitory node in the network of reuse where things can find a second chance.

The spatial diagrams of different supply yards reveal the architectural organization according to size and complexity. Supply yards are multifunctional spaces consisting of display, storage, living, workshop, and office areas. To avoid housing costs, they stay at their depots together in one room or at worker dormitories. In such settings, the human body and the discarded materials are inseparable, existing in a trans-corporal connectivity and relationality (Alaimo 2010). Beyond their practical economic function, supply yards act as living spaces where *çıkmacıs* temporarily reside. The yard becomes a vessel in which not only waste is stored and sold but also where people live on a day-to-day basis. The margins between the social and the material become so thin in these yards that one cannot separate the living beings from the discarded materials. Bell's concept of 'living waste' asserts that there is a coexistence of people and unwanted matter (Bell 2019). This intertwined symbiotic relationship could be better understood by exploring social interactions of other entities nearby but outside this zone, for example, the customers who repair their flats, build secondary houses (e.g. summer houses, cottages, sheds, and etc.) on low budgets.

In the other major cities of Turkey, urban renewal projects are increasing pace. Owing to this, I focused on the industrially developed cities of Ankara and Kayseri. Unlike Istanbul, the *çıkmacıs* in Ankara and Kayseri instituted demolition cooperatives and made efforts to attain legal status in order to gain a more professional status. As in the Global South, with its collaboration of scattered actors such as waste pickers, *çıkmacıs* found ways to adjust to the formal waste management structure (Gutberlet 2015; Dias 2016). Furthermore, local municipalities provided spaces for them outside the city center. This model seems to support the co-functioning or co-production of integration between formal and informal spheres.

The type of materials reclaimed from these areas are different because the cooperatives demolish traditional houses which are built with wood and stone rather than industrial components. Additionally, they sell rare antique building components to touristic establishments in the region. They provide materials to housing constructions—mostly inhabited by refugees—in 'Gecekondu Prevention Zone', which are tracts of land taken and sold by municipalities to promote a more officially recognized dwelling form. Aside from these two cities, I investigated the hometowns of *çıkmacıs*. The supply yards in Nevşehir and Niğde are able to provide materials from Istanbul. All around this area, I discovered Georgian wholesalers visiting the supply yards.

The situation in Georgia is indistinguishable from Turkey in terms of the *gecekondu* housing phenomena. The production of space is based not only on materiality of second-hand materials but also the efforts of residents to find their own solutions for housing after drastic economic and political changes (Chapter 6.4). Due to the fall of the Soviet Union and the lack of housing resources, the people of Gldani were able to appropriate their own dwellings. This, in turn, allowed them to add informal extensions to their apartment blocks by reusing salvaged materials.

Demolition and building salvage are generally excluded from the architectural discourse because they are dirty work and waste represents something unwanted in the capitalist system. Material life cycles of buildings are part of the circular economy but salvage and reuse is practically and economically complex because of requirements for specialized expertise. It requires time and monetary investment. To confront this problem, a better understanding of the relational agency of the materials is required.

Exteriority refers to the ability of assemblage's components to be separated and reassembled in other constellations (DeLanda 2016). Building deconstruction engages in exteriority in which a building assemblage is dismantled and makes available various construction material nodes that can then be reused in other construction projects. This change is a kind of revitalization of material. The materials influence policy-making because of their relationship to earthquake mitigation, environment contamination and rural dwelling construction. Some of these materials are activated through the activities of human beings. Because of industrial production and recycling processes, these materials can harm people and the environment. Production and recycling of low-quality PVC in window frames is one of the environmental health problems in Turkey. One-fourth of the demolished buildings contain asbestos (Odman 2019). The air contaminated by asbestos in the demolition sites and their surroundings endangers çıkmacıs and other nonhuman organisms (Ch. 7.2.4). Hence, the demolition (urban renewal) map coincides with the asbestos risk map of Istanbul.

The act of inhabiting is a process of gathering materials. Informal urbanization is a similar process but on a much larger level (McFarlane 2011b). The 'kinetic city' that exists outside the Global North is assembled with reclaimed materials (Mehrotra, Vera, and Mayoral 2017). For example, gecekondus were built with salvaged materials during the rapid urbanization of Istanbul. At present, reclaimed materials are reused in rural areas for upgrading, adding extensions and repairing houses in slow-paced constructions. The three example houses (Ch.7.3) show how different dwellings are part of incremental construction activities in which second-hand materials are gradually gathered. These materials influence the design of rural dwellings. Such a form of construction is a gray zone that resembles the informality of gecekondus. These houses entail some people bypassing zoning laws. Rather than focusing on large-scale urban projects, this book presents incremental rural construction as a hopeful alternative model.

8.3 The Commons and Material Reclamation

In economically privileged countries, the entire life cycle of a building has become a trending subject. In the Global North, there are new policies that focus on sustainable deconstruction but their implementations are limited and slow:

> Deconstruction is a green alternative to demolition, sending up to 85 percent less material to landfills. Building materials and construction account for just under 10 percent of the world's energy-related global carbon emissions. Using salvaged materials eliminates emissions associated with making and transporting new building materials. Plus, it's not as noisy as knocking down a house and doesn't spew dust or toxic materials, such as asbestos, into the air. (Marshall 2022, 1)

Furthermore, design for deconstruction or disassembly (DfD) is gaining popularity in architectural practices. Architects and engineers may help this initiative by developing dwellings that are equipped with adaptable and reusable materials and components. They could begin using fewer adhesives like glue or foam sealant for details, which also exacerbates the difficulty of pulling apart buildings. More importantly, such professional practices could come to influence urban policy-making processes that create guidelines and safety measures for deconstruction.

To illustrate, Rotor in Belgium is a company and online platform that primarily builds its practice on the recovery of material resources through the deconstruction of buildings. They address the issue of reuse in the context of formal construction. However, it is a complex task since regulations are stringent. As a result, reuse becomes an almost impossible practice when too many middlemen pop up in the process of developing a building; this also occurs when there are large-scale professional responsibilities at stake (Ghyoot, Devlieger, and Billiet 2018). Rotor is trying to challenge this situation by working with public administrations and authorities or sectoral federations to come up with felicitous rules and regulations.

In contrast to policy and innovative developments in the Global North, Turkey does not yet have a formal management strategy; instead, it has informal scrap collectors, demolishers and waste pickers. With the support of these relational infrastructures, the potential of construction waste can be effectively utilized in the second-hand market so that reclaimed materials can support livelihoods and have second lives. This book can be used as a guide for architects, designers, and urban planners because it can show how the *çıkmacıs* are able to organize themselves despite limited material and financial resources.

The *çıkmacıs'* assemblage could be interpreted as an everyday political strategy (Simone 2015; Bayat 2004). Material reclamation is not only an economic and sustainable activity but also has the hidden political stance of survival. *Çıkmacıs* gain their advantage from the gray zone emerging from the regulative absence of waste management. Their strategies are to adapt and interpret absences and possibilities. These gaps also serve to identify a Global South modernism that results from infrastructural absences and unequal distribution of resources. However, they are adapting to changing urban conditions while simultaneously creating sustainable practices of revaluing waste. Architecture and urban design can learn from ad-hoc reuse practices and focus on the socio-materiality of discarded construction materials. At the same time, the authorities can improve the social and technical conditions of *çıkmacıs* instead of integrating them into a formal system or taking over their sector.

As a guide for material reuse, Chapter 7 describes how building parts are used in the incremental processes of dwelling construction. The usage of second-hand components in a rural house affirms that urban renewal waste affects rural construction processes. If this conceptual argument could be understood, the excess of these second-hand materials as a resource could be expanded to the commons.

The commons represent material resources available to whatever members of society they apply to. However, they should be socially constructed and maintained in relation to the environment and livelihoods within that society. Waste, through its recovery, becomes another part of the commons. For instance, Lane argues that things discarded on the street constitute an informal 'waste commons' (Lane 2011). Her research shows that more waste is repurposed by informal salvaging activities (gifting and gleaning) than by the official processes of municipal solid waste management. Regardless of this fact, government officials attempt to make this 'waste commons' unreachable by passing legislation that prohibits salvaging. However, at the end of the day, waste belongs to everyone.

Even though the *çıkmacıs'* activities and rhythms currently exist within capitalism, they are a unique group with unique resources who have the potential to transform CDW into an urban commons. They provide a comprehensive assemblage of materials, supply yards and professional experience. This potential could be strengthened by the creation of new government policies in the construction sector that would stipulate a certain proportion of CDW from each demolition to be held by the common good. It is not hard to imagine each construction company donating some of their scrap materials toward such an endeavor. There is already the precedent of the existing *çıkmacıs* collectives and, if they could extend themselves further in the way described above, they could become a vital support of the right to dwell. This relational infrastructure could be reconstructed by donation, common usage, collective participation and sharing. In short, it could be reassembled through reuse.

To imagine the governance of second-hand being part of the commons involves keeping the exchange "off-limits to the logic of market exchange and market valuations" (Harvey 2019, 73). Then such production could be a form of need-oriented value production instead of another profit-seeking framework of capitalism (Gidwani 2013). The *Çıkmacıs'* transactions are slightly independent from the market dynamics dependent on global prices. One of them mentioned that the price of a window frame did not change for many years even though labor costs did. The prices of second-hand items are negotiable. Governing bodies and housing funds could finance the *çıkmacıs* so that second-hand building materials could be used as a common resource.

Another question is: How can one reimagine the scenario when the physical and economic infrastructure comes to a halt as the result of the next earthquake in Istanbul? The Adhocist Manifesto states:

> At a populist level, *adhocism* is radically democratic and pragmatic, as in the first two stages of the revolution. It is also evident after catastrophes such as Hurricane Katrina or the earthquake in Haiti, when people make do with whatever is at hand. (Jencks and Silver 1972, 19)

Accordingly, it is not hard to imagine that the reconstruction will depend on ad-hoc salvaging practices. In the aftermath of an earthquake, debris clearing will most likely be taken care of by demolishers and *çıkmacıs*. With these experiences, they can respond to such emergencies since they can quickly adapt to burdensome situations. This is because they have the ability to adjust to shifting urbanizations and are able to operate in precarious environments, both socially and physically.

Based on these assumptions, in the following section I will reflect on research limitations and offer suggestions for future research.

8.4 Research Restrictions and Potential Proposals for Future Work

The restrictions of this kind of research are related to geography and time. Nevertheless, a considerable amount of empirical data was collected by conducting multi-sited ethnography. In the beginning, the research questions were based on demolitions and material reclamation in Istanbul. As the fieldwork progressed, the research territory expanded to Ankara, Kayseri, Nevşehir, and Niğde. Based on the ethnographic data, I followed second-hand trade in cities where my informants came from. However, other densely-built urban centers in Turkey need to be rebuilt and urban demolitions continue happening at a considerably high rate. For instance, İzmir is the third largest city in Turkey and in a seismic zone like Istanbul, and there is an urgent need to renew the built environment where *gecekondus* urbanized the city in the past. Besides this, the renovation of tourist facilities is also creating a substantial amount of demolition waste. During holiday visits, I spotted a few second-hand supply yards in the area. Ship breaking (also known as ship recycling) is also practiced on the İzmir coast. The region has a unique potential in terms of salvage practices. However, because of time constraints, I did not widen the fieldwork to the western part of Turkey. My visit to Georgia to investigate incremental construction there was also bounded by a restricted time frame.

Another constraint would be the exponential economic and political changes after the research period, namely from 2015 to 2019. The book covers a time when urban renewal projects and the construction sector were expanding. After 2018, the construction sector experienced a steady decrease during a prolonged recession period. The real estate investments have slowed down and Turkey has experienced an economic and political imbalance after the Covid-19 pandemic (Orhangazi and Yeldan 2021).

Based on these economic thresholds, a comparative analysis of material reclamation and second-hand trade could be undertaken. For further research, it would be crucial to investigate how scrap collectors and demolishers were able to adapt to the recession dynamics. On the one hand, the demand for cheap materials may have increased because of inflation and economic contraction. On the other hand, the excess material may have been reduced. However, building salvage as an infrastructural practice—with its long-lasting presence, adaptability and mobility—can handle fluctuating situations. Further, Design for Deconstruction should be implemented as a part of nationwide urban renewal projects.

The access limitations to some demolition sites were another fieldwork problem. As described in the methodology subchapter 3.3.4, my presence at the demolition sites was often questioned and I had to deal with some restrictions. First, I was not allowed to some sites because the site supervisors thought I was a journalist or someone who would make trouble for them by calling up and complaining to inspectors and controllers. From their perspective, it would result in fines or temporary closures. In some cases, our social differences (class, education, etc.) made it an obstacle to communicate with uncooperative informants.

Time limitation was a problem when visiting the villages. My stay in Engin's village was short but useful in terms of being a witness to their rural lives. As an idea of further research, one could put a higher level of importance on the *çıkmacı*'s agricultural livelihood in the village. Farming activities and personal histories of *çıkmacıs* could be more fleshed out by meeting and interviewing other villagers. This way, one could gather comprehensive empirical data on movement between village and urban centers. In order to reassemble the urban and rural areas, it's critical to develop a deeper understanding of the *çıkmacıs'* circular movement. The empirical focus should not just be on the urban centers. It should also be territorial in terms of the impact of urbanization.

It is my hope that my cross-disciplinary approach can be a unique precedent for researchers who investigate socio-materialities and networked livelihood activities in the context of urban studies. I attempted to establish associations between different research fields: architecture, urbanization, economy, geography, and sociology. During the research, I realized that when 'planning disciplines' like architecture and urban design are associated with social sciences, the outcome is substantial. The perspective should be multi-disciplinary because architecture and urban design are not only very technical but also human oriented when it comes to analyzing relational and complex assemblages. Toward that end, thick description could help to reveal the micro ethnographies that have valuable contributions to the life cycle of materials. Meanwhile, the alliance of disciplines should be improved in the earlier stages of practical and higher education. Architectural production focuses on capitalism rather than analyzing everyday practices and informal means of producing spaces. I have attempted to reveal the difference between 'what is imagined or planned on paper' with what is experienced in everyday livelihoods. An ability to follow the material-human symbiosis at play in construction reclamation can contribute to the establishment of a new sustainable commons and the overcoming of environmental devastation.

Acknowledgements

The creation of this book has been a collaborative work. It has been a long journey in which very many inspirational and obliging people have kindly supported me.

I would like to start by thanking my main supervisor, Prof. Dr. Nina Gribat. She was always there when I needed help. She aided me with elaborate comments on my writing. I am truly grateful for her encouragement and wise guidance. She showed me how academic work can be conducted with solidarity. I consider myself very lucky to receive such strengthening support that includes caring, understanding and sharing.

I would like to acknowledge my gratitude to the Hans Böckler Foundation for providing a scholarship for my Ph.D., conferences, and a perspective-altering summer school that I attended. Their solidarity and attention to my research topic made it possible for me to give it my full attention. In the foundation network, I want to especially thank Prof. Dr. Barbara Schönig for reviewing my research progress.

I am indebted to the participants of our monthly academic colloquium: Dr. Emily Bereskin, Anna Kokalanova, Christoph Muth, Agnès Klöden-Billemont, Natacha Quintero González, Pearl Puwurayire, Christian Rosen, Tülay Güneş, Leonie Plänkers, Jammie A. Titilayo and Erik Hofedank. They not only shared their research and academic knowledge but also made invaluable comments on my presentations. Without their support, I would not have been able to keep up such a regular workflow.

I would like to thank Prof. Dr. Can Altay, Prof. Dr. Nurbin Paker, Prof. Dr. Arda İnceoğlu, and Prof. Dr. İpek Akpınar, who guided me at the very beginning of my Ph.D. journey in Turkey. I am also grateful for the companionship of Mike Nelson, Mari Spirito, Özgür Atlagan, Erdinç Eşref Uslu, Bekir Sak and Kılıçer Family while exploring Turkey in search of my research topic.

I am grateful for the many scholars who influenced me profoundly. The work of Dr. Benedict Anderson, Dr. Sezai Ozan Zeybek, Dr. Özlem Ünsal Kavlak, Dr. Emrah Altınok, Yaşar Adanalı, and Anna Wyss have been very inspirational, and their motivating help is unforgettable. Specially, I am thankful to the researchers who I met in RC21 Summer School Delhi in 2019 for sharing their work and practices.

I am grateful to Vera Ryser, Halil and Sevda Vatansever for their unprecedented generousness in helping me overcome various challenges during my stay in Germany. I am thankful for Charlotte Watermann's support in the scholarship application process. I am indebted to Mark Farrier for the last phase of the writing process. His contribution has had a vitalizing effect on improving the language of the work.

Most importantly, I would like to thank the çıkmacıs who agreed to participate in the research and share their work experiences and life stories. Although their work conditions were extremely demanding and tiresome, they welcomed me as an outsider.

Lastly, I would like to thank my parents, Merih Ege and Ahmet Tevfik Ceritoğlu, for their extraordinary encouragement throughout my education. And foremost, I am grateful to my biggest supporter and life partner, Lia Kraus. With her patience and kindness, she made me believe in myself enough to complete the book.

Bibliography

Abramson, Daniel M. 2017. *Obsolescence - an Architectural History.*

Acuto, Michele. 2011. "Putting ANTs into the Mille- Feuille." *City* 15 (5): 552–62. https://doi.org/10.1080/13604813.2011.609021.

Adaman, Fikret, and Burçay Erus. 2019. "Turkey: Active Labour Market Policies for Syrian Refugees Are Also Supporting the Local Population Affected by the Refugee Influx." ESPN Flash Report 2019/15. European Social Policy Network.

Adanalı, Yaşar. 2012. "Urban Transformation and Law on Disaster Prevention: A Pretext for Lucrative Investment." *Perspective Magazine Heinrich Böll Stiftung* 3–13: 37–39.

Addis, William. 2006. *Building with Reclaimed Components and Materials: A Design Handbook for Reuse and Recycling.* London; Sterling, VA: Earthscan.

Akbulut, Mehmet Rıfat. 1994. "'Kadıköy.'" In *Dünden Bugüne İstanbul Ansiklopedisi [Istanbul Encyclopaedia from Yesterday to Today]*, 4:329–39. Istanbul: Türkiye Ekonomik ve Toplumsal Tarih Vakfı, T.C. Kültür Bakanlığı.

Akın, Günkut. 2010. "20. Yüzyıl Başında İstanbul: Toplumsal ve Mekânsal Farklılaşma [Early 20th Century Istanbul: Social and Spatial Differentiation]." In *OSMANLI BAŞKENTİNDEN KÜRESELLEŞEN İSTANBUL'a: MİMARLIK ve KENT Osmanlı Başkentinden Küreselleşen Istanbul'a: Mimarlık ve Kent*, edited by Ipek Akpinar.

Aksoy, Asu. 2014. "İstanbul'un Neoliberalizmle İmtihanı [Istanbul's Trial with Neoliberalism]." In *Yeni İstanbul Çalışmaları: Sınırlar, Mücadeleler, Açılımlar*, edited by Ayfer Bartu Candan and Cenk Özbay, 1. basım. İstanbul: Metis.

Aktaş, Uğur. 2010. *İstanbul'un 100 Esnafı [100 Tradesmen of Istanbul].* İstanbul Büyükşehir Belediyesi Yayınları.

Alaimo, Stacy. 2010. *Bodily Natures: Science, Environment, and the Material Self.* Bloomington: Indiana University Press.

Allon, Fiona R., Ruth Barcan, and Karma Eddison-Cogan, eds. 2020. *The Temporalities of Waste: Out of Sight, out of Time*. 1 Edition. Routledge Environmental Humanities. New York: Routledge.

Altay, Can. 2013. "Here We Are: The Imagination of Public Space in Gezi Park." Ibraaz. 2013. https://www.ibraaz.org/essays/70.

Altay, Can, and Deniz Altay. 2008. "Counter-Spatialization (of Power) (in Istanbul)." In *Urban Makers: Parallel Narratives of Grassroots Practices and Tensions*, edited by Emmanuele Guidi, 1. Aufl, 77–101. Berlin: b_books.

Amin, Ash. 2014. "Lively Infrastructure." *Theory, Culture & Society* 31 (7–8): 137–61. https://doi.org/10.1177/0263276414548490.

Angell, Elizabeth. 2014. "Assembling Disaster: Earthquakes and Urban Politics in Istanbul." *City* 18 (6): 667–78. https://doi.org/10.1080/13604813.2014.962881.

Angell, Elizabeth, Timur Hammond, and Danielle Van Dobben Schoon. 2014. "Assembling Istanbul: Buildings and Bodies in a World City: Introduction." *City* 18 (6): 644–54. https://doi.org/10.1080/13604813.2014.962882.

Appadurai, Arjun, ed. 1986. *The Social Life of Things: Commodities in Cultural Perspective*. Cambridge: Cambridge University Press. https://doi.org/10.1017/CBO9780511819582.

Arkitekt. 1976. "Tekül Apartmanı [Tekül Apartments]." *Arkitekt*, no. 361: 18–19.

Assche, Kristof, and Joseph Salukvadze. 2013. "Urban Transformation and Role Transformation in the Post-Soviet Metropolis." In *Remaking Metropolis: Global Challenges of the Urban Landscape*, edited by Edward Cook and Jesus J. Lara. New York, NY: Routledge.

Atay, Oğuz. 1991. *Korkuyu beklerken [Waiting for Fear]*. Yeni baskı. Bütün eserleri / Oğuz Atay 4. Istanbul: İletişim.

Ayata, Sencer. 2008. "Migrants and Changing Urban Periphery: Social Relations, Cultural Diversity and the Public Space in Istanbul's New Neighbourhoods." *International Migration* 46 (3): 27–64. https://doi.org/10.1111/j.1468-2435.2008.00461.x.

Ayşe, Pul. 2008. "Osmanlı Sosyal Hayatı Figüranlarından Arayıcı Esnafı [Seeker Tradesmen from Ottoman Social Life Figures]." *Tarih İncelemeleri Dergisi* 23 (1): 211–38.

Bajc, Vida. 2012. "Abductive Ethnography of Practice in Highly Uncertain Conditions." In *Bringing Fieldwork Back in: Contemporary Urban Ethnographic Research; [2010 Yale Conference 'Bringing Fieldwork Back In']*, edited by Elijah Anderson. The Annals of the American Academy of Political and Social Science, 642.2012. Los Angeles: SAGE.

Balaban, Osman. 2011. "İnşaat sektörü neyin lokomotifi [What is the locomotive of the construction sector]." *Birikim, İnşaat Ya Resulullah*, 270: 19–26.

Balamir, Murat. 1994. "Kira Evleri'nden, Kat Evleri'ne Apartmanlaşma: Bir Zihniyet Dönüşümü Tarihçesinden Kesitler [Apartmentisation from Rent Houses to Flats: Cross-Sections from the History of a Transformation of Mentality]." *Mimarlık*, no. 260: 29–33.

Balayannis, Angeliki. 2020. "Toxic Sights: The Spectacle of Hazardous Waste Removal." *Environment and Planning D: Society and Space* 38 (4): 772–90. https://doi.org/10.1177/0263775819900197.

Barnett, Clive, Paul Cloke, Nick Clarke, and Alice Malpass. 2005. "Consuming Ethics: Articulating the Subjects and Spaces of Ethical Consumption." *Antipode* 37 (1): 23–45. https://doi.org/10.1111/j.0066-4812.2005.00472.x.

Bauman, Zygmunt. 2011. *Wasted Lives: Modernity and Its Outcasts*. Reprint. Cambridge: Polity.

Bayat, Asef. 1997. *Street Politics: Poor People's Movements in Iran*. New York: Columbia University Press.

Bayat, Asef. 2000. "From 'Dangerous Classes' to 'Quiet Rebels': Politics of the Urban Subaltern in the Global South." *International Sociology* 15 (3): 533–57. https://doi.org/10.1177/026858000015003005.

Bayat, Asef. 2004. "Globalization and the Politics of the Informals in Global South." In *Urban Informality: Transnational Perspectives from the Middle East, Latin America, and South Asia*, edited by Ananya Roy and Nezar AlSayyad. Transnational Perspectives on Space and Place. Lanham, Md.: Berkeley, Calif: Lexington Books; Center for Middle Eastern Studies, University of California at Berkeley.

Bayat, Asef. 2007. "Radical Religion and the Habitus of the Dispossessed: Does Islamic Militancy Have an Urban Ecology?" *International Journal of Urban and Regional Research* 31 (3): 579–90. https://doi.org/10.1111/j.1468-2427.2007.00746.x.

Bayraktar, Uğur B. 2016. "Restoring the Property: The Land Code of 1858 and Private Property in Ottoman Kurdistan." In . Lisbon.

Bell, Lucy. 2017. "Recycling Materials, Recycling Lives: Cardboard Publishers in Latin America." In *Literature and Sustainability: Concept, Text and Culture*, edited by Adeline Johns-Putra, John Parham, and Louise Squire. Manchester University Press. https://doi.org/10.2307/j.ctt1wn0s7q.

Bell, Lucy. 2019. "Place, People and Processes in Waste Theory: A Global South Critique." *Cultural Studies* 33 (1): 98–121. https://doi.org/10.1080/09502386.2017.1420810.

Bennett, Jane. 2004. "The Force of Things: Steps toward an Ecology of Matter." *Political Theory* 32 (3): 347–72. https://doi.org/10.1177/0090591703260853.

Bennett, Jane. 2010. *Vibrant Matter: A Political Ecology of Things.* Durham: Duke University Press.

Berkmen, Naime Hülya, and Turgut Sırma. 2019. "'Bağdat Street' in The Grip Of Urban Transformation." *MEGARON / Yıldız Technical University, Faculty of Architecture E-Journal.* https://doi.org/10.14744/megaron.2019.35467.

Bernard, H. Russell. 2006. *Research Methods in Anthropology: Qualitative and Quantitative Approaches.* 4th ed. Lanham, MD: AltaMira Press.

Beyond Istanbul. 2017. "80'lerde Gazetelerde Gecekondular ve Mafya İlişkisi [Slums and Mafia Relations in Newspapers in the 80s]." Beyond.Istanbul. September 6, 2017. https://beyond.istanbul/80lerde-gecekondular-ve-ma fya-i%CC%87li%C5%9Fkisi-f44d8bebbbdc.

Bilgin, İhsan. 1988. "Konut Sorunlarının Çeşitlenmesi [Diversification of Housing Problems]." *Defter,* no. 7: 37–49.

Bilgin, İhsan. 2000. "Bedelsiz Modernleşme [Modernisation at no cost]." In *Mübeccel Kıray için yazılar,* edited by Mübeccel Belik Kıray and Fulya Atacan. Cağaloğlu, İstanbul: Bağlam.

Bilgin, İhsan. 2013. "Kentsel Dönüşümün Doğası; Akış mı Zorlama mı? [The Nature of Urban Regeneration; Flow or Coercion?]." In *Milyonluk Manzara: Kentsel Dönüşüm Resimleri,* edited by Semih Akşeker, 1. baskı. İletişim Yayın- ları 1870. Cağaloğlu, İstanbul: İletişim.

Bilsel, Cana. 2011. "İmparatorluk'tan Cumhuriyet'e İstanbul'u Modernleştirme Projesi ve Prost Planı [Istanbul Modernisation Project from the Empire to the Republic and the Prost Plan]." Edited by İpek Yada Akpınar. *Betonart,* no. no.29 (k): 43–28.

Birkbeck, CHRIS. 1979. "Self-Employed Proletarians in an Informal Factory: The Case of Cali's Garbage Dump." In *The Urban Informal Sector,* edited by RAY Bromley, 1173–85. Pergamon. https://doi.org/10.1016/B978-0-08-024 270-5.50015-6.

Blok, Anders, and Ignacio Farias, eds. 2016. *Urban Cosmopolitics: Agencements, Assemblies, Atmospheres.* Questioning Cities. New York, NY: Routledge.

Boggio, Andrea. 2013. *Compensating Asbestos Victims: Law and the Dark Side of In- dustrialization.* Farnham, Surrey, England; Burlington, VT: Ashgate.

Boratav, Korkut, A. Erinc Yeldan, and Ahmet H. Köse. 2001. "Turkey: Globaliza- tion, Distribution and Social Policy, 1980–1998." In *External Liberalization, Economic Performance and Social Policy,* edited by Lance Taylor, 317–64. Ox-

ford University Press. https://doi.org/10.1093/acprof:oso/9780195145465.0
03.0010.

Bouzarovski, Stefan, Joseph Salukvadze, and Michael Gentile. 2011. "A Socially Resilient Urban Transition? The Contested Landscapes of Apartment
Building Extensions in Two Post-Communist Cities." *Urban Studies* 48 (13):
2689–2714. https://doi.org/10.1177/0042098010385158.

Boysan, Burak. 2011. "Genişliğin Azameti, Sağlamın Heybeti, Hendesenin
Güzelliği, Trafiğin Hâkimiyeti [The Greatness of the Width, the Majesty of
the Solid, the Beauty of the Trench, the Dominance of the Traffic]." Edited
by İpek Yada Akpınar. *Betonart*, no. 29 (k): 40–61.

Bozdoğan, Sibel. 2010. "From 'Cubic Houses' to Suburban Villas: Residential
Architecture and the Elites in Turkey." In, 405–24. https://doi.org/10.1057/
9780230277397_22.

Brenner, Neil, David J. Madden, and David Wachsmuth. 2011. "Assemblage Urbanism and the Challenges of Critical Urban Theory." *City* 15 (2): 225–40. h
ttps://doi.org/10.1080/13604813.2011.568717.

Brewer, John D. 2000. *Ethnography.* Understanding Social Research. Bucking-
ham; Philadelphia, PA: Open University Press.

Candan, Ayfer Bartu, and Biray Kolluoğlu. 2008. "Emerging Spaces of Neolib-
eralism: A Gated Town and a Public Housing Project in İstanbul." *New Perspectives on Turkey* 39: 5–46. https://doi.org/10.1017/S0896634600005057.

Cantürk, Emel. 2017. "Konut Üzerinden Bir Mikro-Tarih Anlatısı: İstanbul,
Bağdat Caddesi [A Micro-Historical Narrative through Housing: Istanbul,
Bağdat Street]." İstanbul: Istanbul Technical University.

Çelik, Gözde. 2007. "Istanbul Tarihi Yarımadası'nda Tazminat Dönemi İdari
Yapıları [The Ardministrative Buildings of the Tanzimat Period in the Historical Peninsula of İstanbul]." Istanbul: Istanbul Technical University.

Ceritoglu, Onur. 2011. "Tadilat [Remodel]." Istanbul: Sabanci University. http:/
/research.sabanciuniv.edu/20037/1/ErdoganOnurCeritoglu_422883.pdf.

Ceritoglu, Onur. 2018. "Not Enough Doors but Windows." *Manifold*, 2018. http
s://manifold.press/kadraj-onur-ceritoglu-kapi-yok-pencere-cok.

Ceritoglu, Onur, and Can Altay. 2016. "Kentsel Dönüşümün Artıkları - Çık-
macılar: Enformel Kentleşme İle Yıkımların Arasında [Building Salvage
Scrapyards at the Interface of Informal Urbanisation and Demolitions:
Çıkmacıs]." *Toplum ve Bilim*, no. 138–139: 139–45.

Certeau, Michel de. (1984) 2013. *The Practice of Everyday Life.* 2. print. Berkeley,
Calif.: Univ. of California Press.

Charmaz, Kathy. 2014. *Constructing Grounded Theory*. 2nd edition. Introducing Qualitative Methods. London; Thousand Oaks, Calif: Sage.

Collier, Stephen J., and Lucan Way. 2004. "Beyond the Deficit Model: Social Welfare in Post-Soviet Georgia." *Post-Soviet Affairs* 20 (3): 258–84. https://doi.org/10.2747/1060-586X.20.3.258.

Cook et al., Ian. 2006. "Geographies of Food: Following." *Progress in Human Geography* 30 (5): 655–66. https://doi.org/10.1177/0309132506070183.

Cook, Ian. 2004. "Follow the Thing: Papaya." *Antipode* 36 (4): 642–64. https://doi.org/10.1111/j.1467-8330.2004.00441.x.

Corwin, Julia Eleanor. 2018. "'Nothing Is Useless in Nature': Delhi's Repair Economies and Value-Creation in an Electronics 'Waste' Sector." *Environment and Planning A: Economy and Space* 50 (1): 14–30. https://doi.org/10.1177/0308518X17739006.

Dalgıç, S. 2004. "Factors Affecting the Greater Damage in the Avcılar Area of Istanbul during the 17 August 1999 Izmit Earthquake." *Bulletin of Engineering Geology and the Environment* 63 (3): 221–32. https://doi.org/10.1007/s10064-004-0234-9.

Davis, Mike. 2006. *Planet of Slums*. London; New York: Verso.

DeLanda, Manuel. 2006. *A New Philosophy of Society: Assemblage Theory and Social Complexity*. Annotated edition. London; New York: Continuum.

Deleuze, Gilles, and Félix Guattari. 1987. *A Thousand Plateaus: Capitalism and Schizophrenia*. Minneapolis: University of Minnesota Press.

Demir, Ömer, Mustafa Acar, and Metin Toprak. 2004. "Anatolian Tigers or Islamic Capital: Prospects and Challenges." *Middle Eastern Studies* 40 (6): 166–88. https://doi.org/10.1080/0026320042000282937.

Derviş, Pelin, Bülent Tanju, Uğur Tanyeli, and Atilla Yücel, eds. 2009. "Bağdat Caddesi [Bagdat Street]." İn *İstanbullaşmak: olgular, sorunsallar, metaforlar*, 33–37. Garanti Galeri.

DeWalt, Kathleen Musante, and Billie R. DeWalt. 2011. *Participant Observation: A Guide for Fieldworkers*. 2nd ed. Lanham, Md: Rowman & Littlefield, Md.

Dias, Sonia Maria. 2016. "Waste Pickers and Cities." *Environment and Urbanization* 28 (2): 375–90. https://doi.org/10.1177/0956247816657302.

Dinler. 2016. "A Multi-Sited Analysis of Rules and Regulations in the Recycling Market from Ankara to London." Phd, London,: SOAS University of London. https://eprints.soas.ac.uk/23640/.

Douglas, Mary. 1966. *Purity and Danger: An Analysis of Concept of Pollution and Taboo*. Routledge Classics. London; New York: Routledge.

Dovey, Kim. 2012. "Informal Urbanism and Complex Adaptive Assemblage." *International Development Planning Review* 34 (4): 349–68. https://doi.org/10.38 28/idpr.2012.23.

Dovey, Kim. 2014. "Incremental Urbanism: The Emergence of Informal Settlements." In *Emergent Urbanism: Urban Planning & Design in Times of Structural and Systemic Change*, edited by Tigran Haas and Krister Olsson, 1 edition. Farnham, Surrey, UK; Burlington, VT: Routledge.

Dündar, Özlem. 2001. "Models of Urban Transformation: Informal Housing in Ankara." *JCIT Cities* 18 (6): 391–401.

Duyar-Kienast, Umut. 2005. *The Formation of Gecekondu Settlements in Turkey: The Case of Ankara*. Habitat - International 7. Münster: LIT.

Dwyer, Claire, and Peter Jackson. 2003. "Commodifying Difference: Selling EASTern Fashion." *Environment and Planning D: Society and Space* 21 (3): 269–91. https://doi.org/10.1068/d349.

Easterling, Keller. 2014. *Extrastatecraft: The Power of Infrastructure Space*. London; New York: Verso.

Echanove, Matias, and Rahul Srivastava. 2014. "Mumbai's Circulatory Urbanism." In *Empower!*, edited by Marc Angélil, Rainer Hehl, and Eidgenössische Technische Hochschule Zürich. Essays on the Political Economy of Urban Form, Vol. 3. Berlin: Ruby Press.

Ekdal, Müfid. 2004. *Bizans metropolünde ilk Türk köyü Kadıköy [The first Turkish village in the Byzantine metropolis of Kadikoy]*. İstanbul: Kadıköy Belediyesi.

Elettra, Griesi, and Tinatin Gurgenidze. 2018. "Spatial Transformations." Edited by Sebastian Feldhusen and Eduard Führ. *International Journal of Architectural Theory*, Public Space in Architecture, 23 (37): 179–91.

Erder, Sema. 1996. *İstanbul'a bir kent kondu: Ümraniye [A city has landed in Istanbul: Umraniye]*. 1. baskı. Memleket dizisi 2. Cağaloğlu, İstanbul: İletişim.

Ergur, Ali. 2009. "Shame and Pride in Turkish Collective Memory, Spring 2009." *Turkish Policy Quarterly*. http://turkishpolicy.com/article/309/shame-and-pride-in-turkish-collective-memory-spring-2009.

Erman, Tahire. 2001. "The Politics of Squatter (Gecekondu) Studies in Turkey: The Changing Representations of Rural Migrants in the Academic Discourse." *Urban Studies* 38 (7): 983–1002. https://doi.org/10.1080/00420980 120051620.

Erman, Tahire. 2004. "Gecekondu Çalışmalarında 'Öteki' Olarak Gecekondulu Kurguları [Slum Dweller Fictions as 'Other' in Gecekondu Studies]." *European Journal of Turkish Studies*, no. 1 (September). https://doi.org/10.4000/ejts.85.

Erman, Tahire. 2011. "Understanding the Experiences of The Politics of Urbanization In Two Gecekondu (Squatter) Neighborhoods Under Two Urban
Regimes: Ethnography In The Urban Periphery Of Ankara, Turkey." *Urban
Anthropology and Studies of Cultural Systems and World Economic Development*
40 (1/2): 67–108.

Erman, Tahire. 2013. "Urbanization and Urbanism." In *The Routledge Handbook
of Modern Turkey*, 309–18. Routledge. https://doi.org/10.4324/978020311839
9-39.

Erman, Tahire, Burçak Altay, and Can Altay. 2004. "Architects and the Architectural Profession in the Turkish Context." *Journal of Architectural Education* 58
(2): 46–53. https://doi.org/10.1162/1046488042485394.

Erman, Tahire, and Aslıhan Eken. 2004. "The 'Other of the Other' and 'Unregulated Territories' in the Urban Periphery: Gecekondu Violence in the 2000s
with a Focus on the Esenler Case, Istanbul." *Cities* 21 (1): 57–68. https://doi.
org/10.1016/j.cities.2003.10.008.

EUROSTAT. 2020. *Energy, Transport and Environment Statistics: 2020 Edition.* https://op.europa.eu/publication/manifestation_identifier/PUB_KS
DK20001ENN.

EUROSTAT. 2022. "Amount of Waste Recovered Increases in 2020." 2022. https:
//ec.europa.eu/eurostat/web/products-eurostat-news/-/ddn-20220913-1.

Eyice, Semavi. 1994. "Bağdat Caddesi [Bagdat Street]." In *İstanbul Ansiklopedisi*,
528–31. Istanbul: Türkiye Ekonomik ve Toplumsal Tarih Vakfı, T.C. Kültür
Bakanlığı.

Farias, Ignacio, and Thomas Bender, eds. 2011. *Urban Assemblages: How Actor-
Network Theory Changes Urban Studies.* First issued in paperback. Questioning Cities Series. London New York: Routledge, Taylor & Francis Group.

Fuhr, Lili, and Matthew Franklin, eds. 2019. *Plastic Atlas 2019: Facts and Figures
about the World of Synthetic Polymers.* Berlin: Heinrich Böll foundation.

Galletta, Anne. 2013. *Mastering the Semi-Structured Interview and Beyond: From Research Design to Analysis and Publication.* NYU Press. https://doi.org/10.1857
4/nyu/9780814732939.001.0001.

Geertz, Clifford. 1973. *The Interpretation of Cultures: Selected Essays.* New York: Basic Books.

Gegidze, Mariam, David Manjavidze, and Nicole Opel. 2016. "Everything Not
Forbidden Is Allowed." *Arch+*, no. 225: 72–75.

Ghoddousi, Pooya, and Sam Page. 2020. "Using Ethnography and Assemblage
Theory in Political Geography." *Geography Compass* 14 (10). https://doi.org/1
0.1111/gec3.12533.

Ghyoot, Michaël, Lionel Devlieger, and Lionel Billiet. 2018. *Déconstruction et réemploi: Comment faire circuler les éléments de construction [Deconstruction and reuse: How to get building components moving again]*. Lausanne: Presses Polytechniques et Universitaires Romandes.

Gidwani, Vinay. 2013. "Six Theses on Waste, Value, and Commons." *Social & Cultural Geography* 14 (7): 773–83. https://doi.org/10.1080/14649365.2013.800222.

Gidwani, Vinay. 2015. "The Work of Waste: Inside India's Infra-Economy." *Transactions of the Institute of British Geographers* 40 (4): 575–95. https://doi.org/10.1111/tran.12094.

Gidwani, Vinay, and Rajyashree N. Reddy. 2011. "The Afterlives of 'Waste': Notes from India for a Minor History of Capitalist Surplus." *Antipode* 43 (5): 1625–58. https://doi.org/10.1111/j.1467-8330.2011.00902.x.

Gobo, Giampietro. 2008. *Doing Ethnography*. 1 Oliver's Yard, 55 City Road, London England EC1Y 1SP United Kingdom: SAGE Publications Ltd. https://doi.org/10.4135/9780857028976.

Graham, Stephen, and Nigel Thrift. 2007. "Out of Order: Understanding Repair and Maintenance." *Theory, Culture & Society* 24 (3): 1–25. https://doi.org/10.1177/0263276407075954.

Greene, Margarita, and Eduardo Rojas. 2008. "Incremental Construction: A Strategy to Facilitate Access to Housing." *Environment and Urbanization* 20 (1): 89–108. https://doi.org/10.1177/0956247808089150.

Greenpeace. 2022. "Atık Oyunları: Geri Dönüşümsüz Hayatlar [Waste Games: Unrecycable Lives]." Turkey: Greenpeace Akdeniz. https://www.greenpeace.org/turkey/raporlar/rapor-atik-oyunlari-geri-donusumsuz-hayatlar/.

Gregson, Nicky, M. Crang, F. Ahamed, N. Akhter, and R. Ferdous. 2010. "Following Things of Rubbish Value: End-of-Life Ships, 'Chock-Chocky' Furniture and the Bangladeshi Middle-Class Consumer." *Geoforum* 41 (6): 846–54. https://doi.org/10.1016/j.geoforum.2010.05.007.

Gregson, Nicky, and Mike Crang. 2010. "Materiality and Waste: Inorganic Vitality in a Networked World." *Environment and Planning A: Economy and Space* 42 (5): 1026–32. https://doi.org/10.1068/a43176.

Gregson, Nicky, and Louise Crewe. 2003. *Second-Hand Cultures*. Materializing Culture. Oxford: Berg.

Gregson, Nicky, Helen Watkins, and Melania Calestani. 2010. "Inextinguishable Fibres: Demolition and the Vital Materialisms of Asbestos." *Environment and Planning A: Economy and Space* 42 (5): 1065–83. https://doi.org/10.1068/a42123.

Gutberlet, Jutta, Sebastián Carenzo, Jaan-Henrik Kain, and Adalberto Manto-vani Martiniano de Azevedo. 2017. "Waste Picker Organizations and Their Contribution to the Circular Economy: Two Case Studies from a Global South Perspective." *Resources* 6 (4): 52. https://doi.org/10.3390/resources60 40052.

Güzey, Özlem. 2009. "Urban Regeneration and Increased Competitive Power: Ankara in an Era of Globalization." *Cities* 26 (1): 27–37. https://doi.org/10.1 016/j.cities.2008.11.006.

Hammersley, Martyn, and Paul Atkinson. 2019. *Ethnography: Principles in Practice*. 4 Edition. New York: Routledge.

Harvey, David. 1990. "Between Space and Time: Reflections on the Geographical Imagination." *Annals of the Association of American Geographers* 80 (3): 418–34. https://doi.org/10.1111/j.1467-8306.1990.tb00305.x.

Harvey, David. (2012) 2019. *Rebel Cities: From the Right to the City to the Urban Revolution.*

Hawkins, Gay. 2009. "THE POLITICS OF BOTTLED WATER: Assembling Bottled Water as Brand, Waste and Oil." *Journal of Cultural Economy* 2 (1–2): 183–95. https://doi.org/10.1080/17530350903064196.

Hawkins, Gay. 2010. *The Ethics of Waste: How We Relate to Rubbish.* Lanham: Rowman & Littlefield Publishers.

Hawkins, Gay. 2018. "Plastic and Presentism: The Time of Disposability." *Journal of Contemporary Archaeology* 5 (1): 91–102. https://doi.org/10.1558/jca.33291.

Hetherington, Kevin. 2004. "Secondhandedness: Consumption, Disposal, and Absent Presence." *Environment and Planning D: Society and Space* 22 (1): 157–73. https://doi.org/10.1068/d315t.

Heynen, Nik, Maria Kaika, and E. Swyngedouw, eds. 2006. *In the Nature of Cities: Urban Political Ecology and the Politics of Urban Metabolism.* Questioning Cities Series. London; New York: Routledge.

Hulme, Alison. 2015. *On the Commodity Trail: The Journey of a Bargain Store Product from East to West.* London; NewYork: Bloomsbury Academic.

Hulme, Alison. 2017. "Following the (Unfollowable) Thing: Methodological Considerations in the Era of High Globalisation." *Cultural Geographies* 24 (1): 157–60. https://doi.org/10.1177/1474474016647370.

Imamoğlu. 2019. "İstanbul'da 'Deprem seferberliği' başlatan İmamoğlu: Binaların yüzde 22,6'sı yıkılacak, yolların yüzde 30'u kapanacak [Imamoğlu launched 'Earthquake mobilisation' in Istanbul: 22.6 percent of the buildings will be demolished, 30 percent of the roads will be closed]." *Yeşil Gazete - ekolojik, politik, katılımcı, şenlikli...* (blog). October 14, 2019. https://yesilga

zete.org/blog/2019/10/14/istanbulda-deprem-seferberligi-baslatan-imam
oglu-binalarin-yuzde-226si-yikilacak-yollarin-yuzde-30u-kapanacak/.

Ingold, Tim. 2007. "Materials against Materiality." *Archaeological Dialogues* 14 (1):
1–16. https://doi.org/10.1017/S1380203807002127.

Ingold, Tim. 2008. "When ANT Meets SPIDER: Social Theory for Arthro-
pods." In *Material Agency*, edited by Carl Knappett and Lambros Malafouris,
209–15. Boston, MA: Springer US. https://doi.org/10.1007/978-0-387-74711
-8_11.

Ingold, Tim. 2012. "Toward an Ecology of Materials." *Annual Review of Anthropology* 41 (1): 427–42. https://doi.org/10.1146/annurev-anthro-081309-14592
0.

ISICAM. 1980. "ISICAM TV Advertisement." 1980. https://www.isicam.com.tr
/tr/isicam-nedir/isicam-videolari.

Işık, Oğuz. 1995. "Yapsatçılığın Yazılmamış Tarihi [The Unwritten History of
Build-and-Sell Construction]." *Mimarlık*, no. 261: 43–45.

Işık, Oğuz, and Mehmet Melih Pınarcıoğlu. 2001. *Nöbetleşe yoksulluk: gecekon-
dulaşma ve kent yoksulları: Sultanbeyli örneği [Relocated poverty: squatting and
the urban poor: The case of Sultanbeyli].* 1. baskı. İletişim yayınları Araştırma
- inceleme dizisi, 736 114. İstanbul: İletişim.

Istanbul Metropolitan Municipality (IBB). 2005. "1/5000 Kadıköy E-5 (D-100)
Master Plan." IBB.

Izci, Rana. 2016. "The Impact of European Union on Environmental Policy." In *ENVIRONMENTALISM IN TURKEY: Between Democracy and Development?*, edited by Fikret Adaman. Place of publication not identified: ROUT-
LEDGE.

Jencks, Charles, and Nathan Silver. 1972. *Adhocism: The Case for Improvisation.* 1st
ed. New York: Doubleday.

Kanat, Gurdal. 2010. "Municipal Solid-Waste Management in Istanbul." *Waste
Management* 30 (8–9): 1737–45. https://doi.org/10.1016/j.wasman.2010.01.
036.

Karadag, Sibel. 2021. "Ghosts of Istanbul: Afghans at the Margins of Precarity."
Istanbul: Association for Migration Research (GAR).

Karaman, Ozan. 2008. "Urban Pulse—(RE)Making Space for Globalization in
Istanbul." *Urban Geography* 29 (6): 518–25. https://doi.org/10.2747/0272-363
8.29.6.518.

Karatepe, Şükrü. 2003. *Kendini Kuran Şehir [The City that Founded Itself].* İstanbul:
İz Yayıncılık.

Karayel, Veysel. 2019. "775 Sayılı Gecekondu Kanunu uygulamasının genel ve Kayseri İli Selçuklu Mahallesi örneği yönlerinden değerlendirilmesi [Evaluation of Law No. 775 on Slums in general and in the case of Selçuklu Neighbourhood in Kayseri Province]." https://dspace.ankara.edu.tr/xmlui/hand le/20.500.12575/73607.

Kavak, Sinem. 2016. "Syrian Refugees in Seasonal Agricultural Work: A Case of Adverse Incorporation in Turkey." New Perspectives on Turkey 54 (May): 33–53. https://doi.org/10.1017/npt.2016.7.

Keyder, Çağlar, ed. 1999. "The Setting." In Istanbul: Between the Global and the Local, 3–28. Lanham, MD: Rowman & Littlefield.

Keyder, Çağlar, 2005. "Globalization and Social Exclusion in Istanbul." International Journal of Urban and Regional Research 29 (1): 124–34. https://doi.org/10 .1111/j.1468-2427.2005.00574.x.

Keyder, Çağlar, 2011. "Yirmi Birinci Yüzyıla Girerken İstanbul [Istanbul in the Twenty- First Century]." In İstanbul nereye?: küresel kent, kültür, Avrupa, edited by Deniz Göktürk, Levent Soysal, and İpek Türeli.

Keyder, Çağlar, and Ayşe Öncü. 1994. "Globalization of a Third- World Metropolis: Istanbul in the 1980's." Review (Fernand Braudel Center) 17 (3): 383–421.

Kıray, Mübeccel Belik. 1964. Ereğli: ağır sanayiden önce bir sahil kasabası [Ereğli: a coastal town before heavy industry]. Cağaloğlu, İstanbul: Bağlam Yayıncılık.

Kolektif. 2018. İş Cinayetleri Almanağı [Work Killings Almanac 2018]. Umut.

Korkmaz, Tansel, and Eda Ünlü Yücesoy. 2009. "Living in Voluntary and Involuntary Exclusion." In Living in Voluntary and Involuntary Exclusion, edited by Tansel Korkmaz, Eda Ünlü Yücesoy, and Yaşar Adanalı. Refuge- Diwan.

Kuru, Kutluay Yağmur, and Neval Karanfil. 2021. "Kayseri'ye yerleşen geçici koruma altındaki Suriyelilerin Eskişehir Bağları semtinin gettolaşma sürecinin başlaması üzerindeki etkisi [The impact of Syrians under temporary protection settling in Kayseri on the beginning of the ghettoisation process in Eskişehir Bağları neighbourhood]," February. http://acikerisim .nevsehir.edu.tr/xmlui/handle/20.500.11787/1613.

Kusenbach, Margarethe. 2003. "Street Phenomenology: The Go-Along as Ethnographic Research Tool." Ethnography 4 (3): 455–85. https://doi.org/1 0.1177/146613810343007.

Kuyucu, Tuna, and Özlem Ünsal. 2010. "'Urban Transformation' as State- Led Property Transfer: An Analysis of Two Cases of Urban Renewal in Istanbul." Urban Studies 47 (7): 1479–99.

Lane, Ruth. 2011. "The Waste Commons in an Emerging Resource Recovery Waste Regime: Contesting Property and Value in Melbourne's Hard Rub-

bish Collections." *Geographical Research* 49 (4): 395–407. https://doi.org/10.1
111/j.1745-5871.2011.00704.x.

Latour, Bruno. 1988. *The Pasteurization of France*. Harvard University Press, Cambridge Mass.

Latour, Bruno. 2007. *Reassembling the Social: An Introduction to Actor-Network-Theory*. Clarendon Lectures in Management Studies. Oxford: Oxford Univ. Press.

Latour, Bruno. 2015. *Science in Action: How to Follow Scientists and Engineers through Society*. Nachdr. Cambridge, Mass: Harvard Univ. Press.

Latour, Bruno. 2016. "From Realpolitik to Dingpolitik or How to Make Things Public." In *New Critical Writings in Political Sociology*, edited by Alan Scott, Kate Nash, and Anna Marie Smith. London: Routledge. https://www.taylorfrancis.com/books/e/9781315264530.

Law, John. 1992. "Notes on the Theory of the Actor-Network: Ordering, Strategy, and Heterogeneity." *Systems Practice* 5 (4): 379–93. https://doi.org/10.10
07/BF01059830.

LeCompte, Margaret Diane, and Jean J. Schensul. 2013. *Analysis and Interpretation of Ethnographic Data: A Mixed Methods Approach*. 2nd ed. Ethnographer's Toolkit, Book 5. Lanham: AltaMira Press.

Lynch, Kevin, and Michael Southworth. 1990. *Wasting Away*. San Francisco: Sierra Club Books.

Marcus, George E. 1990. "The Modernist Sensibility in Recent Ethnographic Writing and the Cinematic Metaphor of Montage." *Society for Visual Anthropology Review* 6 (1): 2–12. https://doi.org/10.1525/var.1990.6.1.2.

Marcus, George E. 1990. 1995. "Ethnography in/of the World System: The Emergence of Multi-Sited Ethnography." *Annual Review of Anthropology* 24 (1): 95–117. https://doi.org/10.1146/annurev.an.24.100195.000523.

Marcus, George E., and Erkan Saka. 2006. "Assemblage." *Theory, Culture & Society* 23 (2–3): 101–6. https://doi.org/10.1177/0263276406062573.

Marshall, Aarian. 2022. "Why Cities Want Old Buildings Taken Down Gently." *Wired*, February 22, 2022. https://www.wired.com/story/why-cities-want-old-buildings-taken-down-gently/?utm_source=facebook&utm_social-type=owned&utm_medium=social&mbid=social_facebook&utm_brand=wired&fbclid=IwAR3OP4HBFDAtQa2VZ4umB4bCtVLnRC-umpsq_NuT HksFFi9eAoJrsaqoQPk.

Masona, Edimus. 2014. "Land Use/ Land Cover Changes and Stakeholders: Investigating Sustainable Natural Resources Management Options for an A1

Farm a Case Study of Essexdale Farm in Marondera District, Zimbabwe."
http://hdl.handle.net/10646/2566.

Mauss, Marcel. 2002. *The Gift: The Form and Reason for Exchange in Archaic Societies*. Routledge Classics. London: Routledge.

Mazzeo, Agata. 2018. "The Temporalities of Asbestos Mining and Community Activism." *The Extractive Industries and Society* 5 (2): 223–29. https://doi.org/10.1016/j.exis.2018.02.004.

McFarlane, Colin. 2011a. "Assemblage and Critical Urbanism." *City* 15 (2): 204–24. https://doi.org/10.1080/13604813.2011.568715.

McFarlane, Colin. 2011b. "The City as Assemblage: Dwelling and Urban Space." *Environment and Planning D: Society and Space* 29 (4): 649–71. https://doi.org/10.1068/d4710.

McFarlane, Colin. 2011c. "Encountering, Describing and Transforming Urbanism: Concluding Reflections on Assemblage and Urban Criticality." *City* 15 (6): 731–39. https://doi.org/10.1080/13604813.2011.632901.

Mehrotra, Rahul, Felipe Vera, and José Mayoral. 2017. *Ephemeral Urbanism: Does Permanence Matter?* Edited by Richard Sennett and Richard Burdett. First edition. Trento: LISt Lab.

Michael, Kavya, Tanvi Deshpande, and Gina Ziervogel. 2019. "Examining Vulnerability in a Dynamic Urban Setting: The Case of Bangalore's Interstate Migrant Waste Pickers." *Climate and Development* 11 (8): 667–78. https://doi.org/10.1080/17565529.2018.1531745.

Mintz, Sidney W. 1986. *Sweetness and Power: The Place of Sugar in Modern History*. Reprint edition. New York: Penguin Books.

Morrison, Susan Signe. 2015. *The Literature of Waste: Material Ecopoetics and Ethical Matter*. https://search.ebscohost.com/login.aspx?direct=true&scope=site&db=nlebk&db=nlabk&AN=1075587.

Müller, Martin. 2015. "Assemblages and Actor-Networks: Rethinking Socio-Material Power, Politics and Space: Assemblages and Actor-Networks." *Geography Compass* 9 (1): 27–41. https://doi.org/10.1111/gec3.12192.

Nader, Laura. 2011. "Ethnography as Theory." *HAU: Journal of Ethnographic Theory* 1 (1): 211–19. https://doi.org/10.14318/hau1.1.008.

Odman, Aslı. 2019. "Asbest Tehlike Haritası: Ortalık Toz Duman [Asbestos Hazard Map: Dust and Dust]." *Beyond.Istanbul*, no. 4: 70–77.

Öncü, Ayşe. 1988. "The Politics of the Urban Land Market in Turkey: 1950–1980." *IJUR International Journal of Urban and Regional Research* 12 (1): 38–64.

Orhangazi, Özgür, and A. Erinç Yeldan. 2021. "The Re-making of the Turkish Crisis." *Development and Change* 52 (3): 460–503. https://doi.org/10.1111/dec h.12644.

Özçevik, Ö., and P. Tan. 2013. "Do We Have the Right Toolbox? A Process of Mixed Methods: A Research Case from an Urban Transformation Site in Istanbul." In, 437–50. Putrajaya, Malaysia. https://doi.org/10.2495/SC1303 71.

Özdemir, Nihan. 1999. "The Transformation of Squatter Settlements into Authorised Apartment Blocks: A Case Study of Ankara, Turkey."

Öztürk, Deniz. 2019. "Istabul'da Hafriyatın Izini Sürmek: Aktörler, Ağlar ve Akışlar [Tracing Excavation in Istanbul: Actors, Networks and Flows]." Istanbul: Mimar Sinan University.

Öztürk, Murat, Beşir Topaloğlu, Andy Hilton, and Joost Jongerden. 2018. "Rural–Urban Mobilities in Turkey: Socio-Spatial Perspectives on Migration and Return Movements." *Journal of Balkan and Near Eastern Studies* 20 (5): 513–30. https://doi.org/10.1080/19448953.2018.1406696.

Parnet, Claire, and Gilles Deleuze. 2002. *Dialogues II*. 2nd ed. New York: Columbia University Press.

Payne, Geoffrey K. 1982. "Self-Help Housing: A Critique of Gecekondu of Ankara." In *Self-Help Housing: A Critique*, edited by Peter M. Ward, 117–39. London: Mansell.

Pérouse, Jean-François. 2004. "Deconstructing the Gecekondu." *European Journal of Turkish Studies*, no. 1 (September). https://doi.org/10.4000/ejts.195.

Pérouse, Jean-François. 2013. "Kentsel Dönüşüm Uygulamasında Belirleyici Bir Rol Üstlenen Toplu Konut İdaresi'nin Belirsiz Kimliği Üzerine Birkaç Saptama [A Few Remarks on the Ambiguous Identity of the Housing Development Administration, Which Assumes a Decisive Role in the Implementation of Urban Regeneration]." In *İstanbul: Müstesna Şehrin Istisna Hali*, edited by Ayşe Çavdar and Pelin Tan, 1. baskı. KentSel 03. İstanbul: Sel Yayıncılık.

Pérouse, Jean-François. 2014. *İstanbul'la yüzleşme denemeleri: çeperler, hareketlilik ve kentsel bellek [Attempts to confront Istanbul: peripheries, mobility and urban memory]*. İstanbul: İletişim.

Pimapen. 2000. "Dr. Pimapen." 2000. https://www.pimapen.com.tr/tr.

Pink, Sarah. 2013. *Doing Visual Ethnography*. 3rd edition. Los Angeles: SAGE.

Portes, Alejandro, Manuel Castells, and Lauren A. Benton, eds. 1989. *The Informal Economy: Studies in Advanced and Less Developed Countries*. Baltimore, Md: Johns Hopkins University Press.

Rankin, Katharine N. 2011. "Assemblage and the Politics of Thick Description." *City* 15 (5): 563–69. https://doi.org/10.1080/13604813.2011.611287.

Roy, Ananya. 2011. "Slumdog Cities: Rethinking Subaltern Urbanism: Rethinking Subaltern Urbanism." *International Journal of Urban and Regional Research* 35 (2): 223–38. https://doi.org/10.1111/j.1468-2427.2011.01051.x.

Saraçoğlu, Cenk. 2010. "The Changing Image of the Kurds in Turkish Cities: Middle-Class Perceptions of Kurdish Migrants in İzmir." *Patterns of Prejudice* 44 (3): 239–60. https://doi.org/10.1080/0031322X.2010.489735.

Scanlan, John. 2005. *On Garbage.* Repr. London: Reaktion Books.

Secchi, Roberto, and Leone Spita, eds. 2018. *Architettura Tra Due Mari: Radici e Trasformazioni Architettoniche e Urbane in Russia, Caucaso e Asia Centrale [Architecture between Two Seas: Roots and Architectural and Urban Transformations in Russia, Caucasus and Central Asia].* Quodlibet. https://doi.org/10.2307/j.ctv1142p5.

Şen, Alper and Artıkişler Kolektifi. 2014. *Istanbul'un Artığı = Surplus of Istanbul.*

Şentürk, Burcu. 2013. "Planning, Development and Community: Transformation of Gecekondu Settlements in Turkey." Phd, University of York. http://etheses.whiterose.ac.uk/5597/.

Şentürk, Burcu. 2016. *Urban Poverty in Turkey: Development and Modernisation in Low-Income Communities.* Library of Modern Turkey 21. London New York: I.B. Tauris.

Şenyapılı, Tansı. 1981. *Gecekondu çevre işçilerin mekanı [Squatters' neighbourhood as a place for labourers].* Orta Doğu Teknik Üniversitesi Mimarlık Fakültesi.

Şenyapılı, Tansı. 2004. *Baraka'dan Gecekonduya: Ankara'da Kentsel Mekânın Dönüşümü: 1923–1960 [From Shacks to Shantytowns: The Transformation of Urban Space in Ankara: 1923–1960].* 1. baskı. Memleket Kitapları 173. İstanbul: İletişim.

Sesetyan, Karin, Ufuk Hancilar, Erdal Safak, and Eser Cakti. 2020. "Avcılar Olası Deprem Kayıp Tahminleri Kitapçığı [Avcılar Potential Earthquake Loss Estimates Booklet]." Istanbul: IBB & Kandilli Rasathanesi ve depram arastirma enstitusu. https://depremzemin.ibb.istanbul/wp-content/uploads/2020/11/Avcilar.pdf.

Sewell, Granville H. 1966. *Squatter Settlements in Turkey: Analysis of a Social, Political and Economic Problem.* Cambridge.

Silver, Jonathan. 2014. "Incremental Infrastructures: Material Improvisation and Social Collaboration across Post-Colonial Accra." *Urban Geography* 35 (6): 788–804. https://doi.org/10.1080/02723638.2014.933605.

Simone, AbdouMaliq. 2004. "People as Infrastructure: Intersecting Fragments in Johannesburg." *Public Culture* 16 (3): 407–29.

Simone, AbdouMaliq. 2006. "Pirate Towns: Reworking Social and Symbolic Infrastructures in Johannesburg and Douala." *Urban Studies* 43 (2): 357–70. ht tps://doi.org/10.1080/00420980500146974.

Simone, AbdouMaliq. 2008. "Emergency Democracy and the 'Governing Composite.'" *Social Text* 26 (2): 13–33. https://doi.org/10.1215/01642472-2007-02 7.

Simone, AbdouMaliq. 2009. *City Life from Jakarta to Dakar: Movements at the Crossroads.* Routledge. https://doi.org/10.4324/9780203892497.

Simone, AbdouMaliq. 2011. "The Surfacing of Urban Life: A Response to Colin McFarlane and Neil Brenner, David Madden and David Wachsmuth." *City* 15 (3–4): 355–64. https://doi.org/10.1080/13604813.2011.595108.

Simone, AbdouMaliq. 2015. "Relational Infrastructures in Postcolonial Urban Worlds." In *Infrastructural Lives: Urban Infrastructure in Context*, edited by Stephen Graham and Colin McFarlane, 17–38. London; New York, NY: Routledge, Taylor & Francis Group.

Soderman, Braxton, and Roxanne Carter. 2008. "The Auto Salvage: A Space of Second Chances." *Space and Culture* 11 (1): 20–38. https://doi.org/10.1177/12 06331207310702.

Standing, Guy. 2014. *The Precariat: The New Dangerous Class.* London, UK; New York, NY: Bloomsbury.

Stuart, Forrest. 2018. "Reflexivity: Introspection, Positionality, and Self as Research Instrument-Toward a Model of Inductive Reflexivity." In *Approaches to Ethnography: Analysis and Representation in Participant Observation*, edited by Colin Jerolmack and Shamus Rahman Khan, 211–38. New York, NY: Oxford University Press.

Tan, Elif, Ömer Kanıpak, and Dilek Safer, eds. 2016. *Sarı Işık: Kentsel Dönüşüme Hazırlan [Yellow Light: Prepare for Urban Regeneration].* Istanbul: Serbest Mimarlar Derneği.

Tavory, Iddo, and Stefan Timmermans. 2014. *Abductive Analysis: Theorizing Qualitative Research.* Chicago: The University of Chicago Press.

Tekeli, İlhan. 1978. "Kapitalistleşme Süreci İçinde Türkiye'nin Konut Üretimine Bir Bakış [An Overview of Housing Production in Turkey in the Process of Capitalisation]." *Mimarlık* 16: 34–38.

Tekeli, İlhan.1996. "19. Yüzyılda İstanbul Metropol Alanının Dönüşümü [19th Century Transformation of Istanbul Metropolitan Area]." In *Modernleşme sürecinde Osmanlı kentleri Villes ottomanes à la fin de l'empire*, edited by Paul

Dumont, François Georgeon, and Ali Berktay. Tarih Vakfı Yurt yayınları. İstanbul: Türkiye Ekonomik ve Toplumsal Tarih Vakfı.

Tekeli, İlhan.2011. *Türkiye'nin Kent Planlama ve Kent Araştırmaları Tarihi Yazıları [Historical Writings on Urban Planning and Urban Research in Turkey]*. 1. basım. Toplu Eserler 15. Eminönü, İstanbul: Tarih Vakfı.

Thompson, Christian. 2005. "Window of Opportunity." UK: WWF-UK. https://www.wwf.org.uk/sites/default/files/2017-06/windows_0305.pdf.

Thompson, Michael. 1979. *Rubbish Theory: The Creation and Destruction of Value*. New edition. London: Pluto Press.

Thornton, Joe. 2002. "Environmental Impacts of Polyvinyl Chloride Building Material." Healthy Building Network. Washington, D. C.

Thorton, Joe, Healthy Building Network, and Institute for Local Self-Reliance. 2002. *Environmental Impacts of Polyvinyl Chloride Building Materials*. Washington, D.C.: Healthy Building Network.

Tonkiss, Fran. 2011. "Template Urbanism: Four Points about Assemblage." *City* 15 (5): 584–88. https://doi.org/10.1080/13604813.2011.609026.

Tuçaltan, Gül. 2018. *Metabolic Urbanization of Waste in Ankara. A Governance Perspective*. Delft: Uitgeverij Eburon.

Tuçaltan, Gül. 2019. "Waste and Metropolitan Governance as Vehicles of Eviscerating Urbanism: A Case from Ankara." *Capitalism Nature Socialism* 0 (0): 1–15. https://doi.org/10.1080/10455752.2019.1692050.

Türeli, Ipek. 2014. "Heritagisation of the 'Ottoman/Turkish House' in the 1970s: Istanbul-Based Actors, Associations and Their Networks." *European Journal of Turkish Studies. Social Sciences on Contemporary Turkey*, no. 19 (December). https://doi.org/10.4000/ejts.5008.

Türk, Şevkiye Sence, Sezen Tarakçi, and Nevra Gürsoy. 2020. "A Large-Scale Urban Renewal Project in a Vicious Cycle of Commons and Anticommons: The Fikirtepe Case (Istanbul, Turkey)." *Habitat International* 102 (August): 102209. https://doi.org/10.1016/j.habitatint.2020.102209.

Turkish Parliment (TBMM). 1956. *Orman Kanunu No. 6831 [Forest Law]*. https://www.mevzuat.gov.tr/MevzuatMetin/1.3.6831.pdf.

Turkish Parliment (TBMM). 1966. *Gecekondu Kanunu No: 775 [Squatter Law]*. https://www.mevzuat.gov.tr/MevzuatMetin/1.5.775.pdf.

Turkish Parliment (TBMM). 1985. *Planız Alanlar Yönetmeliği [Unplanned Areas Zoning Regulations]*. https://www.mevzuat.gov.tr/mevzuat?MevzuatNo=4882&MevzuatTur=7&MevzuatTertip=5.

Turkish Parliment (TBMM). 2012. *Afet Riski Altındaki Alanların Dönüştürülmesi Hakkında Kanun No: 6306 [Disaster Prevention and Transformation of High-Risk Areas Law]*. https://www.mevzuat.gov.tr/mevzuatmetin/1.5.6306.pdf.

Turkish Parliment (TBMM). 2021. "Depreme Karçı Alınabilecek Önlemlerin ve Depremlerin Zararlarının En Aza İndirilmesi İçin Alınması Gereken Tedbirlerin Belirlenmesi Amacıyla Kurulan Meclis Araştırması Komisyonu Raporu [Report of the Parliamentary Investigation Committee Established to Determine the Precautions to Be Taken Against Earthquakes and the Measures to Be Taken to Minimise the Damages of Earthquakes]." TBMM. https://www5.tbmm.gov.tr/sirasayi/donem27/yil01/ss278.pdf.

Turkish Statistical Institute (TÜIK). 2020. "Waste Statistics 2020." 2020. https://data.tuik.gov.tr/Bulten/Index?p=37198&dil=2.

Union of Turkish Engineers and Architects Chambers (TMMOB). 2017. "İstanbul Asbest Raporu [Istanbul Asbestos Report]." İstanbul: TMMOB.

Union of Turkish Engineers and Architects Chambers (TMMOB). 2019. "Yıkılan Kentler Raporu [Destroyed Cities Report]." Ankara: Türk Mühendis ve Mimar Odaları Birliği. http://www.tmmob.org.tr/yayin/tmmob-yikilan-kentler-raporu.

Ünsal, Özlem. 2011. "(Yıkılarak) Yeniden Kurulan Kent: 2000'li Yılların İstanbul'u [The City Reconstructed (by Demolition): Istanbul of the 2000s]." *Betonart*, no. no.29 (k): 55–59.

USA Environmental Protection Agecy, OLEM. 2018. "Sustainable Management of Construction and Demolition Materials." Overviews and Factsheets. 2018. https://www.epa.gov/smm/sustainable-management-construction-and-demolition-materials.

Varda, Agnes, dir. 2000. *Gleaners and I*. Documentary.

Viney, William. 2014. *Waste: A Philosophy of Things*. London; New York: Bloomsbury Academic.

Vinyl Plus. 2021. "PVC Recycling Technologies." Brussels. https://vinylplus.eu/.

Wainwright, Oliver. 2018. "Vanity Projects and Kamikaze Loggias: Tbilisi's Architectural Disaster." *The Guardian*, November 15, 2018, sec. Cities. https://www.theguardian.com/cities/2018/nov/15/vanity-projects-and-kamikaze-loggias-tbilisi-architectural-disaster.

Yalçıntan, Murat Cemal, Çare Olgun Çalışkan, Kumru Çılgın, and Uğur Dündar. 2014. "İstanbul'un Dönüşüm Coğrafyası [Istanbul's Transformation Geography]." In *Yeni İstanbul Çalışmaları: Sınırlar, Mücadeleler, Açılımlar*, edited by Ayfer Bartu Candan and Cenk Özbay, 1. basım. İstanbul: Metis.

Yazıcıoğlu Halu, Zeynep. 2010. "Kentsel Mekan Olarak Caddelerin Mekansal Karakterinin Yürünebilirlik Bağlamında Irdelenmesi Bağdat Caddesi Örneği [Analysing the Spatial Character of Streets as Urban Spaces in the Context of Walkability Bagdat Street Example]." İstanbul: Istanbul Technical University.

Yazıhüyük Municipality. 2021. "Genel Bilgiler." 2021. http://www.yazihuyuk.b el.tr/.

Yönder, Ayşe. 1998. "Implications of Double Standards in Housing Policy: Development of Informal Settlements in Istanbul, Turkey." In *Illegal Cities: Law and Urban Change in Developing Countries*, edited by Edesio Fernandes and Ann Varley. London; New York: Zed Books: Distributed in the USA exclusively by St. Martin's Press.

Yuan, Hongping, and Liyin Shen. 2011. "Trend of the Research on Construction and Demolition Waste Management." *Waste Management* 31 (4): 670–79. htt ps://doi.org/10.1016/j.wasman.2010.10.030.

Zeybek, Sezai Ozan. 2020. *Türkiye'nin Yakın Tarihinde Hayvanlar: Sosyal Bilimleri İnsan Olmayanlara Açmak [Animals in Turkey's Recent History: Opening Social Sciences to Non-Humans]*. 1. baskı. İstanbul: Notabene Yayınları.

[transcript]

PUBLISHING.
KNOWLEDGE. TOGETHER.

transcript publishing stands for a multilingual transdisciplinary programme in the social sciences and humanities. Showcasing the latest
academic research in various fields and providing cutting-edge diagno-
ses on current affairs and future perspectives, we pride ourselves in the
promotion of modern educational media beyond traditional print and
e-publishing. We facilitate digital and open publication formats that can
be tailored to the specific needs of our publication partners.

OUR SERVICES INCLUDE

- partnership-based publishing models
- Open Access publishing
- innovative digital formats: HTML, Living Handbooks,
  and more
- sustainable digital publishing with XML
- digital educational media
- diverse social media linking of all our publications

Visit us online: www.transcript-publishing.com

Find our latest catalogue at www.transcript-publishing.com/newbookspdf